DramaContemporary

HUNGARY

IN PRINT:

DramaContemporary: Hungary
DramaContemporary: Czechoslovakia
DramaContemporary: Spain
DramaContemporary: France
DramaContemporary: Latin America
DramaContemporary: Scandinavia

IN PREPARATION:

DramaContemporary: Poland
DramaContemporary: Germany
DramaContemporary: Russia
DramaContemporary: India

DramaContemporary
HUNGARY

plays by

András Sütő
Géza Páskándi
István Csurka
György Spiró
Mihály Kornis

Edited, with an Introduction, by
Eugene Brogyányi

PAJ Publications
New York

Published in cooperation with Corvina Press, Budapest

The Palm Sunday of a Horse Dealer (Egy lócsiszár virágvasárnapja)
© 1976 András Sütő; English translation © 1989 Eugene Brogyányi.
Sojourn (Vendégség) © 1984 Géza Páskándi; English translation © 1989 Gabriel John Brogyányi.
Cheese Dumplings (Túrógombóc) © 1980 István Csurka; English translation © 1989 Eugene Brogyányi
Chicken Head (Csirkefej) © 1987 György Spiró; English translation © 1989 Eugene Brogyányi
Kozma © 1986 Mihály Kornis; English translation © 1989 Eugene Brogyányi

First Edition
All rights reserved
No part of this publication may be reproduced or transmitted in any form or by any means, electronic or mechanical, including photocopy, recording, or any information storage or retrieval system now known or to be invented, without permission in writing from the publishers, except by a reviewer who wishes to quote brief passages in connection with a review written for inclusion in a magazine, newspaper, or broadcast.

All rights reserved under the International and Pan-American Copyright Conventions. For information, write to PAJ Publications, 131 Varick Street, Suite 902, New York, N.Y. 10013

Library of Congress Cataloging in Publication Data
DramaContemporary: Hungary
CONTENTS: *The Palm Sunday of a Horse Dealer; Sojourn; Cheese Dumplings; Chicken Head; Kozma*
ISBN: 1-55554-053-8 (cloth)
ISBN: 1-55554-054-6 (paper)

All inquiries concerning texts appearing herein should be addressed to ARTISJUS H-1364 Budapest, P.O.B. 67

For performance rights, please refer to copyright holders.

Publication of this book has been made possible in part by grants received from the National Endowment for the Arts, Washington, D.C. a federal agency, and the New York State Council on the Arts. Translations were made possible in part through grants from The Wheatland Foundation and the Central and East European Publishing Project.

Design by Gautam Dasgupta

Printed in Hungary, 1991

General Editors of the DramaContemporary series:
Bonnie Marranca and Gautam Dasgupta

Contents

INTRODUCTION
by Eugene Brogyányi — 9

THE PALM SUNDAY OF A HORSE DEALER
by András Sütő — 17

SOJOURN
by Géza Páskándi — 65

CHEESE DUMPLINGS
by István Csurka — 103

CHICKEN HEAD
by György Spiró — 129

KOZMA
by Mihály Kornis — 201

The DramaContemporary Series

DramaContemporary is a series specializing in the publication of new foreign plays in translation, organized by country or region. The series developed in response to the increasing internationalism of our age that now links world societies more closely, not only economically, but culturally as well. The last twenty years, in particular, are characterized by cross-cultural references in writing and performance, East and West and throughout the Americas. The new drama series is designed to partake of this movement in world patterns of culture, specifically in the area of our specialty, theatre.

Each volume of DramaContemporary features a selection of recent plays that reflects current social, cultural, and artistic values in individual countries. Plays are chosen for their significance in the larger perspective of a culture, as a measure of the concerns of its artists and public. At times, these plays may find their way into the American theatrical repertoire; in other instances, this may not be possible. Nevertheless, at all times the American public can have the opportunity to learn about other cultures — the speech, gestures, rhythms and attitudes that shape a society — in the dramatic life of their plays.

The Publishers

Introduction

Eugene Brogyányi

I

The modern Hungarian theatre is, for the most part, *terra incognita* to English-speaking readers and playgoers. New Hungarian dramas are seldom performed and even more seldom published in our language. The present volume is, in fact, the first anthology in English devoted entirely to contemporary Hungarian playwrights. Our Western view of this body of literature is so incomplete that the five authors represented here, all considered major figures in Central Europe, are probably unknown to most readers even by name.

One must, in fact, go back to the authors of two generations past to find—in Ferenc Molnár—a Hungarian playwright whose work now enjoys unquestioned international fame. To this day, such Molnár plays as *Liliom*, *The Play's the Thing*, and *The Guardsman* continue to be revived in their English versions, thanks to their wit, sophistication, and masterly construction. Among more recent Hungarian playwrights, however, only one, István Örkény, reaches our stages with even moderate frequency. Örkény's success is well deserved: The charm of *Catsplay* and the sardonic wit of *The Tóth Family* amply explain and justify the attention accorded this master of the grotesque. Unfortunately, similar justice has not been done to Örkény's most gifted contemporaries, some of whom are playwrights of manifest importance. For them, recognition by English-speaking audiences is long overdue.

What stands in the way of recognition? The explanation is both complex and instructive. To begin with, these plays are products of a minor-language culture. Hungarians today number about 16 million, of whom 10.6 million live in Hungary, while most of the rest live in the surrounding states as a result of territorial annexations following the World Wars. Furthermore Hungarian does not belong to any of the major European language groups, i.e., Slavic, Germanic, or Romance. As a Finno-Ugric language, Hungarian is related to Finnish and Estonian; this, however, does not make for mutual intelligibility. The Hungarian nation's relative smallness and obscure language have contributed to the fact that its literature in general is not more widely known. An even more formidable barrier has been Hungary's unfortunate status in recent centuries as a pawn in larger regional conflicts and strategies. Western perceptions have tended to place Hungary in the easily ignored category of small nation buried in a large political bloc. Earlier in this century certain writers succeeded in transcending these obstacles to establish flourishing reputations in English-speaking countries. Molnár, of course, is the most conspicuous example, but other playwrights such as Menyhért Lengyel and Lajos Bíró also contributed to the commercial theatres of England and America. Their work, sometimes referred to by literary historians as export drama, mirrored a middle-class cosmopolitanism that Budapest shared with the big cities of the West, a factor which surely contributed to the success of these plays abroad.

With the advent of the cold war, however, the steady flow of Hungarian plays to America ground to a halt, partly because Hungarians ceased to write plays for export to the West. This change, however, was but one factor in a major alteration of the world's political climate: Central Europe virtually ceased to exist in these years, insofar as the continent was divided rigidly along East–West lines. Americans now regarded Hungary primarily as a member of the Eastern bloc, and East-West hostility was now added to the barrier of linguistic isolation that had always impeded the international circulation of Hungarian plays. Small wonder, then, that many of Hungary's finest playwrights remain unknown to us.

Yet it is precisely this condition of double isolation that lends Hungarian literature much of its own highly individual color and informs the plays in this volume with a significance that transcends the provincial.

As a consequence of their tragic and complex past, Hungarians regard national survival as a major accomplishment. A national obsession with history, accordingly, is highly apparent in Hungarian literature. For Hungarians, the past speaks urgently and questioningly to the present. But while Hungarians feel a strong connection to the historical continuum of their particular cultural community, they feel, at the same time, a lack of connection to the greater European whole. By virtue of their obscure origins and highly unusual language,

Hungarians feel unrelated to their neighbors. In his book, *Hungary*, Paul Ignotus writes that speaking Hungarian imparts "the feeling of having ... no relatives at all; that, or being related to everybody." Indeed, this very sense of ontological solitude, like that of the residents of Camus's plague-stricken Oran, points to an all-embracing human solidarity, hence connection.

Friedrich Dürrenmatt speaks of the problems faced by playwrights of small nations in creating dramas of universal human significance. Dürrenmatt distinguishes between *Kleinstaat* (Small-State) and *Grossmacht* (Great-Power) literature. In a speech cited in George Wellwarth's *Three Catalan Dramatists*, Dürrenmatt stated that the degree of interest the world takes in the everyday affairs of a given country is proportionate to the political prominence of that country. Therefore the Great-Power dramatist need write only about everyday life in his society in order to engage the interest of the rest of the world. The Small-State dramatist does not have this option if his work is to be of any interest beyond his own society. He must use his society as a model for the world as a whole. The plays contained herein fulfill Dürrenmatt's condition for Small-State drama of universal significance. In them the peculiar Hungarian feeling of solitude emerges as a metaphor for the existential crisis: the individual's confrontation with the collective world.

In an essay entitled *The Transformation of the Individual in the Modern Theatre*, Robert Corrigan points out that collective social order has swallowed up an earlier type of organization — the communal society. Communal life was defined by shared traditions, values, habits, beliefs, customs — in other words, by a common heritage. An individual's place in the community was guaranteed simply by virtue of his having been born into it. By contrast, modern mass society is collective, regardless of the economic or political system that provides its outward trappings. The collective is based on shared goals for the future; the common past that its members share is at best irrelevant. An individual's sense of identity — that is, his connection to his fellow man, to his society, to his very self — is defined entirely by his function. He is, in fact, an intersection of impersonal interests. A central concern of many contemporary dramatists is the individual's need to face and combat the dehumanizing forces of the collective world. The struggle often takes the form of an assertion of identity: The individual, especially in times of crisis, realizes and acts upon the organic totality of his being.

But whereas Corrigan's essay may be read in part as an epitaph for the community, in Central Europe the community survives, albeit under threat. Evidence of this survival is provided by Sándor Csoóri, a pre-eminent Hungarian poet. In a speech entitled "Writer, State, Nation," delivered to the 1986 P.E.N. Congress in New York, Csoóri spoke of the crucial importance to Hungarians of the distinction between the concepts of nation and state. These concepts are by and large synonymous to Americans (indeed, the Swiss Dürrenmatt's use of the adjective *Kleinstaat* also betrays such an equational tendency). Csoóri's analysis can be seen as a Central European version of Corrigan's distinction between communal and collective social organization. In Csoóri's words, "There was a time when culture was the source of all creation, from the leather whip to a political theory. The first great division in European history was between the state and the church. Subsequently, intellectual activity and art became separated from the modern state in a similar manner." It follows that the nation, a historical formation, is the wellspring of the Hungarian writer's inspiration; the state is merely an economic and foreign-policy unit. Csoóri claimed that "in the face of external constraints and realities, the nation represents internal independence," and he concluded that "without national cultures, no form of freedom is imaginable."

Csoóri's implication that a cultural context is the *sine qua non* of freedom of expression is a notion with a long legacy in Hungary. In the 18th century, an Enlightenment-inspired movement for national resurgence, led by the writer György Bessenyei, sought to establish a canon of native literature of the past in order to provide the present with a sense of literary continuity. In the *Oxford History of Hungarian Literature* Lóránt Czigány writes of this sense of continuity, in its ultimate manifestation known as literary consciousness *(irodalmi tudat)*, thus: "Both tradition and innovation guarantee the growth of literature, but innovation — which brings about originality — may only be forthcoming if an awareness of the accumulated traditions exists ... *Irodalmi tudat* is a sense of belonging, of being part of a tradition." Another aspect of this resurgence was the idea that writers ought to devote their efforts to improvement of the country's social structure and intellectual climate. To this day, the Hungarian writer's traditional role involves a conscious defense of communality.

For the Hungarian writer the route from palpable realities to the predicament of modern man is very direct. The crisis of identity is to Hungarians not so much a generalized angst as it is a part of everyday experience: Hungary is a country where jailers and their victims have switched places repeatedly in this century; and through no choice of their own, one-fourth of the Hungarian people in their ancestral homeland live as national minorities in Czechoslovakia, the Soviet Union, Rumania, Yugoslavia, and Austria. This division by political borders is widening the gap between beneficiaries and victims of historical circumstances. As of this writing, Hungary is evolving into a democratic and pluralistic society as the ruling party, having renounced Communism, is preparing to compete in open elections with opposition parties. Thus the inhabitants of that state are in the process of seizing control of their own destiny, while the 2.5 million Hungarians across the border to the east must endure an ever more virulent form of nationalist oppression as Rumania sinks deeper into its Stalinist morass. The Hungarian condition, given expression — even allegorical expression — by the nation's literary artists, can and often does become a paradigm of the condition of universal modern man.

II

This volume can offer only a sampling of contemporary Hungarian drama. These plays, dating from 1970 to 1986, represent a cross-section of styles, regional origins, and generations. Due to lack of space, many worthy playwrights, among them István Eörsi, Péter Nádas, and of course István Örkény, had to be left out. The five plays included do, however, provide an inkling of the remarkable diversity that characterizes Hungarian drama today.

It is no coincidence that the two historical dramas in this volume are by Transylvanian writers, András Sütő (b. 1927) and Géza Páskándi (b. 1933). Transylvania is a province of historical Hungary that now forms part of Rumania. Repressive minority policies have forced Hungarian writers of the region to treat social and national problems in allegorical terms. Indirect expression of specific issues can, however, go very directly to the heart of universal themes, as the first two plays printed here demonstrate.

The play that represents Sütő in this volume is *The Palm Sunday of a Horse Dealer*, the first play in a trilogy written during the 1970s. Like its two companion dramas, it deals with the individual's rebellion against identity-threatening forces. These plays may fruitfully be examined in the light of Jean-Pierre Vernant's observations on Greek tragedy. According to this Marxist classicist, a single basic concern underlies all prototypical Greek tragedies (i.e., the works of Aeschylus and Sophocles, but not those of Euripides). This is the necessity of preserving the recently established, and hence precarious, new social order of the Athenian city-state. Thus, every Aeschylean and Sophoclean play deals in some way with the problem of a remarkable individual of admirable accomplishments whose continued existence, however, is seen as a threat to the existing order. In the end, the individual is sacrificed or neutralized, albeit with regret, so that the social order may survive.

The Palm Sunday of a Horse Dealer closely conforms to this model. Based on the novella *Michael Kohlhaas* by Heinrich von Kleist, it deals with a law-abiding Saxon supporter of the new Lutheran movement who, having suffered an abuse of feudal privilege for which he cannot get lawful redress, turns to open rebellion. At the behest of Luther himself, the hero ultimately receives just compensation for his injuries, but also just punishment for fomenting a criminal uprising that has grievously imperiled the stability of Luther's new accommodation with the nobility. At his moment of triumph, with his identity and dignity intact, the rebel Kohlhaas steps onto the gallows.

In the second play of Sütő's trilogy, *Star at the Stake*, the new order is John Calvin's theocracy in Geneva and the beleaguered hero is Calvin's friend, Michael Servetus. As students, Calvin and Servetus were intellectual comrades-in-arms, glorying in their own unorthodoxy and frequently exchanging theological speculations. Later, however, Servetus's continued speculations threaten to undermine Calvin's claim to absolute truth — the claim upon which the survival of his regime depends. Clutching the "heretical" book he refuses to renounce, Servetus in the end is burned at the stake at Calvin's command. In *Cain and Abel*, the last play of the trilogy, the new order is, provocatively, the creation of Genesis. When the servile and guilt-ridden Abel claims God as his authority for introducing the practice of human sacrifice, Cain kills him in protest, in what is, itself, an act of sacrifice that ensures the survival and preserves the dignity of mankind.

Géza Páskándi's *Sojourn*, the second play in this anthology, is a very different kind of historical drama from Sütő's, exhibiting an abstract quality that contrasts strongly with Sütő's poetic naturalism. *Sojourn* begins with the above-discussed prototype as status quo: The remarkable individual, in this case a 16th-century reformer, the founder and first Bishop of the Unitarian Church, must be sacrificed to the new power structure of Transylvania. The instrument of his undoing is Socino, an itinerant theologian quartered in the Bishop's house. Socino is a typical Páskándi protagonist, an individual who, rightly or wrongly, believes himself threatened by a powerful entity. Rather than confronting power head on, he attempts to insulate himself from it and, in the process, creates a situation in which he becomes his own prisoner. Socino, the unwilling informer who reveres his victim and fancies he can save him by playing both ends against the middle, thus allows himself to be led step by step into betrayal. His debased actions are ultimately shown to be implicit in the debased role he has accepted, however reluctantly: having once compromised himself by saying yes, he cannot, at any later point, find a logical reason for saying no. Therefore he cannot locate himself among the nuances of inscrutable power, even the power that his victim, the betrayed, wields over him. By the end it is uncertain who laid what sort of trap for whom. Páskándi, though not an absurdist, does allow for the absurd, which is an *aspect* of the author's world, not an all-encompassing condition. Thus, Páskándi characterizes much of his writing for the theatre as "absurdoid."

With *Cheese Dumplings* by István Csurka (b. 1934), playwright-in-residence of the *Vígszínház* (Comedy Theatre) of Budapest, we move into the realm of open social criticism, deployed with the author's characteristic grotesque humor. The setting of this one-act play is a radio studio where talk-show guests, leading intellectuals of the day, are expected to discuss social issues that are of importance to lowbrows, in this case, the role of stupidity in society. As in Páskándi, no compromise is possible between integrity and lack of integrity. The talk-show guests find themselves tongue-tied. Trapped in a prison of their own making, they must confront the fact that their lives have involved a bargaining away of principles. They are thus guilty of betraying their duty as intellectuals: to be the conscience of society. While their inarticulateness ruins the show, it also reveals them in their appointed roles as stooges for vacuity. Thus the blame for the broadcast's failure is placed on the traditional scapegoat, the technician, who will not be missed by society since he has no value as a front man. The intellectuals' promise to intercede for him is merely the half-hearted gesture of the impotent.

György Spiró (b. 1946) and Mihály Kornis (b. 1949) belong to the new generation of Hungarian playwrights whose work has been designated theatre of privation *(hiánydramaturgia)*. These plays are characterized by an absence of rational action, the modern world having robbed the individual of the conditions for such action.

Set in the depths of urban social decay, Spiró's *Chicken Head* takes to task the paternalistic system, represented by the often-referred-to Council. But the play's significance lies in its exposing of modern man's catastrophic want of connection to others and to himself. Rife with casual profanity, the play revels in a sordid naturalism. The opening image of severed chicken heads is emblematic of severed human bonds: The characters are suffering from the disease of spiritual privation. Insofar as their actions stem from trying to find a cause in the causeless, their longing for a connection is real and holds out hope. It is significant — and very Hungarian — that solace in this play is derived from a literary source: in this case, from the (alas untranslatable) verses of the great poet Endre Ady (1877–1919), whose literary quest also involved the search for a spiritual connection.

In Kornis's play, three women, drinking and sunbathing in a restricted resort for those with the right connections to power, are unexpectedly confronted by an enigmatic stranger, Kozma. He comes from "above," which could refer to the Party hierarchy or, as his name implies, to the cosmic sphere. All around these characters are the now-living/now-dead bodies of anonymous, forgotten victims of the recent past. The dionysian Kozma elicits confused and contradictory confessions of self-justification from the women as each in turn reincarnates him as someone significant from her past. Furthermore, the women do not perceive the victims as anything more than annoying natural debris, while for their part the members of this latter-day Greek chorus do not recognize either the "tragedy" they were gathered to investigate, or the bonds they share with each other. The victims are, in the words of critic Zsuzsa Radnóti, "the ruins of an erstwhile community." The irony of this lack of awareness on both sides is heightened by the fact that the vacationing women are beneficiaries of historical circumstances and conditions that account for the demise of the victims. In the striking conclusion, the victims reassemble on a now-driverless truck that is stuck in the sand.

With this image of despair we are a long way from Sütő's hopeful hero on the gallows. Indeed these five plays offer a glimpse into a literature marked by vitality and diversity; they demonstrate the far-reaching capacity of contemporary Hungarian drama to forge man's image out of the world's inhumanity.

* * *

Thanks are due Pamela Billig of the Threshold Theater Company, János Benyhe and Tünde Vajda of Corvina Press, Leslie Billig, Zsuzsa Berger, and Károly Nagy, for valuable editorial advice. I am indebted to Benjamin Folkman for his general editorial help and, in particular, for pointing out to me Jean-Pierre Vernant's views on Greek tragedy. I gratefully acknowledge the Threshold Theater Company and the Literature Program of New York State Council on the Arts for their support of my translating efforts and those of the late Gabriel John Brogyányi.

The Palm Sunday of a Horse Dealer

András Sütő

A drama in three acts after the novella of Heinrich von Kleist

translated by Eugene Brogyányi

Béla Ilovszky (MTI)

THE PALM SUNDAY OF A HORSE DEALER
[Madách Theatre, Budapest, Hungary]
Directed by Ottó Ádám

CHARACTERS:

Michael Kohlhaas
Lisbeth
Nagelschmidt
Herse
Maria
Baron Wenzel von Tronka
Baron Günther
Franz Müller
Kallheim
Hinz
Kunz
Zauner
Eibenmeyer
Toll-keeper
Castellan
Sister Antonia
Martin Luther
Henrik
Mann
Castle Guard
Bailiffs, serfs, citizens

(Takes place in the first half of the sixteenth century.)

Trouble once came on horse's back
Galloping on a gleaming black
To Kohlhaasenbrück
Where a horse dealer
Named Michael Kohlhaas took the attack

Trouble appears with unthought speed
Mounted on a galloping steed
O how suddenly
Unexpectedly
Trouble rides in on its battle-steed

But O how passing Trouble slows
It came on horse on foot it goes
So slowly passing
Creeping in the dust
For departing is what Trouble loathes

But consolation will abound
For everyone whose hope is sound
Good Michael Kohlhaas
As warring angel
Will battle Trouble into the ground

And justice will prevail some day
If there is one to show the way
Of fire and sword
With the pluck and grit
That Michael Kohlhaas dared to display

ACT ONE

The house of Michael Kohlhaas in Kohlhaasenbrück. The door and windows are open as when, after a bad night, people begin a better day; or when, after a severe winter, spring has arrived; or when the deceased has been removed from the house and buried; or when—for some reason—one can place one's trust in the outside world. The sounds of a Lutheran service can be heard: singing, organ music. Maria joins in now and then by singing and praying with reverence, her attention divided between housework and the service. After a short time noise breaks out in the main square of the town: the barking of dogs and the cries, "Catch him! Tie him up! Flog him! Trample his guts out! Lord Günther, I don't see him!" Presumably the voice of Lord Günther: "You brainless peasant yokels!" With this, the yellers move on. Maria is so absorbed in her conversation with God that she does not even hear the voices. She does her best to follow the singing coming from the church. Nagelschmidt appears in the doorway opening onto the town square, disheveled, panting. He hesitates for a moment. Maria has her back to him. On hearing new steps, he enters with quick, stealthy strides, and hides behind the curtain of the wash-alcove. As the singing from church gets louder, so does Maria's. A mercenary Castle Guard with a whip in his hand stops at the door, then enters. With due respect, he waits till Maria finishes her singing.

CASTLE GUARD: Where's Nagelschmidt?
MARIA: Nagelschmidt?
CASTLE GUARD: He must have run in here.
MARIA: I didn't see him. But why must he have run in here?
CASTLE GUARD: Because he's no longer the servant of the lord of this house, your pious master, but his bosom friend.

MARIA: You are mistaken.
CASTLE GUARD: I may be mistaken, but my master, Baron Günther, is not. The Baron said that this horse thief...
MARIA: Horse dealer...
CASTLE GUARD: ... horse thief. This horse thief is one of Thomas Münzer's men. At the time of the uprising he stole two of the Baron's plough-horses. The Baron's serfs testify...
MARIA: Baron Günther's serfs were hanged.
CASTLE GUARD: Yes, they testified there beneath the gallows that Nagelschmidt stole the plough-horses for Münzer.
MARIA: Münzer was beheaded.
CASTLE GUARD: I saw it. I was there when they beheaded Münzer in Mülhausen. I stood at the side of Baron Günther and saw close up when that Antichrist's head fell to the dust and rolled away, and Münzer grabbed for it as if he could somehow hurl his own skull among us. *(Laughs.)*
MARIA: My God, why do you tell me this?
CASTLE GUARD: I tell you because Baron Günther said that this Nagelschmidt was a supporter of the Antichrist, that he stole the Baron's plough-horses, and is now the bosom friend of a respectable horse dealer.
MARIA: My master, Michael Kohlhaas, does not befriend horse thieves. As God is my witness, he did not sympathize with the peasant revolt or with Thomas Münzer. Mr. Kohlhaas is a believer in lawful order, and he never advocated anything but tolerance. Only Christ our Lord was more patient and peace-loving, which your master knows well, after all, he's a long-time customer of my master, as is Baron Wenzel von Tronka. Mr. Michael Kohlhaas listens only to the word of Reverend Doctor Martin Luther, and has always stood by him, whenever that Münzer insulted Doctor Luther and called him a sneak, a dimwit, or a jackass.
CASTLE GUARD: And Nagelschmidt?
MARIA: Please leave me alone. Mr. Kohlhaas will come home at any moment, and as kindhearted as he is, will even offer you a glass of wine ... for your insolence. Throw bread back at him who throws stones at you, that's my good master: if you want to know him, read the Bible. If you want to know the Bible, cast a single glance at the life of Michael Kohlhaas. He is the embodiment of the ten commandments and their fulfillment in one person.
CASTLE GUARD: Then I'll leave. You've become very smart as a nanny...
MARIA: Smart enough not to tolerate your stupid slander in Mr. Kohlhaas's house.
CASTLE GUARD: How about a glass of wine?
MARIA: Get one from your master, with whom you share an interest in severed heads. And now, if you don't clear out of here, I'll put a curse on you.
CASTLE GUARD: *(Frightened.)* You're not a witch, are you?
MARIA: Heavenly Father, Who dwells on high ...

CASTLE GUARD: *(Stopping up Maria's mouth.)* Shut up, or I'll shut you up ... I beg of you ...
MARIA: *(Freeing herself from the grip of the Castle Guard.)* Just this: May you be clobbered by gentleness and patience ...
CASTLE GUARD: Just that and no more ... *(Runs away.)*

(There was too much confidence. The door and windows must be closed. After that, Maria hurries back into the kitchen. Nagelschmidt comes out from behind the curtain and sits at the table. Maria brings wine, places it before him. Nagelschmidt prepares to pour himself some.)

MARIA: That's Mr. Kohlhaas's glass. Actually, I brought the wine for him too. *(Places another glass on the table. Nagelschmidt pours, drinks. Maria watches.)* So, you're here after all.
NAGELSCHMIDT: Uh-huh. *(Drinks.)*
MARIA: And what will happen to you if the door doesn't happen to be open sometime? *(As Nagelschmidt casts a glance toward the window.)* Or the window. *(As he looks around more.)* Or the chimney chute. Or the keyhole.
NAGELSCHMIDT: Your heart will always be open.
MARIA: That's right, but it would be smarter if you tried settling your quarrel with Baron Günther.
NAGELSCHMIDT: Isn't that what I'm constantly doing? Yet for his part, he stops somewhere and yells, catch the horse thief! So I kick the Castellan in the groin. While you ...
MARIA: ... while I say: All Kohlhaasenbrück knows where you run to hide. You don't even try to make sure your boots aren't showing beneath the curtain. You never consider how much damage your behavior could do to the good name of Mr. Kohlhaas. You're often seen together. Somewhere by mistake they'll confuse the two of you ...
NAGELSCHMIDT: The two of us? Sin and virtue? The upholder of the law and the trampler of the law? Lord Günther recently yelled that my serf-rage reeks far and wide. But even my father was no longer a serf — he was a horse dealer.
MARIA: Unfortunately Lord Günther speaks the truth. And that stench overpowers Mr. Kohlhaas's aroma of Palm Sunday when he's around you.
NAGELSCHMIDT: Those are the words of the gracious Lisbeth: that Michael's disposition has the aroma of Palm Sunday! You quoted her word for word to that louse as well.
MARIA: I'm not ashamed to be my mistress Lisbeth's echo. Because she is the echo of Christ our Lord ...
NAGELSCHMIDT: And I?
MARIA: You?
NAGELSCHMIDT: When I say the princes are not the masters but the servants of the sword, of the power of the state, and should not do whatever happens to strike their fancy—whose echo am I then, Maria?

MARIA: When you say this, you're the echo of your own head fallen to the dust, of the nape of your neck in the hangman's noose, my dear.

NAGELSCHMIDT: And if I said it not in my own name, but according to the command of God ... *(Michael Kohlhaas enters, a rocking horse under his arm, listens to the haranguing Nagelschmidt with a smile.)* ... if I said it like this: The power of the sword belongs to the entire community, not to a single man, Daniel seven, Revelation six, and if some judgment is not just, the community of Christians must reject it, Moses four, verse seventeen ... and if they fleece and extort everyone, Micah three ...

KOHLHAAS: ... if they fleece and extort, ask, and it shall be given you; seek, and ye shall find; knock, and it shall be opened unto you, Matthew seven ... my dear friend, Nagelschmidt.

NAGELSCHMIDT: Welcome, Michael.

(They embrace.)

KOHLHAAS: You're setting fires again. You wish to incite Maria to rebellion?
MARIA: Really now ...
KOHLHAAS: Are you all in good health?
MARIA: Thank God, we are well, sir. My mistress Lisbeth is in church with the child, the servants are at the stables ... and everything is in order. And ...
KOHLHAAS: Your son Herse ...
MARIA: Yes, sir. My only son ...
KOHLHAAS: He should be arriving soon. I sent him toward Tronka with the two blacks. They left yesterday from Leipzig, I came by way of Dresden.
NAGELSCHMIDT: You didn't sell the blacks?
KOHLHAAS: I couldn't sell them for less than thirty gold florins. What do you think of those horses, my friend?
NAGELSCHMIDT: They're worth forty ...
KOHLHAAS: They're more than horses, they're cotton-wrapped ebony statues. I bought marvelous bells in Leipzig to go around their necks.
MARIA: I bet my son asked you to buy the bells.
KOHLHAAS: He didn't have to. I knew how much he liked them. A lover doesn't pine for a girl the way your son pines for the sound of beautiful bells.
MARIA: When we were still papists, my little darling often did altar-service. He'd say traveling with belled horses was like religious service.
NAGELSCHMIDT: He, on the other hand, does horse-service. Gratias agamus Domino Deo nostro ... *(Laughs.)*
MARIA: Godless wretch! *(To Kohlhaas.)* Sir, do something for this man. Before our very eyes he's ambling straight to hell, or at least to the gallows.
KOHLHAAS: What did he do this time?
MARIA: Don't you hear the filthy way he speaks about sacred things? I can't judge his actions, for instance that he hit the Castellan on the head again, but

I'm witness to his words. You heard them yourself when you stepped in. He provokes the established power with them — not only against himself, but against us as well, since he's a friend of your house. Don't be so lenient toward him, I beg of you! Leniency is sin ... Lenient goodness is also sin ... *(Exits.)*
NAGELSCHMIDT: Sin!
KOHLHAAS: You take it lightly. But listen here, Karl, the uprising is over; may God rest the souls of the dead. Consider yourself lucky that no one has to say about you, may God rest your soul. You owe your life to Doctor Luther, because like me, you heeded him instead of Thomas Münzer.
NAGELSCHMIDT: I heeded the devil.
KOHLHAAS: If that's what you call reason, the peaceful solution of problems ...
NAGELSCHMIDT: ... the glossing over of problems.
KOHLHAAS: Communication instead of a firebrand, the strength of love instead of killing, the lawful enforcement of justice instead of the trampling of the law; if that is the devil, so be it. The devil saved you.
NAGELSCHMIDT: And did Doctor Luther always proclaim this? Hack them, strangle them, stab and slash them, in open and in secret, wherever you can ... because there can be nothing more pestilential, injurious, or diabolical than a rebel. It is just the same as with a mad dog: If you do not destroy it, it will destroy you, and the whole people as well. Pity and tolerance are of no avail here, for this is the time for the sword and for wrath, not for grace. Whoever sheds his blood for the higher powers is a true martyr before God ... Whoever dies on the side of the peasants will burn forever in hell. Who said this? Wasn't it Doctor Luther?
KOHLHAAS: I know. That was when you turned away from him. Desperation made him say it.
NAGELSCHMIDT: A fine thing. Strike them, slash them, stab them, strangle them according to the command of love, Letter to the Romans thirteen. Fodder, a wand, and burdens are for the ass; and bread, correction, and work for the servant. Strangle them like mad dogs, without selection, because even if there are innocent ones among them, God will save and protect them as He did Lot and Jeremiah. Well, I'm Lot and Jeremiah. He saved me. Because besides stealing Lord Günther's two horses for the rebels, I didn't do anything. I pondered and hesitated.
KOHLHAAS: I see you cling to the thought that you foolishly missed the gallows, or being broken on the wheel, or the red-hot iron between your ribs.
NAGELSCHMIDT: My brother and my uncle are dead and buried! If I'd taken the horses in time they could have escaped.
KOHLHAAS: They could have stayed in peace. The uprising was defeated. Therefore the rebels were wrong.
NAGELSCHMIDT: Of course, justice always belongs to the victors.
KOHLHAAS: What sort of justice is it that brings its own advocates to the gallows? Irresponsible. Or at least premature. What sort of reason, what sort of wisdom

proclaims premature justice capable of survival? What would you say about a Nature that bamboozles the doves into laying their eggs in the snows of February, the does into dropping their young in the frost? Wouldn't you say Nature went crazy?

NAGELSCHMIDT: Revolution is not some popular custom that must conform to dates.

KOHLHAAS: It must conform to its own readiness. Doctor Luther could have posted his ninety-five theses in Wittenberg sooner. Indulgences were sold before 1517. Wesel called the Pope a monkey dressed in purple a hundred years earlier, still the name-calling brought about no reformation. It had to wait for the Holy Year, for Tetzel's swinish deeds in Saxony. The right moment! The opportunity! And it did not fail because the time was ripe. He that keepeth his mouth keepeth his life: but he that openeth wide his lips shall have destruction. Remember the Proverbs of Solomon.

NAGELSCHMIDT: Hope deferred maketh the heart sick. That's also from Solomon.

KOHLHAAS: Nevertheless, how could Münzer think the world could be turned upside down every other day? Didn't he realize that first Luther's victory must be consolidated? Luther never looked down on the peasants; for whom did he translate the Bible into our national tongue, if not the peasants? Even when he turned against them, he defended their interests, our reformed faith. If Luther had not won the support of the higher powers by distancing himself from Münzer, then those powers would have been compelled to rely on the Pope's forces, and our national cause would have been lost once and for all. You would now be sitting in the prison of the papists.

NAGELSCHMIDT: The free are those who sit in prison. They did what they had to do. We are the prisoners, Michael, prisoners of bad conscience. When my brother was being interrogated with hot pincers, he told his executioners they would come to know my vengeance. But I'm not capable of anything. I have neither money nor armed troops; if occasionally I can hit some lordly dog, some castellan in the mouth ...

KOHLHAAS: You must be more patient, Karl. Lisbeth!

(Lisbeth enters with Henrik, who is about eight years old.)

LISBETH: Michael!
HENRIK: Father!
KOHLHAAS: My dear ones! How you've grown, Henrik!
HENRIK: What did you bring me from the market?
KOHLHAAS: First close your eyes.
LISBETH: In church also, he kept asking that: what did father bring from the market? Well, close your eyes.
KOHLHAAS: *(Brings in the rocking horse he left in the antechamber, sits Henrik on it.)* Gallop!

LISBETH: Giddyup! Berlin's not far away ...
HENRIK: Hack them, strangle them, stab them ...
LISBETH: *(With her hand fastened to his mouth.)* Not that. We do not hack.
KOHLHAAS: We do not slash.
LISBETH: This is Mr. Nagelschmidt's story. Only he doesn't have a horse for it ...
KOHLHAAS: He doesn't have a horse for it ...
NAGELSCHMIDT: I don't, but I will. *(Begins to leave.)*
LISBETH: Stay, Karl. Dine with us.
NAGELSCHMIDT: Another argument would come of it. I already got my portion from Maria. *(Laughs.)*
LISBETH: Since today is Sunday, I won't allow arguing. Today the two of you will be at peace.
KOHLHAAS: I promise ...
NAGELSCHMIDT: So do I ...
KOHLHAAS: I brought this for you, Lisbeth. *(Hangs a locket on a silver chain around her neck.)*
LISBETH: An amulet! A silver amulet! Thank you. How do I open it? Good fortune dwells inside it. I can't open it.
KOHLHAAS: Wait, I'll show you ... But guess what's inside.
LISBETH: Not good fortune?
KOHLHAAS: Besides that. What's visible?
LISBETH: What's visible inside?
KOHLHAAS: A legion. My legion.
NAGELSCHMIDT: An armed one?
KOHLHAAS: An angelic one. *(Opens it, looks at it.)* My one-person angelic legion.
NAGELSCHMIDT: Then we won't get far with that either.
KOHLHAAS: Only with this will we get anywhere. *(Musing.)* After God, only with this. *(Turns the locket toward Lisbeth.)*

(Lisbeth looks at it silently, while Maria's voice is heard from the kitchen.)

MARIA: Nagelschmidt, a soldier on horseback! *(Nagelschmidt steps out impetuously, the child follows him with curiosity.)*
LISBETH: *(After a long silence.)* Who painted me so beautifully?
KOHLHAAS: A master of Dresden.
LISBETH: It's beautiful. More beautiful than I am.
KOHLHAAS: A faint copy of the original.
LISBETH: How did he do it? He never saw me.
KOHLHAAS: Isn't it enough that I see you?
LISBETH: For me, yes. For the painter it's little.
KOHLHAAS: I dictated your features into his brush.
LISBETH: Don't play the rogue. Blond, twenty-six years old. Generalities.
KOHLHAAS: Oh, that's not what I said. I said: Lisbeth ... her eyes are doves behind her veil ...

LISBETH: I don't even wear a veil ...
KOHLHAAS: Her eyes are as the eyes of doves by the rivers of waters ...
LISBETH: Doves enough for a whole pigeon coop ...
KOHLHAAS: More too, I said. Her eyes are like the fishpools in Heshbon by the gate of many peoples. Her hair is as a flock of goats that appears from Mount Gilead. Her teeth are like a flock of sheep which came up from the washing, and none is barren among them. Her head, the shape of her head is like the Carmel, her face looketh forth as the morning, as fair as the moon, clear as the sun, as long as it does not get sad, then it is terrible as an army with banners ... *(They laugh.)*
LISBETH: *(Playing at coquetry.)* And beyond that? Her neck, her shoulders, her stature?
KOHLHAAS: After that I said: how beautiful are her feet with shoes, O prince's daughter! The joints of thy thighs are like jewels, the work of the hand of a cunning workman.
LISBETH: You mean the master's or the Shulamite's?
KOHLHAAS: Thy two breasts are like two young roes that are twins ... and thy stature is like to a palm tree ...
LISBETH: You skipped a lot, you're forgetting some parts.
KOHLHAAS: And the roof of thy mouth like the best wine for my beloved, that goeth down sweetly, causing the lips of those that are asleep to speak ...
LISBETH: King Solomon would call you to account for your omissions ...
KOHLHAAS: Thy lips are like a thread of scarlet, and thy speech is comely, like a piece of pomegranate ...
LISBETH: Again you skipped ... Thy navel ...
KOHLHAAS: Thy navel is like a round goblet ... thy belly is like an heap of wheat set about with lilies ...
LISBETH: Careful, the continuation applies to you rather than me: thy nose is as the tower of Lebanon which looketh toward Damascus ... That's what I'll say if ever I order a picture of you. My beloved is white and ruddy, the chiefest among ten thousand.
KOHLHAAS: His head ...
LISBETH: ... is as the most fine gold, his locks are bushy, and black as a raven ... His cheeks are as a bed of spices, as sweet flowers ... How does it go on?
KOHLHAAS: With what applies to both of us: Set me as a seal upon thine heart, as a seal upon thine arm: for love is strong as death; jealousy is cruel as the grave: the coals thereof are coals of fire, which hath a most vehement flame ...
LISBETH: Make haste, my beloved, and be thou like to a roe or to a young hart upon the mountains of spices ... make haste, my Michael, and see what Nagelschmidt is up to.
KOHLHAAS: I make haste.

(They laugh a long time. Kohlhaas disengages himself from Lisbeth's arms, and is about to start outward. At this moment violent pounding and yelling begin outside. Beating on the windows and doors. First Maria runs in, frightened, with the child, then Nagelschmidt with some heavy object.)

MARIA: O, my God! Mr. Kohlhaas, the bailiffs.
HENRIK: Father, the bailiffs. Strike them, slash them ...
KOHLHAAS: We will not strike them, we will not slash them. Maria, take the child out.
MARIA: Come, my dear. Let's go and pray.
LISBETH: Open it before they smash it in.
NAGELSCHMIDT: I'll smash in their snouts!
KOHLHAAS: What do they want? *(Opens the door.)*
NAGELSCHMIDT: *(Seizing the chest of the Toll-keeper, behind whom stand two soldiers.)* How dare you ... How dare you break into the house of an honorable man, you scoundrel?!
TOLL-KEEPER: Baron Wenzel von Tronka ... Take your hand off me ...
KOHLHAAS: Nagelschmidt!
LISBETH: Karl!
TOLL-KEEPER: I was sent by Baron Wenzel von Tronka. Remove your hand!
NAGELSCHMIDT: I'll remove it together with your cheek pouch, you gopher-face!
TOLL-KEEPER: The soldier will shoot ...
KOHLHAAS: Nagelschmidt!
LISBETH: Karl, calm down.
KOHLHAAS: Be so kind as to come in, sir.
TOLL-KEEPER: You see what a decent tone of voice is?
NAGELSCHMIDT: And that pounding?
TOLL-KEEPER: Could it be that I'm gopher-faced?
NAGELSCHMIDT: Definitely.
TOLL-KEEPER: But you seem Münzer-faced ... which is not at all stylish ... to be Münzer-faced ... Dózsa-faced ...
NAGELSCHMIDT: Leave the dead alone, you worm!
TOLL-KEEPER: ... Such fashions are not advisable.
NAGELSCHMIDT: Thank you for the tribute. Coming from a weasel ...
KOHLHAAS: Nagelschmidt! ...
NAGELSCHMIDT: I've finished. A fine thing, coming from a rat.
TOLL-KEEPER: Are you Mr. Kohlhaas?
KOHLHAAS: At your service.
TOLL-KEEPER: As I started to tell this one ... *(Nods toward Nagelschmidt.)* I am the new Toll-keeper of Baron Wenzel von Tronka. Please forgive the impatience.
KOHLHAAS: You must have had good reason.
TOLL-KEEPER: I'm on an urgent assignment.
KOHLHAAS: And what is that?

TOLL-KEEPER: The pass.
KOHLHAAS: What pass?
NAGELSCHMIDT: The one that's making my knuckles itch.
TOLL-KEEPER: Mr. Kohlhaas, please. I can't speak amid threats.
NAGELSCHMIDT: And not only my knuckles, my foot is also itching.
TOLL-KEEPER: There he goes again ...
KOHLHAAS: The Toll-keeper is on assignment. Let him carry it out. Now then, what pass?
TOLL-KEEPER: Concerning the horses ... A certain servant of yours named Herse is there.
KOHLHAAS: Where?
TOLL-KEEPER: At Tronka Castle. Detained. He came from Leipzig with two black horses. Horses with bells.
KOHLHAAS: That's right.
TOLL-KEEPER: He has no pass.
KOHLHAAS: Who requires it?
TOLL-KEEPER: Baron Wenzel. He recently received this manorial privilege.

(Lisbeth, in the meantime, finds some papers in a small chest, hands them to Kohlhaas.)

KOHLHAAS: There was some word of this last month already. The Chancellery in Dresden said that according to our laws, the lord of Tronkenburg has no right to demand a pass of any honest dealer.
TOLL-KEEPER: That, in fact, is the case.
KOHLHAAS: Well then?
TOLL-KEEPER: It is my personal opinion that he may not demand it. My father is also a horse dealer.
NAGELSCHMIDT: His father also. His mother ...
TOLL-KEEPER: Unfortunately, I am in service. So are my opinions. If there is no pass, the two blacks are to remain on the far side of the toll gate, in custody.
LISBETH: That's illegal! They cannot do it.
KOHLHAAS: Calm yourself, my dear. The Toll-keeper can't help it ...
TOLL-KEEPER: Unfortunately.
NAGELSCHMIDT: Unfortunately. He's sorry for you on top of it. He breaks down the door out of pure pity. The tearful hangman, God damn it! My God, when will You finally hang the tearful hangmen?! Visit honest hangmen upon us, Lord ...
KOHLHAAS: Do not take the Lord's name in vain.
NAGELSCHMIDT: Then bless me, Lord, with Kohlhaas's equanimity.
TOLL-KEEPER: Do you see how rash he is? Sir, I must ask you either for the pass, or the remittance, fifty farthings in cash. Otherwise the horses remain there. Those magnificent horses.
KOHLHAAS: But I won't let this go at that ...

NAGELSCHMIDT: Finally!
LISBETH: Here's the money. Set that poor servant free. He's been on the road a week.
TOLL-KEEPER: The problem is, my lady, that the servant also has this Münzerrage. He assaulted the armed guard with his fists.
LISBETH: Was he being mistreated?
KOHLHAAS: Hurry with that money, sir. Set that poor Herse free. Give him these twenty farthings, he must have run out of sustenance by now. He should bring the horses here first. I want to see them.
TOLL-KEEPER: I'll tell him, sir. May God remain with this house.
NAGELSCHMIDT: You mean He isn't going with you?
TOLL-KEEPER: Do you see? He's starting again.
KOHLHAAS: May God bless you.
NAGELSCHMIDT: God? May my boot bless the scoundrel's rump! The seat of his servile conviction.
TOLL-KEEPER: *(Deftly jumps out of the way of the kick, out the door.)* Next time I'll do the kicking! *(Exits.)*
NAGELSCHMIDT: Horse tick! Running away brings out his courage.
LISBETH: Steady, Karl. Nowadays there's no need for courage. *(Exits into the kitchen.)*
KOHLHAAS: *(After a long pause.)* Truly, there's no need for courage ...
NAGELSCHMIDT: It's the nature of courage that it always finds a toll-keeper worthy of a wallop. Whichever way you turn, there's always some insolent, grinning face you just have to whack. And all of them harp on the law.
KOHLHAAS: They harp on it, we should lay claim to it. Your hot-headedness blinds you to our rights.
NAGELSCHMIDT: Our rights?
KOHLHAAS: Our rights! Do you think the words of the Dresden Chancellor came out of the blue? The Elector, as you well know, is a believer in lawful order. You don't know it because ...
NAGELSCHMIDT: ... because while writing the law with his hand, he kicks it over with his foot. He kicks it in the pants every day, every hour, and every moment. That famous lawgiving hand is a servant hand. It serves the interests of the Emperor and of the kicking feet, the scoundrels of Tronka.
KOHLHAAS: Wenzel von Tronka is not the Electoral Council, or the Imperial Assembly. The Elector wishes to ensure peace ...
NAGELSCHMIDT: Peace!
KOHLHAAS: Let there be an end to all the conflagrations. Münzer should have realized that. He won fifty thousand gallows for himself — the soul of your brother is in heaven — whom did Münzer redeem with them?
NAGELSCHMIDT: Himself.
KOHLHAAS: Christ redeemed us all.
NAGELSCHMIDT: Not in equal measure.

KOHLHAAS: You cried equality. They leveled your house. Of course now you'd want everybody to join you in your grievance. You're selfish, Karl. The people have grown weary of religious disputes, of uprisings, of burying the dead. They want to live, to work, to raise children, to go to the market-place; after so much upheaval, they want to catch their breath, to forge doors and window gratings instead of weapons. To celebrate a Christmas in peace. Just look, we've hardly reformed our faith, and already newer reformers are arising: Anabaptists and Libertines. What sort of peace will come of this?

NAGELSCHMIDT: I am come not to send peace on earth, but a sword ...

KOHLHAAS: Yes. Christ said that. But Nagelschmidt should not confuse himself with the Son of God. Put up again thy sword into its place: for all those that take the sword shall perish with the sword. He said this too. May I ask you for something? If possible, spare the honor of my house. You hit a bailiff in the mouth, naturally you flee to us. Don't misunderstand, come here as you would to your own home. But every bailiff with a bloody mouth tells his superior that Michael Kohlhaas's friend did it. They chase you, and then take it out on me, and on my horses. Last time one of them burnt the ear of my bay. You provoked Baron Günther, he is Wenzel's friend.

NAGELSCHMIDT: In other words, the pass money was on account of me, too.

KOHLHAAS: I can't be sure ...

NAGELSCHMIDT: Then I'll pay the penalty. Here are the fifty farthings.

KOHLHAAS: I didn't mean to offend you.

NAGELSCHMIDT: I didn't mean to inflict a loss on you.

KOHLHAAS: For God's sake, Karl, don't twist the meaning of my words. I only said it in the interest of the two of us, and for the peace of Lisbeth and my son. Don't insult me by insinuating that I'd fret over a miserable fifty farthings.

NAGELSCHMIDT: You're fretting over your fifty farthingsworth of tranquility.

KOHLHAAS: Is that the value you put on my principles?

NAGELSCHMIDT: That's the value the lords of Tronka put ...

KOHLHAAS: *(Bursting forth.)* Enough! That's enough now, Karl! At least in the relations between the two of us, cut out your lawlessness! Put an end to this trampling of rights!

NAGELSCHMIDT: *(Laughing.)* What?! I, Nagelschmidt, the trampler of rights, the offender of the law?

KOHLHAAS: My lawful rights guarantee my honor against your offenses! It is my God-given right to preserve my family's peace, even from you. Do you think I'm alone? Do you think dead people live with me here? Ghosts?

NAGELSCHMIDT: My God! You gave him a voice!

KOHLHAAS: May you have a hundred lives, may you risk them all at every moment; but mark my words, Lisbeth has but a single life; so does this innocent child; as God is my witness I am responsible for them. Or did God entrust you with their well-being?

NAGELSCHMIDT: An archangel's proclamation!

KOHLHAAS: If this is fifty farthingsworth of honor to you ...
NAGELSCHMIDT: I said tranquility!
KOHLHAAS: It comes to the same! If it's fifty farthingsworth, so be it. How many farthingsworth is yours? How many souls' fates do you carry? The handcuffs of how many persons who depend on you? You may risk your neck every day; you're free — to be irresponsible. To beat your head against a wall!
NAGELSCHMIDT: And what else?
KOHLHAAS: To have yourself hacked to pieces! To have yourself strung up! To have yourself broken on the wheel! But only yourself! Don't play with the lives of others. That villain said you were Münzer-faced. You have that Münzer-rage, that's the problem! Nothing can be gained by rage alone.
NAGELSCHMIDT: Nor by prayer either!
KOHLHAAS: Nor by prayer either. Nor by your thirst for vengeance. Hack them, strangle them, stab them! You say this to others, even to my son! To that innocent! Hack them, stab them! Just like your Münzer: Let the people run headlong into disaster, into the fool's paradise of irresponsible promises. After all, the people disdain the fifty farthingsworth of tranquility. After all, they prefer to be impaled, to have their guts hung out on the gateposts by the superior power! The superior power, Nagelschmidt! By the underestimated adversary, and by stupidity. Do not lay a hand on your enemy until you're sure you can take his head! Remember? At whom is this directed if not the thickheaded, the adventurers who failed military studies and arithmetic, the toll-keepers of credulousness?
NAGELSCHMIDT: That's how I like you. Raise that voice!
KOHLHAAS: Stop jeering! Widows and orphans are mourning the credulous by the tens of thousands. Mark my words, Nagelschmidt, he who incites uprising and does not take it to victory is a mass murderer.
NAGELSCHMIDT: *(This time also flying into a rage.)* You lie!

(Lisbeth enters.)

KOHLHAAS: I lie? This can only be answered with a sword ... Out! Out of my house!
LISBETH: Michael! What happened? Karl, for God's sake ...
NAGELSCHMIDT: He's lost his mind.
LISBETH: This argument will never come to an end! What do you expect of Baron Wenzel von Tronka when you devour each other this way? Michael, my dear, calm down. I've never seen you this upset. A glass of water ... A calmative ... *(Exits.)*
NAGELSCHMIDT: Forgive me, Michael.
KOHLHAAS: You know well, Karl, that while I criticize Münzer, I don't accuse him, though my soul weeps. You yourself saw on the way to Leipzig, and even more around Frankenhausen, the tear-soaked eyes of those left behind

by the murdered peasants. It is said that to this day crowds of women and children rove the battlefields ...

(Lisbeth enters with a glass of water, places it before Kohlhaas silently.)

KOHLHAAS: ... weeping, they gather the little mementos of the fallen ... You know well, after all, your brother was there. Do you still remember Melanchthon's account? The poor people just stood there and sang. We Beseech You, O Holy Ghost! As if insane, they neither defended themselves nor fled. Out of eight thousand the army of the Princes massacred six thousand. Münzer told them just not to be afraid, he would stay every bullet, according to God's promise. Whereas God never made a promise like that to anybody.

NAGELSCHMIDT: *(Indicates with a gesture that Melanchthon did not tell the truth.)* Then what is to be done?

KOHLHAAS: The way of the law, the Sanctity of the Law. We must cling to the promulgated laws, Karl, no matter how inadequate.

(Distant dog barking, then two little bells are heard to the rhythm of a limping walk. Kohlhaas and Lisbeth hurry to the window. Nagelschmidt remains seated, despondent.)

LISBETH: It's Herse! He's arrived ...

KOHLHAAS: With my cotton-wrapped ebony steeds. Let's take a look at the horses, Karl.

LISBETH: Maria! Your son is back, Maria!

(Herse enters, beaten half to death, with the horses' bells in his hand.)

LISBETH: Dear God! Maria!

MARIA: *(Rushes in.)* Herse! What's wrong with you, my son? Did you go mute? Are you mute or drunk?

NAGELSCHMIDT: Both ...

LISBETH: He's covered with mud! He's all black and blue.

KOHLHAAS: Where are the horses? Where did you leave the horses?

MARIA: It's as if you'd strayed in from among the pigs ... Speak, what happened to you? Let me take your coat off ... Sit down here, you poor thing. He's staggering. Please don't be angry with him, sir. You know him ... He doesn't do this sort of thing ... Herse ... Herse, my son!

KOHLHAAS: Where are the horses? I entrusted you with the horses. Why did you take the bells off them?

LISBETH: Drink a little tea, son.

MARIA: Curses on him. Why don't you answer the gentleman? Where did they get you drunk, you curse of God? My dear sir, please don't be angry with him. You know he doesn't drink. Only when others make him. Only then does he drink. You know that he never drinks on his own. *(She rubs Herse's head.)* His whole head is one big bruise, honorable lady. Where did you get all the bruises on your head, my son? Not from drink. Speak, did you fall off the horse?

KOHLHAAS: Take a look, Karl, are the horses in the yard?

NAGELSCHMIDT: If they didn't slip down his throat, they're somewhere. *(Exits.)*

LISBETH: Let's lay him down. A wet pack, Maria.

MARIA: Come on, son. Such shame you've brought on our heads ...

KOHLHAAS: Where did you leave the horses, Herse?

MARIA: He'll tell us tomorrow, sir. He's become very tight-lipped. You haven't gone deaf, have you? *(Into Herse's ear.)* Where did you leave the horses? The horses! What happened? Answer the gentleman.

HERSE: *(Falteringly.)* They beat me up.

MARIA: They beat you up. You didn't go mute. You're just hanging your head down. *(Pats his face, then suddenly slaps him in anger.)* Come to! Holy Mother of God! Sir ... Lady ... Please look here! There's blood coming from his mouth ... From his lungs ... My dear son!

KOHLHAAS: I'll send for the doctor. Lisbeth ... be careful ... he should lie motionless ...

MARIA: Herse, my son ... My dear child ...

CURTAIN

ACT TWO

Scene 1

The setting is the same as in the first act. Lisbeth is preparing for a trip. Henrik is on his rocking horse. It is a summer day. The door is open.

HENRIK: Hack them! Hack them!
LISBETH: We do not hack.
HENRIK: Strangle them!
LISBETH: We do not strangle.
HENRIK: Strangle them! Stab them!
LISBETH: How often must I tell you, Henrik? Now stop the strangling! Dismount, go and eat.
HENRIK: Mother, where are you going?
LISBETH: I'm going away, but I'll be back soon.
HENRIK: Soon? From where?
LISBETH: From nearby. I'm going to fetch your father's horses.
HENRIK: Father can't get them?
LISBETH: He has other things he must do.
HENRIK: What are you bringing me?
LISBETH: What you asked for. A bell to go around your horse's neck. Go eat, my little son.
HENRIK: Take me too, Mother.
LISBETH: Where should I take you? Where would you like to go?
HENRIK: Nowhere, nowhere! Just take me with you.
LISBETH: Oh, that's not possible. The horsemen ride about wildly there. Like that...

(From the distance yelling, the sound of horses' hooves, then Nagelschmidt jumps in the door and goes straight behind the wash-alcove curtain.)

HENRIK: Karl...
LISBETH: Ssh!
CASTLE GUARD: *(Enters.)* Excuse me, Madam...
LISBETH: I will not. How dare you barge in here like that?
CASTLE GUARD: A horse thief...
LISBETH: No horse thief! Don't look for a horse thief in the house of an honorable man.
HENRIK: Hack them... *(Lisbeth clasps his mouth.)*
LISBETH: Stop bothering us.
CASTLE GUARD: Hack them... The child too...
LISBETH: Out there the servants hack carrots, that's where he learned it.
CASTLE GUARD: Uh-huh.
LISBETH: But if you'd like your head to get hacked into the forage, just wait here till my husband returns.
CASTLE GUARD: My regards to the honorable gentleman. *(Exits hastily.)*
NAGELSCHMIDT: *(Appears, laughing.)* You gave him a good scare, Lisbeth. If he knew that Michael would have thrown bread at him. Don't be angry. I promised I wouldn't create my own laws. This was my last disturbance.
LISBETH: What did you do this time?
NAGELSCHMIDT: Certain noble individuals tore Herse's shirt and pants off, gnawed his feet, chewed up his ear. I, in turn, poisoned them.
LISBETH: Oh, no...
NAGELSCHMIDT: Eight corpses... eight and a half, since one of them crawled away.
LISBETH: God in heaven!
NAGELSCHMIDT: Hear how quiet it is around the castle? No more barking, no more howling. The pack of hounds passed on to a better fate. Don't you find the atmosphere more peaceful? *(A dog howls.)*
LISBETH: God giveth dogs in place of dogs.
NAGELSCHMIDT: That's the half-dead one. That's only fifty-percent dog. It's cursing me, using its right to a last howl.
LISBETH: And from me, a last warning, Karl...
NAGELSCHMIDT: I swear that from this day forth, only the law... That which His Holiness the Law says.
HENRIK: Who is the law? Where does the law live?
NAGELSCHMIDT: His Holiness the Law? Mr. Law? I'll explain.
LISBETH: *(Seizes the child, hurrying outward.)* We won't make a brigand out of the child.
NAGELSCHMIDT: Brigand? But it's precisely to avoid crime that he should know: Mr. Law is the Emperor, the Elector, Wenzel von Tronka, and the Chancel-

lery. Mr. Law regulates behavior, work, love, in Geneva, as we've heard, the length of skirts, and morality, while he locks the lecherous women in the tower; Mr. Law sees to it that we observe the days of fast, that we deliver our quota of wine, wheat, geese, pigs, and occasionally our daughters to the lord of the land; what sacred images we may have in our houses; what we should dream, what we should read, what we should hold opinions about and what they should be ... In a word, Mr. Law determines the path we are to follow. On that path he chases us with a stick all the way to paradise.

LISBETH: *(Who listens to this from the door.)* Every one of your words is an offense. If I go to Berlin with you, the sovereign's Bodyguard will arrest both of us.

NAGELSCHMIDT: I'll be silent.

LISBETH: Your dog-poisoning impulses are written all over your face.

NAGELSCHMIDT: In the vicinity of our rulers, I'll put on my most gentle face. I'll behave in the most shameful way possible: with humility and enthusiasm. I'm seriously preparing for this trip, Lisbeth. Just this morning I practised emperor-loyalty instead of sword-fighting.

LISBETH: With your own hands you're building your gallows as if it were some ceremonial gate. And the coach is not yet ready.

NAGELSCHMIDT: *(Humbly exits, singing.)* How fanciful the gallows-tree, its windows face eternity ...

(Kohlhaas enters with Franz Müller.)

KOHLHAAS: Lisbeth! Our savior, Mr. Franz Müller, Brandenburg's foremost authority on the law ...

LISBETH: Franz!

MÜLLER: There now. Lisbeth doesn't insult me for having asked for her hand in marriage once. Michael is always calling me *Mr.* Müller.

LISBETH: Surely just out of respect.

KOHLHAAS: Of course out of respect! He's the chief advisor to the Electoral Chancellery, indeed, he even frequents the Court of Berlin ... He, that is to say, Franz, will draft our petition.

MÜLLER: Franz will draft it, and Mr. Müller will get Lisbeth before the Elector.

LISBETH: We'll be eternally grateful, Franz. Make yourself comfortable, and talk to us ... My God, how many years has it been since we've seen you?

MÜLLER: It's been exactly eight years since you turned me down, albeit with soft words, because, as you say, this rascal is a King Solomon ...

LISBETH: He was my Song of Songs ...

MÜLLER: ... the Song of Songs. Mr. Müller, on the other hand, O, Mr. Müller! The possessed of the legal disciplines, of dry niceties. Finally, as you know, I got engaged to jurisprudence. Without a wife and children my life is dreary, but ... how shall I say it? ... I freely pass judgment on all that I was once a prisoner of. Suffer the little children to come unto me, as well as revenge, jealousy, love, suffer unto me the young, the old, the widows and the stolen donkeys, vengeance, mourning, the chicken thieves, the quacks and the false prophets, the persecuted and the persecutors, the cheaters and the cheated, the master and his servant, husband, lover, the unpaid debt and the neglected prayer, the straying priest and the stray dog, all that lives, that breathes, and therefore sins. Because there is no more fallible being than man. Judging from our present system, if he opens his mouth, he runs foul of the law with every hundredth, hundred and third word. And do you have any idea how much people chatter from morning to night? How much sign-language the deaf-mutes engage in?

LISBETH: And who found all this out? About every hundredth word ... hundred and third word?

MÜLLER: Those whose profession it is.

LISBETH: That's terrible.

MÜLLER: How can we exonerate someone if we don't keep track of his offenses? Society is like goose liver in the frying pan. If it's not watched, it burns.

LISBETH: Suffer unto me ... Before the law. Nagelschmidt said the same thing.

MÜLLER: Who?

LISBETH: Oh, nothing. I just remembered something. But you have tremendous power in your hands!

MÜLLER: Not really. There's someone above me, who says, suffer Mr. Müller to come unto me. And higher still, suffer Mr. Kallheim to kowtow unto me. And he's just an extension of the highest hand, into which Lisbeth, we hope, will place the complaint of the upright horse dealer. My friend Michael has become gloomy.

LISBETH: What's wrong, my dear?

KOHLHAAS: I got to thinking. I was counting up my sins.

LISBETH: Your sins ... Tell me, Franz, when your observers indict all of humanity, all of the goose liver, what will Michael's fate be?

MÜLLER: Naturally exoneration. With him we will begin again the days of Eden. And I, like Lucifer, because of Eve's beauty, will continue to envy him. *(They laugh.)*

LISBETH: For that compliment, I'll bring a little something to drink. And I'll send Herse to help with the petition. *(Exits.)*

MÜLLER: Justice comes about through complaint. Out of the small eggs of complaint hatch the sparrows of satisfaction. So it started when Baron Wenzel von Tronka detained your servant with the two blacks. *(Writes.)*

KOHLHAAS: He's been vomiting blood ever since.

MÜLLER: That's for the end. The dramatic climax must be saved for then. Like Greek drama, misery must also be structured. Otherwise it loses its effect. So they unjustifiably demanded a pass from your servant ... *(Herse enters.)* ... whereas the Chancellery in Dresden ... yes ... What happened after that?

KOHLHAAS: Tell what happened next, Herse.

HERSE: After the beating?
MÜLLER: The beating also remains for the end.
HERSE: I got it right at the start.
MÜLLER: How did it start?
HERSE: The Castellan asks me where I'm coming from. I tell him I'm going home.
MÜLLER: For an answer like that I would have beaten you too. Tell us, after your master, Mr. Kohlhaas, paid the fifty farthings, why did they place the horses in confinement?
HERSE: The horses? Confinement? They put them in the stable.
MÜLLER: Confinement. The Elector is a great horse-lover, so we have to make him feel sorry for the horses. Did they beat the horses?
HERSE: They beat me!
MÜLLER: That's another story. Did they mistreat the horses?
HERSE: On the contrary. Lord Wenzel and his friend Günther galloped over. How much? Forty in gold. That's too much. Show the pass. There's no pass. The Toll-keeper set out for the fifty farthings. Lord Wenzel says take the horses to the stable. The stable was full; then take them to the pigsty. But I can't take them in there. The pigsty's full of fleas. They tell me to keep my mouth shut. Fine, but I won't ruin the horses, they hold their heads high, they'd hurt themselves in the pigsty. I hold my nose high, says the Castellan, and he hit me on the back a few times with the flat of the sword. I had enough of that, so I mounted and made for the main gate. The Castellan whistled, they closed the gate, two bailiffs threw me down, kicked me, one of them stepped on my stomach, the dogs came, they bit and mauled me, look here, and then, so I wouldn't die in their yard, they threw me over the fence. I fainted. And now I'm here. *(Shouting.)* Look here!
MÜLLER: Thank you. You may go.
HERSE: I forgot to tell you I strangled two dogs.
MÜLLER: Let's not bring that up.
KOHLHAAS: The Elector loves dogs too.
HERSE: Then our conversion would have been much better if it could have made us dogs. *(Exits.)*
MÜLLER: And he wonders about having been beaten.
KOHLHAAS: Don't you wonder?
MÜLLER: To wonder is itself a minor form of transgression. So the horses remained there.
KOHLHAAS: I had written proof that the demand of the castle was groundless. That part of the suit I won. It cost as much as six horses. Baron Wenzel summoned me to take back my two blacks. From the pigsty.
MÜLLER: *(Writes quickly.)* From the pigsty ...
KOHLHAAS: In the course of six months, my two beautiful horses were virtually annihilated. I could not accept those two matted, skin-and-bones nags. My

demand in the second part of the suit was that I get back what was taken from me. My appeal was suppressed at the Prosecutor's Office in Dresden.

MÜLLER: It was not suppressed. It was judged incorrectly. The Office, my dear friend, is a unified, close-knit family. It is not advisable to cast aspersions on any member of that family. Therefore ...

KOHLHAAS: ... they suppressed it!

MÜLLER: ... as a consequence of errors in filing ...

KOHLHAAS: Two relatives of Baron Wenzel interfered in my case: Lord Hinz, Cupbearer to the sovereign, and Lord Kunz, the Court Chamberlain. *(Müller does not write this. Later on also, he writes only what he deems appropriate.)* That's how it happened that they sent my complaint back for judgment to precisely the one against whom I complained: the lord of Tronka Castle. This form of abuse of rights is commonplace nowadays. As a result, the plaintiffs fall into the hands of the defendants. Instead of receiving lawful redress, the victim once again falls into the claws of the offender. Is it true you killed this man? Slander, insinuation, cries the murderer, while the corpse is hit in the mouth.

MÜLLER: You've wandered far afield ...

KOHLHAAS: What does Lord Wenzel claim? The servant was not beaten, he injured himself during his escape. My horses were in good condition, but captious man that I am, I left them there to be fed by the lord of the castle, so I have no grounds for demands. And after all these lies, when I requested the protection of the Principality of Brandenburg, Chancellor Kallheim, related by marriage to the lord of Tronka, sent word to me that instead of engaging in false accusations and groundless suits, I should immediately take possession of my horses, otherwise he'll have me thrown in jail for unruly behavior. Me, about whose honesty and respect for the law even Dr. Martin Luther himself could testify? Michael Kohlhaas in prison? I have no choice now but to pursue this case if it takes me the rest of my life. I would pursue it even if it weren't over two horses worth a fortune, but over a mangy cat.

MÜLLER: Let that remain between the two of us.

KOHLHAAS: What?

MÜLLER: The cat. This attitude springs from an exaggerated sense of justice. Justice as a great gold-weighing balance. In other words, naiveté.

KOHLHAAS: A sense of justice is naiveté?

MÜLLER: Definitely, if you think that justice is tailor-made according to each person's measurements. The justice of the law is general, and unfortunately approximate. Like army boots. Its purpose is not justice for the individual, which is impossible to realize, in other words, not the defense of the individual hangnail, but the protection of the entire body, order, the tranquility of society. *(Writes.)* For my fallible nature, conceived in sin, and disposed toward disorder ...

KOHLHAAS: I am not disposed toward disorder!

MÜLLER: Even your raised voice disproves that claim.

KOHLHAAS: I'm not asking for forgiveness! I'm demanding justice, and the punishment of all those who ...
MÜLLER: Stop, stop! We started with a humble request, you continue with demands, and you top off the whole appeal with punishment. Your grievance — this is how we'll word it — is a tiny scratch on the clean countenance of justice, the Emperor's justice. Given this, your demand is an exaggeration, which therefore raises suspicion. If I put myself in the place of the Imperial Attorney I would ask: What is it that feeds Michael Kohlhaas's temper, what sort of dissatisfaction, when the ostensible cause, the fifty farthings, the temporary detention of the two horses, is ultimately of no consequence? Does not this passionate sense of justice veil a secret discontent with the existing order?
KOHLHAAS: Is this an indictment? The indictment of the right to defend oneself?
MÜLLER: This isn't my opinion. I'm just thinking with the head of the adversary.
KOHLHAAS: If you so easily switch your own head with that of the adversary, we might as well give up the case right now. With your mind so at home in contradictory interpretations, you'll turn the grievance against me in the end.
MÜLLER: Someone could do so if he wanted to interpret it that way.
KOHLHAAS: Does the written word no longer have any meaning?
MÜLLER: Only interpretations, my dear friend. The meaning of our words is in the heads of those who read them.
KOHLHAAS: So it makes no difference what we write.
MÜLLER: If what emerges from our petition is that your justice is the sovereign's justice, then your grievance is his grievance; if we reveal convincingly that Lord Wenzel's outrages cast a bad light on His Highness, then our case is won.
KOHLHAAS: So let's report to His Highness that they stole two of his horses, that they fined him fifty farthings, that they beat His Highness, and I, Michael Kohlhaas, having heard of this, protest ...
MÜLLER: Don't be sarcastic; we won't get anywhere this way.
KOHLHAAS: Nor will we get anywhere if I drown my faith in the sovereign in flattery. Perhaps you know best which are those false roads that lead toward justice. All I can say is that in spite of Hinz, Kunz, and Kallheim, I believe in the law, and in the benevolence and impartiality of the sovereign. *(Müller writes.)* If I'm passionate, explain it as the consequence of this conviction, which I must hold, because I don't want to create laws for myself with my own hands. The sad fate of Münzer's people should suffice as an example. I want to see my wife and child happy, and all I wish for is to delight in my horses rather than engage in litigation. It is among my fruit trees and at marketplaces that I feel well, and with Christ our Lord I say to those wronged: Ask, and it shall be given you; seek, and ye shall find; knock, and it shall be opened unto you.
MÜLLER: Not even I could have said it better. Here is your justice, Michael, in the words of Jesus. *(Lisbeth enters with a bottle of wine and glasses.)* Lisbeth, beautiful lady! Your husband outdid me with his eloquence. If I ever get into trouble, I'll ask him to defend me.

LISBETH: He'll terrify his adversaries with his gentleness.
KOHLHAAS: *(Pours.)* Let's thank Franz for the prayerful petition.
LISBETH: And for getting me before the sovereign.
MÜLLER: We'll meet in front of the main gate of Berlin at the arranged time. I must go. Michael has given a motto to my lifework in the law: Knock and it shall be opened unto you ... Let's find each other in peace and joy. Knock. *(Exits.)*
KOHLHAAS: May God bless you.
LISBETH: May God bless you. *(Pause.)* When do I have to be there?
KOHLHAAS: Saturday morning at nine o'clock.
LISBETH: And truly before the sovereign?
KOHLHAAS: Perhaps even the Emperor will be there. Just hear how high our case is going. *(Reads.)* To Charles, Holy Roman Emperor through the grace of God, King of Germany, Spain, the two Sicilies, Jerusalem, Hungary, Dalmatia, Croatia, etc., Archduke of Austria, Prince of Burgundy, Count of Habsburg, Flanders, and Tyrol ... Frightening?
LISBETH: My God ... To have to crawl through the barbed wire of so many titles, so much honor.
KOHLHAAS: I'll go with you.
LISBETH: Unnecessary. Mr. Müller told you they don't look upon you with favor at the castle. A woeful, helpless woman ... according to Franz ... would charm even a tyrant's heart. Look after Henrik.
KOHLHAAS: Look after yourself.
LISBETH: Don't brood. Whatever happens, don't do anything.
KOHLHAAS: I'll just wait for you. Nagelschmidt swore to me he'd control himself. Still I'm worried about you.
LISBETH: My patron saint, the amulet, will be with me always. *(Reads the text inscribed on the back of the locket.)* "I will rise now, and go about the city in the streets, and in the broad ways I will seek the one my soul loveth" ... The child is sleeping ... Kiss him in my place. I'm speaking like a poet, like King Solomon. *(They laugh.)* Why did you have this inscribed with: I will rise now and go about the city?
KOHLHAAS: Remember those days when I was always on the road? In Dresden, Leipzig, Brandenburg.
LISBETH: But you always came back. It was but a little that I passed from them, but I found the one whom my soul loveth. Here I sat with Henrik, we waited for you every evening. We just watched the road, like two statues. The mother statue sang, too. I set to music the sixth verse of chapter three. Henrik laughed at me. You're watching for the pillars of smoke, he'd say, I'm watching for my father. *(Sings.)* Who is it that cometh out of the wilderness like pillars of smoke? Do you like it?
KOHLHAAS: Doctor Luther could count it among his hymns.
LISBETH: The King of the Song, of course, did not think of your poor Lisbeth. Who is this that goeth into the wilderness like pillars of smoke?

KOHLHAAS: My four white horses will fly her hither and back. Nagelschmidt's whip will be the pillar of smoke.

LISBETH: Where do I find my shawl from Leipzig? Because my lord brought that as well. I sought it but I found it not. I called for it but it answered not.

KOHLHAAS: It answered me, because here it is. *(Spreads the shawl over Lisbeth's shoulders.)* Don't catch cold on the trip.

LISBETH: For lo, the winter is gone, the rain is gone. Lisbeth has gone also. And when you say to yourself I sought her, but I found her not, I called to her, but she answered me not! — here I'll be with the sovereign's justice.

NAGELSCHMIDT: *(Steps in.)* Or with his head. *(Upon Kohlhaas's gesture of disapproval.)* Just kidding.

KOHLHAAS: Lisbeth and your life.

NAGELSCHMIDT: So help me God!

KOHLHAAS: If they speak to you with stones, with what do you answer?

NAGELSCHMIDT: With bread, sir. And cake.

KOHLHAAS: Correct. What do you keep shut, even if they confiscate all four of your horses?

NAGELSCHMIDT: My mouth, sir. My face. I'll suggest this course of action to everyone.

(All three exit. The bells of the horses can be heard, while the stage goes dark.)

Scene 2

The setting is the same, one week later. Sunday. Soft, distant organ music. Kohlhaas sits at the window with Henrik in his lap.

KOHLHAAS: Do you see something?

HENRIK: No.

KOHLHAAS: Neither do I.

HENRIK: Now *you* sing the song that'll bring her home.

KOHLHAAS: I don't know it.

HENRIK: *(Sings.)* Who is it that cometh out of the wilderness like pillars of smoke? Is Berlin far?

KOHLHAAS: Very far. But a week has passed already. Your mother should be here soon.

HENRIK: What is she bringing us?

KOHLHAAS: Punishment. Now don't get scared. For the two of us it's a kind of ... present. For us it's a joy. For the Baron von Tronka, on the other hand, a rap ...

HENRIK: A rap?

KOHLHAAS: Over the knuckles. Your mother is bringing the Elector's decision,

which orders that the Baron return my two black horses right away. Fattened up.
HENRIK: Can he fatten them up right away?
KOHLHAAS: *(Startled.)* Not right away. In due course.
HENRIK: Then why did you say right away?
KOHLHAAS: I forgot that everything happens only in due course.
HENRIK: Everything?
KOHLHAAS: You see, I made another mistake. Not everything. Because trouble comes all at once. They took away my horses, they beat up Herse, nobody wanted to deliver justice. Only good comes in due course.
HENRIK: Does it come in a big way?
KOHLHAAS: Little by little.
HENRIK: Father, who brings trouble?
KOHLHAAS: The troublemakers.
HENRIK: And the troublemakers? Who brings them?
KOHLHAAS: Who brings them? Trouble. Did you get a bug in your ear?
HENRIK: I just wanted to get it straight in my mind.
KOHLHAAS: Didn't you have it straight?
HENRIK: Not about what you said.
KOHLHAAS: When you're bigger I'll explain it. By then everything around us will be calm. The colts will be grown up too. We'll be able to come and go to the cities. The bailiffs won't pound the door, they'll probably retire to tend fields. We'll go to Berlin; we'll have nothing to complain to the Emperor about; we'll just take walks along the riverbanks, row in the lakes, eat spit-roast meats, watch the jugglers ... what a place!
HENRIK: Hm. It would be good to grow up right away.
KOHLHAAS: It would. But then I'd get old right away. Your mother too. You wouldn't want that, would you?
HENRIK: Either way it's no good.
MARIA: *(Runs in anxiously.)* Sir! Nagelschmidt ... Alone and on horseback ... Across the field ... not even on the highway ...
KOHLHAAS: My little son, go on out with Maria ... Go on ...
MARIA: My God! What could have happened?
HENRIK: Father! Don't send me away! Don't ...
KOHLHAAS: You may come back right away, Henrik.
HENRIK: Right away? Not in due course?
KOHLHAAS: Right away, son. Go on. *(Maria and Henrik exit.)*
NAGELSCHMIDT: *(Enters.)* We have to go to Schwerin, Michael, urgently!
KOHLHAAS: To Schwerin? Why?
NAGELSCHMIDT: To Lisbeth. Mr. Müller had her taken there.
KOHLHAAS: Had her taken?
NAGELSCHMIDT: We laid her on pillows, a doctor from Berlin accompanied her to Schwerin, to her parents' house. He gave strict orders not to stop till we

reached home, but she fainted at Potsdam. The doctor said if it's closer to Schwerin, she must be taken there immediately.

KOHLHAAS: What happened?

NAGELSCHMIDT: A member of the Elector's Bodyguard hit her in the chest with the butt of his lance.

KOHLHAAS: Why?

NAGELSCHMIDT: She pressed too close to the Elector.

KOHLHAAS: Where was Mr. Müller?

NAGELSCHMIDT: A few steps from her. He had arranged things the day before with the commander of the Bodyguard so that she would be allowed to hand over the petition personally. But there were so many petitioners that the Bodyguard before the Brandenburg Gate panicked, and began pushing the crowd back with lances. Poor Lisbeth, holding her Leipzig shawl in one hand, waving the petition in the other, unsuspectingly approached the Elector according to the arrangements. He didn't notice her since he had to acknowledge the cheers of the crowd. According to Mr. Müller, they replaced the commander of the Bodyguard with another, who didn't know about the agreement. It is the habit of this one to permit the people nothing on such festive occasions except enthusiastic acclamation or singing, and even that with the cheeks turned, so that no one should be able to harm His Highness with an evil eye. Lisbeth fainted from the blow. We can thank Mr. Müller that she wasn't trampled to death by the crowd. The petition was taken out of her hand by a kindhearted knight. Maybe he got it to the Elector.

KOHLHAAS: And where were you during all this?

NAGELSCHMIDT: On Lisbeth's instructions, I was waiting for her in the coach in the courtyard of the inn, ready for our return.

KOHLHAAS: What did the doctor say?

NAGELSCHMIDT: That her recovery would be very lengthy.

KOHLHAAS: A month? A year?

NAGELSCHMIDT: That's all he said. When we laid her in the wagon she came to. She sat up among the pillows, addressed you, then asked me about Henrik — why I didn't seat him next to her too. She was bleeding from the nose and mouth, but it didn't last long. The doctor said the movement did her good, otherwise she would have suffocated from dried blood.

KOHLHAAS: *(After a long silence.)* On the day of her recovery I'll issue that guard's death warrant.

NAGELSCHMIDT: With whose signature?

KOHLHAAS: The Elector's. The Emperor's. I'll engage every attorney in Europe.

NAGELSCHMIDT: That'll take a fortune.

KOHLHAAS: I'll have it. I'll have a fortune. Send the magistrate, Mr. Mann, here ... Tell him I request him to be so kind as to come over in a matter of importance to him. We're leaving for Schwerin in half an hour. In a quarter of an hour!

NAGELSCHMIDT: *(Meeting Mr. Mann at the door.)* Mr. Mann! *(Exits.)*
MANN: I only came, dear neighbor, since I saw Mr. Nagelschmidt galloping home like crazy, and alone. Nothing happened this time ... please tell me anything, just not more trouble. Let's hope the wrath of God went elsewhere.
KOHLHAAS: The wrath of God moved into my house. Have a seat, Mr. Mann. I'd like to make an agreement with you within a few minutes. *(Places pen and inkwell before him.)* Write, compute: How much is my farmstead along the Havel worth to you?
MANN: I don't know ... this suddenly ... all of a sudden ...
KOHLHAAS: How much did you offer me last year?
MANN: Last year? If I remember correctly, fifty. But please, dear neighbor ... what happened?
KOHLHAAS: I'll tell you. How much will you pay for my house in Dresden?
MANN: I don't know. I have no idea. You have me totally confused.
KOHLHAAS: Is it worth a hundred to you?
MANN: I don't know its location, in what part of the city. And how large it is, and the condition ...
KOHLHAAS: Outskirts, six rooms, land, orchard. Write fifty if it's too much. Please write! Onward! Are you willing to buy twenty of my forty pair of horses? They're worth thirty gold florins a pair, take them at twenty, how much is that altogether?
MANN: I can't calculate this way! Please don't consider me a usurer. I wouldn't deprive you of a farthing that's rightly yours ...
KOHLHAAS: I know. Write: twenty pair of horses ... four hundred. My last offering: my house. My home. This house. Don't be surprised, Mr. Mann. How much will you give me for this house?
MANN: For God's sake, dear neighbor ... don't be angry, but you're not in your right mind ... you're pale and your hand is shaking ... Maria! Maria, a glass of water for Mr. Kohlhaas! Where do you wish to move? Do you mean to become a world-wanderer? At least tell me what happened! Did some great enterprise of yours collapse? Tell me, please, I'll help you out with a loan.

(Maria enters with a glass of water, places it on the table without uttering a word, then leaves as she came, weeping.)

KOHLHAAS: I cannot take on a loan. It's not certain I'll be able to pay it back. I'm bringing another suit.
MANN: Whom are you suing, and why?
KOHLHAAS: Whom? Wenzel von Tronka, the Bodyguard of Berlin, the Court of Dresden, Lords Hinz and Kunz, Saxony, Brandenburg, the whole Empire. And why? For any kind of meager satisfaction, Mr. Mann; for a drop of trust I can place in Saxony; for a spark of faith that will keep me from becoming an outlaw.

MANN: This is incomprehensible to me.

KOHLHAAS: I bought the house for four hundred, I'll give it for three, draft the contract afterward, I'll sign these blank pages.

MANN: Don't do such a thing. Anyone could cheat you. Don't place blank signed pages in people's hands. God Himself would not do such a thing, though He sees to the bottoms of our hearts. He subjected even Abraham, His loyal son, to a test. He asked for Isaac's blood as proof.

KOHLHAAS: The One Whose hands we're in can allow Himself to doubt. He can allow Himself the luxury of our not believing in Him. His power depends only on His power, not on our devotion. I have no power. I have the need not to doubt your honesty. What is the sum?

MANN: As an advance, a thousand in gold, in the bank of Dresden. We won't draw up the contract till you've calmed down, Mr. Kohlhaas.

KOHLHAAS: Thank you. I'll send a wagon from Schwerin for the furniture. I'll take the little pine from the garden. Lisbeth had me plant it when our son was born.

MARIA: *(Enters, alarmed.)* Sir ... the Toll-keeper from Tronka with two soldiers ...

KOHLHAAS: If I see them here I'll shoot them dead! *(Takes a firearm from the wall.)* I'll shoot the villains dead! *(Puts down the weapon.)*

(Knocking at the door to the street. Kohlhaas again seizes the weapon. Mann grabs his arm in desperation.)

MANN: Dear neighbor, my dear friend, calm yourself! You are not yourself. Where is your Christian patience?

KOHLHAAS: Is there still Christianity? Can there still be patience?

MANN: What happened to the gentle Michael Kohlhaas of old?

KOHLHAAS: What happened to him? You're asking this of me? *(Upon further knocking.)* Come in, you scoundrels! By now I'm also free to do my will.

MANN: You're not free. You have a family. You have honor.

KOHLHAAS: I had. If that's what it was. With one bullet I can still get it back. *(Müller steps in.)* Mr. Müller! Franz! What does Lisbeth say? What does the doctor say? Can we bring her right home? Not in a wagon on those bumpy roads. In a carriage! Quietly ... On the good road ... In a covered carriage it's not risky, is it?

MÜLLER: Lisbeth says ...

KOHLHAAS: Tell me!

MÜLLER: ... forgive those who have trespassed against you.

KOHLHAAS: That's all? Only this handcuff?

MÜLLER: These were her last words.

KOHLHAAS: Her last words?

MÜLLER: And her last wish was that I give this to you.

KOHLHAAS: *(Takes the locket.)* Lord God! When?

MÜLLER: She died at four in the morning. The doctor was unable to stop the internal bleeding.
KOHLHAAS: He wasn't able to ... He couldn't see it ... Or perhaps he wasn't even the doctor ... but the accomplice of the Bodyguard. But what am I saying ... *(To Nagelschmidt, who has just stepped in.)* Karl ... I killed my wife ... I shouldn't have let her go. She became the victim of my cowardice. A gentle lady ... with a prayerful petition. I threw her to the villains in an act of supplication.
MÜLLER: You know well, she insisted ...
KOHLHAAS: To spare me. And she believed that they'd be more kindly disposed toward her gentleness. That they'd take pity on the sacrificial lamb. The Lord God asked for Isaac's blood only as a test. He accepted Lisbeth's from me. He forgot about the angel who was to have held back my hand in time.
NAGELSCHMIDT: Don't take another's sin upon you, Michael.
KOHLHAAS: No saving angel turned up for me. Perhaps He was right. If God is compassionate, He cannot tolerate our sending petitioning women instead of armed men to pursue our justice, the mere semblance of which would have satisfied us ultimately.

(Maria enters with Herse. She presses the locket in Kohlhaas's hand to her face, then kisses it. She begins sobbing out loud.)

KOHLHAAS: We fell from grace with God, Maria. We no longer satisfy His intentions. *(From the garden, Henrik is heard singing, "Who is it that cometh out of the wilderness ...")* Who is it that cometh out of the wilderness, like pillars of smoke? Who?

(From outside, organ music marking the end of a religious service can be heard. Nagelschmidt suddenly steps to the window, then is about to seize the firearm on the table. Kohlhaas stops him.)

MARIA: *(Frightened.)* The bailiffs!
A VOICE: *(From without.)* Nagelschmidt!
KOHLHAAS: *(Takes the weapon, opens the window.)* I'll answer. *(Shoots. The bailiff cries out, Kohlhaas turns to Nagelschmidt.)* How many grooms do we have here?
NAGELSCHMIDT: Seven.
KOHLHAAS: Seven men, seven guns, seven horses. From the cemetery we head for Tronka.

CURTAIN

ACT THREE

Scene 1

Setting: Tronka Castle, several rooms of which can be seen. In the middle, the large dining hall; to the right, the outpost of the Castellan; to the left, the small domestic chapel. When the curtain rises, Sister Antonia is praying in the chapel, while the gentlemen are reveling in the large dining hall. Present are Baron Wenzel, Baron Günther, Hinz, Kunz, Kallheim, the Advocates Zauner and Eibenmeyer. In the small room to the right, the Castellan is playing cards with the Toll-keeper.

GÜNTHER: My friends! My lords, honorable Advocates, attention please.
WENZEL: *(At the head of the table.)* Speak, Günther!
SEVERAL: Speak, speak!
GÜNTHER: My friends, I must admit to you the secret of today's hunt, of every one of our hunts, the real incentive behind Baron Wenzel's zeal...
SEVERAL: But we know it. We know. It's an open secret. Not deer, not rabbit.
GÜNTHER: Not deer, not rabbit. But amazon. Did you see her?
SEVERAL: Who didn't see her? Who didn't admire her? Who wasn't delighted by her?
GÜNTHER: Of course we saw her. But which of you noticed our host? Did he once fire at fleeing game?
HINZ: As a matter of fact, we never heard a shot.
GÜNTHER: Because the only fire was in his heart. They settled down in the pleasant clearing, and ... what did they sing?
KUNZ: To part with her now I no longer can do... *(Laughter.)*
GÜNTHER: And why? Because: *(Sings.)*
   I came to know her, O rapturous hour...

ALL: My body and spirit both danced with delight.
Now I languish in love, the slave of her power.
With my heart so ensnared I cannot take flight.
To part with her now I no longer can do ...
KUNZ: To part with her now I no longer can do ...
WENZEL: Lord Kunz knows only this one line. *(They laugh.)*
KUNZ: The result of an acquaintance. The most important one.
GÜNTHER: But how much nicer this little get-together would be, my friends, if a little of that result could be enjoyed by each of us. Wenzel, where are the wenches from last time?
HINZ: *(Enthusiastically.)* The girls!
WENZEL: *(Sings.)* Where can the women be?
ALL: Where can the women be,
That I so long to see?
Whether morning, noon or night
Their kiss is pure delight.
KUNZ: Their kiss is pure delight!
WENZEL: Lord Kunz is once again concentrating on the essence!
KUNZ: With great anticipation.

(They laugh, toast each other with their goblets, drink.)

CASTELLAN: *(Throws down his cards, gets up, takes his coat.)* Our game just went to the devil. I can go gather in the womenfolk.
TOLL-KEEPER: What if they forget this time ...
CASTELLAN: As if you didn't know them. When they start in with where can the women be, I can start racking my brains which ones to get from where in the fields. But that's nothing yet. The man whistles, they come. As far as the wagon. But when it comes to getting on it, such screeching, like piglets, one or another gets stubborn, won't even budge without the whip, then calls for her father. Then comes the father, or the brother, foaming with rage, he has to be thrown in the slammer, and the work suffers. That song costs us a lot.
WENZEL: Castellan!
CASTELLAN: *(Enters.)* Yes, sir.
WENZEL: Where can the women be, that I so long to see?
CASTELLAN: How many do you wish, your Lordship?
WENZEL: Let's count ... Günther, Hinz, Kunz, Kallheim, Eibenmeyer ...
CASTELLAN: Please count so that some will be left in the fields.
WENZEL: That's how I'm counting.
CASTELLAN: We'll be left without grain. Allow me to point out that this song could deprive us of all our grain.
WENZEL: Worrying again?
CASTELLAN: Will three be enough?

WENZEL: A cartful!
CASTELLAN: Urgently, or after bathing?
WENZEL: The way they are. With mother earth on them.

(Castellan leaves.)

CASTELLAN: *(In the small room to the Toll-keeper.)* You stay here in case they think of something else. *(Starts down the long staircase. Toll-keeper opens the window, then prepares for sleep.)*
GÜNTHER: But till then, isn't there a female appetizer in the whole residence?
KUNZ: Where can the women be? Their kiss is pure delight.
WENZEL: We could honor Sister Antonia with a spot of wine ...

(Sister Antonia, who has been annoyed already by the revelry, now begins to listen at the door while praying.)

HINZ: Whether morning, noon or night, sister's kiss is pure delight.

(They laugh.)

KUNZ: *(Sings.)* The priest, enraptured by her charms,
　　　　Entwined the prioress in his arms.
　　　　That was in May, hip-hip hooray!
WENZEL: *(As a reminder.)* She's Jesus's bride.
GÜNTHER: Jesus is far away. We're closer. *(Laughter.)*
WENZEL: Sister Antonia!
ANTONIA: *(Enters, frightened.)* I was praying just now ...
WENZEL: Just a drop ... a spot ... beauteous bride of Jesus.

(He strokes her, at which the others throw themselves on her, tear at her clothing. Kissing her neck and shoulders, opening her mouth by force, they pour in wine, pull her about from arm to arm. Voices: Jesus's bride! Her dewy body! Her chastity! Her purity! The priest enraptured by her charms, entwined the prioress in his arms!)

ANTONIA: Let me go! Help! Jesus, help!
WENZEL: Where is Jesus? Far away!
ANTONIA: Help! Jesus, help! Doctor Luther! Doctor Luther! Help! Beasts! You'll all end up in hell.

(Voices: Hell must be sweet with Sister Antonia! We'll all go to hell! With her and through her!)

WENZEL: *(Seeing the sister seize a knife.)* The knife! Take the knife away from her!

ANTONIA: May God forgive you! *(Stabs herself in the heart.)*
WENZEL: *(After they cover the corpse in stunned silence.)* I forgot about Doctor Luther. He's supposed to enroll us all in the reformed faith tomorrow.
KALLHEIM: They'll find out up at the Court.
EIBENMEYER: You'll pledge a few of your papist relatives to the Reformation.
ZAUNER: Even the Elector will hear about it right away through people whose ears are continuously on duty.
EIBENMEYER: Then you can immediately begin increasing the number of relatives to be pledged. We'll bury her in the garden.
GÜNTHER: Advocate Zauner, let's hope your ears aren't on duty.
ZAUNER: I hope Advocate Eibenmeyer's aren't either.
EIBENMEYER: Only God can tell which ears are on duty here. Perhaps precisely those of the one who accuses another of having eager ears. Or just the one *to whom* he makes the accusation. Or both. Or neither, but an absent third party. Perhaps your best, or supposedly best, friend, your drinking buddy. Or not even him, only his ears, which, estranged from their owner, work — that is, listen — independently, without his consent. I'll give you an example. How did our friend, Advocate Franz Müller, who, of course, isn't present, outdo all of us and recently become Imperial Attorney? We can't know yet, but could it be that he climbed to prominence on our backs?

(A spear flies in and lodges in a beam. Wenzel takes a note from it.)

WENZEL: Attention, dutiful ears! We don't have to intimidate each other. Here's something that's supposed to intimidate us all. *(Reads.)* "To Baron von Tronka and his friends. Listen here, you degenerate plundering son of a bitch! I demand that in twenty-four hours you return my two confiscated horses, the fifty farthings stolen from my pocket, my servant Herse Hutten's expropriated coat, hat, satchel and its contents, to wit: one clay pipe, twelve farthings, flintstone, tinder, and pipetool. Otherwise I will burn your castle down to the ground, and, in a manner befitting you, I will chop you and yours up, together with your friend Günther, and feed you to the pigs." Dated Schwerin, anno Domini, so on, signed: the Archangel Michael Kohlhaas.

(Stunned silence. The sound of steps from somewhere.)

KUNZ: *(Alarmed.)* The girls are coming.

(Günther is seized by hysterical laughter. They all start laughing by degrees. During this time, Nagelschmidt and Herse jump in the window of the small room. They grab the sleeping Toll-keeper.)

HERSE: Beat him up?

NAGELSCHMIDT: *(Signals that they will throw him out the window.)* He's about to dream that he's flying. If, in the course of his flight, he grows wings, he'll survive.

(They throw him out. After a short time, a scream is heard.)

HERSE: No wings.

(The sound of steps. The lords laugh. Two armed grooms come up the stairs.)

WENZEL: The pipetool too! *(They laugh.)*
GÜNTHER: The tinder too!
HINZ: The flint! *(They are drowning in laughter.)*

(Kohlhaas appears at the back door. The lords become petrified. Only Wenzel continues laughing, since he does not see Kohlhaas. Nagelschmidt, Herse, and the two grooms step in from the small room. Another three grooms appear behind Kohlhaas.)

KOHLHAAS: *(Comes forward, Wenzel draws his sword, Kohlhaas knocks it out of his hand with a single gesture.)* I don't need your life, sir. But I insist on the pipetool, and on my horses... fattened.
WENZEL: The knacker took the horses.
KOHLHAAS: The knacker took the horses? That's too bad, Baron. You'll follow them on Saint Michael's horse.
NAGELSCHMIDT: To the joy of the knackers, we'll have to make dog food out of you. The only thing is, I don't know according to what recipe: mixed with gruel or with bran?
KOHLHAAS: Forgive him if his language is a bit rough.
WENZEL: Your proclamation is no different.
KOHLHAAS: He helped me draft it. Unfortunately I'll have him make public the news of your death, also. Don't count on a polished style, Baron.
WENZEL: *(In desperation.)* Castellan!
KOHLHAAS: Don't count on the guards either. They're sleeping — over in the other kingdom. The Castellan also.
WENZEL: Don't forget, Mr. Horse Dealer, that all the landowners of this area made a pact of mutual assistance. We have armed troops...
KOHLHAAS: You had.
HINZ: I have fifty troops in Lützen...
KOHLHAAS: Dispersed.
NAGELSCHMIDT: Together with your castle, my lord.
KUNZ: And Pleissenburg?
KOHLHAAS: Burnt to the ground.
KALLHEIM: My bailiff in Wittenberg will somehow get wind of this.

KOHLHAAS: We spared Wittenberg. The only thing that disappeared, Advocate Kallheim, was your castle.
EIBENMEYER: And Leipzig?
KOHLHAAS: In Leipzig Advocate Eibenmeyer's house appeared to be superfluous.
EIBENMEYER: And my family? The inhabitants of my house?
KOHLHAAS: The way it happens at such times. Some were lucky, others not. Mr. Zauner may be at ease. We didn't harm Dresden. Any more inquiries?
GÜNTHER: We do not engage ordinary serf-rebels, highwaymen, child murderers in conversation. In Jassen I have an armory and mercenary troops.
KOHLHAAS: In my service. I pay more, dear sir. I converted everything I owned to cash, since Lord Wenzel bereaved me of everything. Of my peaceful intentions and the mother of my child.
GÜNTHER: My father will find out.
NAGELSCHMIDT: Only in heaven. That is if he got in.
GÜNTHER: You murdered him too! Dogs!

(Günther dashes at Kohlhaas, who is attacked from behind by Wenzel. A brawl breaks out. The lords run in all directions, the grooms in pursuit. Nagelschmidt stabs Günther, then casts himself on Zauner.)

KOHLHAAS: Don't hurt Zauner.
ZAUNER: Thank you, Mr. Kohlhaas. I'll reciprocate. *(Exits.)*
KOHLHAAS: *(Seizing Wenzel by the chest.)* Bring rope, Karl!
NAGELSCHMIDT: Iron would be more fitting. *(Running out.)* Herse! Some rope for the Baron!
WENZEL: We'll divide it between us. One end will go around your neck.
KOHLHAAS: You flatter yourself. We hang dogs only with other dogs. But first I'll have you tied to a wagon and paraded before the people; before the advocates; before the law courts; before the powers that dispense justice; first I'll exhibit you to the law in the name of the law ... *(Releases Wenzel, who backs toward the chapel entrance, tries to open it, but the door is locked.)*
WENZEL: Which will strike you down.
KOHLHAAS: You're mistaken, you vermin! By now I'm outside the law. Outside everything I ever held obligatory, of divine origin. Outside my death, also. I live where my wife does: in Nothingness, in the graveyard.
WENZEL: The rebels, church-plunderers, and the Hussites were dragged to the stake even from the grave. Don't count on a single fortunate hour, Kohlhaas. You don't have an army the size of the Prince of Meissen's or the Elector's.
KOHLHAAS: They did not suffer a loss and bereavement as great as mine, which trampled me, but also armed me. Loss can be a weapon, in case you didn't know ... But how would you know? Nothing was ever taken from you. And when you robbed, other hands did it for you. My horses were snatched from me by bailiffs ... My lawful rights were denied me with lies, my patience was worn away in the name of God ...

WENZEL: I'll give you twelve horses in place of your two ...
KOHLHAAS: You're offering me a deal? It was while bargaining that I lost everything. While honoring the laws. While praising the authorities. While humbly pleading and hoping. Now I am taking the law into my own hands, the law which should have protected my rights. *(Throws a flaming torch out the window.)*
WENZEL: The rights of an incendiary?
KOHLHAAS: *(Throwing out another torch.)* Protected my home, my wife. *(After the third torch.)* My love of peace.
WENZEL: Which, as we see, was a lie.
KOHLHAAS: Because I built on sand. On the lies of the Office. On my gullibility! *(Smoke rises from the castle yard.)* Isn't it nice, this smoke? The smoke of my entreaties. Of my expectations. Of the petition that they knocked out of Lisbeth's hands with lances. Lisbeth! Who will forgive me for pushing her into the lances of the Bodyguard?! And what could I do with that forgiveness? What, von Tronka? On your knees, scoundrel! Say your last prayer!
WENZEL: Have mercy, Kohlhaas! You too are in God's hands.
KOHLHAAS: No longer. Now I *am* His hand.

(The women who fled to the chapel sing.)

> Pity me, O Lord,
> A sinner full of woe.
> Lift up my poor heart,
> Which has sunk O so low.

NAGELSCHMIDT: *(Rushes in, rope in hands.)* The barns are burning.
KOHLHAAS: Let them!
NAGELSCHMIDT: Shall I tie him up?
KOHLHAAS: Unnecessary. I condemned him to death.
WENZEL: Have mercy on me! Jesus is nearby! Jesus on the cross. Here near you ...
NAGELSCHMIDT: Contemptible hypocrite!
KOHLHAAS: His cross is a soft cushion compared to the one on which I was hung by you, murderer of my Lisbeth!
NAGELSCHMIDT: First let's roast him a little.
KOHLHAAS: It only pains me to see him alive. He should die as soon as possible!
NAGELSCHMIDT: Out of here with the moneychangers!

(At this moment Martin Luther steps in.)

LUTHER: Michael Kohlhaas! Kohlhaas! How low have you sunk? How dare you break in here with weapons? Blind man, open your eyes: before Whom do you stand?
KOHLHAAS: Before the person more dear to my heart than anyone: Doctor Luther.

LUTHER: Look upon the wounds of the Nazarene, not me, you ruinously straying wretch! How could you have proclaimed yourself an emissary of celestial wrath? Who handed you the sword of justice, that in a frenzy of blind passion you should pass judgment on Christians according to your own mind in the drunkenness of vengeance? How can you seek justice on your own when you are infected with injustice down to the marrow of your bones?
KOHLHAAS: With sorrow, your Reverence.
LUTHER: There is solace for human sorrow, damnation for injustice.
KOHLHAAS: It was me the injustice struck.
LUTHER: You? It struck through you. You attacked peaceful communities day and night, like the wolves of the wilderness. You drove your sword through innocents entrusted to the protection of God, on the excuse of a lawsuit started over a useless trifle. Don't you, Michael Kohlhaas, belong under the Governor and the Elector? Who deprived you of your right to attain lawful satisfaction through the higher authorities?
KOHLHAAS: I tried, your Reverence ...
LUTHER: Irresolutely and impatiently, distrustfully from the beginning, disrespectfully confusing clerks with governors, identifying the existing order with the court orderlies who suppressed your complaint. Are you still so nearsighted that you cannot see before you the Calvary you set out upon in this world and in the next? This way there will never be an end to your case. In heaven, how will you be able to accuse the earthly authority that to this day has no idea of your trifling complaint? That higher authority could say before the throne of God: my Lord, I never even saw, much less hurt this man whose hands are dripping with blood. And this would be true. Instead of being high-handed, why weren't you more humble and diligent in your pursuit? And the army of serfs following your lead — these new rebels after so much bloodshed — what has this to do with your case, your horses, your servant's satchel? Are you aware that in the region of Pleissenburg and Lützen they're spreading word of Münzer's resurrection, they're saying that you are the one who proclaimed the new uprising? Ah, my dear lords, how prettily the Lord will go smashing among the clay pots with His rod of iron. Münzer said these words, and now, lo, they are attributed to you.
KOHLHAAS: I never said these words, sir.
LUTHER: Your deeds foretold them. Your skirmishes, your incendiarism, your proclamations nailed to the walls of castles. Your entire hopeless venture. Michael Kohlhaas, most fervent of my followers, how could you have turned your back so thoroughly on God?
KOHLHAAS: Hopelessness has buttressed my faith, your Reverence.
LUTHER: What an expression! Hopelessness! Your hopelessness deserves a pyre. You use this pagan word now that our liberated faith is being consolidated once and for all?
KOHLHAAS: Everything is falling together. Only my life has fallen to pieces.

LUTHER: Because you are selfish; in your sorrow you became blind, and an enemy of our reformed faith. If you don't happen to know, Rome is preparing a new assault; the cause of all of us is in the balance, not just your horse and satchel. We need unity, not divisiveness.

KOHLHAAS: That is the way it should be.

NAGELSCHMIDT: Your Reverence! Did not you yourself call the Emperor a tyrant and the Prince of Saxony the pig of Dresden? That in piling one toll on top of another, one tax on top of another, they behave in a way that would be excessive even for robbers and crooks – did not you yourself say this before the great uprising?

LUTHER: All things have their time. Whoever does not understand that each hour has its own requirement, and that a hitherto unimportant thing can take on importance, should not have the impudence to cut into my words. The Reformation is our common duty, Rome our common enemy. In Paris and Venice they dragged our brethren in the faith to the stake! The papists do not distinguish between lords and serfs. The hell of counter-reformation is threatening our entire nation, while you, thinking on the level of four-legged creatures, are here at home killing believers who have returned to the pure gospel.

KOHLHAAS: My wife, my wedded companion, also returned. Do you know what happened to her?

LUTHER: I know. I personally asked the sovereign for the punishment of the guilty. I wept over Lisbeth's death, Michael Kohlhaas. But our tears must not wash away the cause on which our lives and our salvations rest. Promise me, my brother in faith, Michael my son, that you will put down the sword, which is the weapon of robbery and bloodlust. You will put it down now, and Baron Wenzel will also put aside his wrath. The Lord speaks to you with the last wish of your wife: forgive those who trespassed against you ...

(Wenzel steps beside Kohlhaas upon Luther's gesture.)

KOHLHAAS: I cannot do it, your Reverence. Not even at the cost of my salvation.

(Trumpets sound at the four corners of the castle.)

LUTHER: The combined forces of the Prince of Meissen and the Elector. It was not I who brought them upon you, though I should have done just that. Won't you give him your hand, Kohlhaas?

KOHLHAAS: Many years ago, they summoned before the Imperial Diet of Worms a man, a young man with an inflamed soul, who turned the world upside down with his courage. They summoned him before strict and hostile judges, so he would take back his doctrines before the Emperor. His life, or his death at the stake, depended on a single nod, nevertheless he said: I neither can nor will retract anything; for it cannot be right nor courageous to do anything against the conscience. Far be it from me to compare myself to that man, before whom I now stand, to whom I opened my heart from the start: Doctor Martin Luther. I have no doctrines; I gave the people nothing — small, large, valuable — that anyone could ask me now to take back. But as insignificant as my person is, so enormous and irreplaceable is my loss. You may be right that all this is but a speck of dust on your colossal truth. But who can help the fact that we received life, the only one, as specks of dust? Who ordered things in such a way that without the justice of specks of dust, universal justice and truth become meaningless? Universal justice and truth, which we should not have to seek, as children do rainbows, but which ought to be wherever they are proclaimed. Justice proclaimed and not carried out, the Constitutions of Dresden and Brandenburg, sir, are more foul than open lies, because they are like bait; a dog will run from me or show its teeth if I hurl a pitchfork at it, but it will perish from a poisoned piece of bread, licking the hand of its murderer. Gullibility and petitionary hope put an end to Lisbeth's life. It is possible that the child waiting for me in Schwerin, after losing his mother, will now lose his father as well. I can leave him nothing except an orphanhood that will raise him from hope on its knees to hope standing upright. That young man, the onetime Doctor Martin Luther at the Imperial Diet of Worms himself stood upright and said: Here I stand, I cannot do otherwise, so help me God, Amen.

LUTHER: *(More gently.)* The erstwhile Martin Luther is prepared even today to die for the truth of the Son of Man. However, the command of life is not death, but the avoidance of it, not suicidal hopelessness, but wise actions. A prudent man foreseeth the evil, and hideth himself, but the simple pass on and are punished. For to him that is joined to all the living there is hope, for a living dog is better than a dead lion. Our awareness of death is punishment enough. Courage is necessary to serve out that sentence, for the dead know not anything, neither have they any more a reward.

KOHLHAAS: For me, this has already come to pass.

LUTHER: You will be led back to life by the one whose good intentions you doubted with weapon in hand. Read this, Baron. *(Hands a paper scroll to Wenzel.)*

WENZEL: "We, the Elector of Saxony, having considered the intercession that Doctor Martin Luther made before Us on his behalf, have personally examined the complaint of Michael Kohlhaas, horse dealer, and found it to be completely just. Consequently, We order the reopening of his case and the punishment of all those who have violated peaceful trade and the laws of Our realm. To facilitate the administration of justice, We grant Michael Kohlhaas safe-conduct to Dresden, and We grant amnesty to all his troops, on condition that he lay down all arms within three days of receipt of this decree, furthermore, that all booty be surrendered to the Court at Lützen as Electoral

property." Date as above ... And my grievance? What about that, your Reverence?
LUTHER: Ask, and it shall be given you ... Knock, and it shall be opened unto you. Kohlhaas, put down the weapon! *(Kohlhaas plunges his sword into the beam.)*
NAGELSCHMIDT: *(Shouting.)* Michael! You deceived me! You betrayed me!
LUTHER: Ask, and it shall be given you ... Knock, and it shall be opened unto you. *(Exits.)*

(The scene becomes dark, the din dies away.)

Scene 2

The main square of Dresden. Jubilant crowd, judicial table. In the background, a platform veiled with a white cloth. Kohlhaas, Nagelschmidt, Herse, and a few grooms proceed in. Voices: Long live Kohlhaas! Justice for Kohlhaas! Punishment for von Tronka! To the fire with him! Kohlhaas and his companions take seats on the bench before the platform. Wenzel enters amid the crowd's jeers, Nagelschmidt offers him his seat, but he refuses it and remains standing. The members of the court proceed onto the platform: Zauner, Eibenmeyer, Müller, Kallheim, Hinz, and Kunz sit on the side.

EIBENMEYER: Brethren! Quiet and order, please! It was to set an example, not for rowdiness, that the Elector ordered a public pronouncement of judgment here on the main square of Dresden. Our armed guards will arrest the troublemakers on the spot. The honorable Baron Wenzel von Tronka, present?
WENZEL: Present.
EIBENMEYER: Michael Kohlhaas, horse dealer. *(Kohlhaas rises.)* Yes. Please remain standing. We must hear the judgment of the Elector and the Emperor. Advocate Zauner ...
ZAUNER: Lo, Michael Kohlhaas, the day has come on which your justice will be delivered. After assuring you of safe-conduct from Tronka, We took under close scrutiny the purposes which had taken you there. We determined that you were led neither by the intent to rob, nor by a serf's impulse to stir up our peaceful social order, but exclusively by the desire to reclaim your own petty possessions, the crumbs of your justice. He who clings to his proclaimed justice honors his sovereign, the Higher Power ordained of God. He who squanders its crumbs becomes deprived of his bread. For this reason, on this day We order: your two black horses, in the condition you rightfully demand, and with bells, be returned to you. Similarly, your illegally exacted fifty farthings, and your servant Herse Hutten's coat, hat, satchel and the personal items therein, to wit: clay pipe, flintstone, tinder, twelve farthings, and one bone-handled pipetool. Written in Brandenburg, Elector Frederick ... Who,

as another sign of his graciousness would have wanted to convey the decision in person. The Elector asks your indulgence, Michael Kohlhaas, but he must be host this day to our Emperor. The Emperor also asks you to excuse him, for due to a special engagement, he is forced to convey his decision on the petition of your wife, Lisbeth Kohlhaas, through the Imperial Attorney, Franz Müller. Mr. Müller...

MÜLLER: Charles the Fifth, Holy Roman Emperor through the grace of God, King of Germany, Spain, the two Sicilies, Jerusalem, Hungary, Dalmatia, Croatia, etc., Archduke of Austria, Count of Habsburg, Flanders, and Tyrol, signs by his own hand the following additional ruling in the litigation elucidated by the just hand of the Elector of Brandenburg: The rod and reproof give wisdom, but a child left to himself bringeth his mother to shame. Since Lords Hinz, Kunz, and Kallheim defiled the impartiality of the Chancellery of Brandenburg, this day they are dismissed from their offices. *(The crowd cheers.)* And since any violation of law is an affront to the Person of the Highest Lawmaker, the Baron Wenzel von Tronka is sentenced to two years' imprisonment for his transgressions.

(Stunned silence. At this moment trumpets sound, then cannon fire is heard. In a corner of the square that cannot be seen, the sound of Kohlhaas's horses' bells becomes intermingled with the noise. A court orderly hands Kohlhaas Herse's coat, hat, and satchel. The crowd quickly breaks up. Cries of: "The Emperor is here!", "Let's go see the Emperor!", "Long live the Emperor!" Only a few armed guards remain with Kohlhaas in strict formation. Kohlhaas recovers gradually from the weight of his unexpected victory. He stares after the crowd rushing toward the sound of the cannon fire.)

KOHLHAAS: Good people! You leave me now? Is no one curious anymore about the arrogant lord of Tronka? People! Long live the Emperor! He brought my Palm Sunday... Long live the Emperor! *(To Nagelschmidt as if in final reply to all their arguments.)* Long live the Emperor! *(Nagelschmidt remains motionless.)* Even if late, he brought me my Palm Sunday. Do you hear, Karl? Wenzel von Tronka is sentenced to two years' imprisonment! *(Deliriously tastes the word.)* Sentenced... Sentenced... Lisbeth sends this spark of comfort from the grave: Sentenced! *(Triumphantly.)* Repeat, Müller, my dear friend, let your tongue, like an empty mill, turn the word over: sentenced.

MÜLLER: *(Shaken and perspiring.)* Sentenced.

KOHLHAAS: Oh, if only Lisbeth could hear it, Karl! *(Embraces Nagelschmidt.)*

NAGELSCHMIDT: She hears it, surely.

KOHLHAAS: She was going to bring me... us... this message. How can man and satisfaction be torn so far apart? Thank you, Karl, for standing beside me... We've won back our refuge with this single torch of a word: sentenced!

NAGELSCHMIDT: It's not enough.

MÜLLER: The Emperor's text is not over, Michael. No matter how short life is,

and no matter how long and agonizing the path of justice, no one has the right to seek it on one's own authority on side roads.
KOHLHAAS: Like the swine of Tronka!
MÜLLER: For justice turns away from the one who approaches it in an unjust way; for rights can only be gained rightfully, salvation only through humility. You regained everything that is your due, Michael Kohlhaas, but do not forget that as man pursues justice, he runs into debt.
KOHLHAAS: I sacrificed everything I owned.
MÜLLER: It is your turn now to pay.
NAGELSCHMIDT: His? You mean that of the Antichrist of Tronka! All of Kohlhaas's losses should be made good!
MÜLLER: *(Becoming gradually sterner, freeing himself from the painful bonds of friendship.)* It is your turn now to pay.

(Kohlhaas watches Müller with increasing trepidation.)

NAGELSCHMIDT: We do not pay. We demand!
EIBENMEYER: The Emperor's teaching is a true teaching.
NAGELSCHMIDT: The Emperor's teaching is a false teaching!
MÜLLER: *(Reads.)* You set fire to castles, you extinguished human life, you walked the path of lawlessness in pursuit of your rights ...
NAGELSCHMIDT: What else could he have done? How are we to approach crucified justice, when the knaves of Pilate guard it — against us? How can rights be freed from their sealed grave without the defeat of the Pharisees? Mr. Attorney, did our highest justice, to Whom we build churches, approach Caiaphas or the Judases with humble appeals? Did God not free His only begotten Son with earthquake and splintering rocks to raise Him up? Does the Emperor point us to one path? Is the unwalkable path the only one?
EIBENMEYER: Nagelschmidt confuses himself and his incendiary friend with the Law and ...
NAGELSCHMIDT: Man begins when he confuses himself with all that has been taken from him!
EIBENMEYER: Guard!

(Two soldiers silence Nagelschmidt.)

MÜLLER: Michael Kohlhaas, resident of Kohlhaasenbrück, born on June 17, 1502 in Schwerin, is sentenced to death by hanging on this day. Date as above, with the Emperor's personal signature.
NAGELSCHMIDT: Lord God! They tricked him! They deceived him! You rogues, you tricked him, you ensnared him, you lured him into a trap. Why did we listen to you? Oh, how foolish I was, outdone only by Michael Kohlhaas! I should have known ... each one of their words reeks of hyena, and with every

one of their favors, every one of their shrewd concessions, they veil their final purpose. Mr. Müller, you lent your tongue to this heinous judgment ... tear out your tongue! You lent it your voice — cut your throat!
MÜLLER: The voice was mine ... the verdict the Emperor's, Michael. Forgive me.
KOHLHAAS: Is that your last request? *(Laughs hysterically.)* The last request of the deliverers of judgment, that we forgive them. *(His laughter is interrupted by the triumphant jeering laughter of Wenzel, whom the lords are accompanying outward. Kohlhaas looks toward him.)* I'll meet with you again! *(To Müller.)* But never again will I meet with you. We have no more accounts to settle ...
MÜLLER: You know well ... I did all I could. It was the unfortunate constraint of circumstance that ...
KOHLHAAS: May power lie lightly upon you. Rest in peace.

(Müller exits. Only those involved in hanging remain on the scene. Armed guards, hangman, the supervisor in charge of the execution, etc. As they set the gallows in place, Nagelschmidt in desperation observes Kohlhaas with a burnt-out stare.)

KOHLHAAS: You'll raise Henrik, won't you? *(Hangs the locket around Nagelschmidt's neck.)* The argument between the two of us is over. The executioner is putting the period on it. Move the little pine tree from the corner of our garden to Schwerin. I planted it on Lisbeth's request when our child was born. Be careful not to harm the roots. Water it so it will gain new strength. How gentle your face is now, Karl. I never saw you this gentle. As if you'd used Jesus's towel. The one on which His features remained. We could have used His patience — toward each other in the common peril. *(Nagelschmidt wipes his tears.)* Don't let Henrik see your tears. Do you think that little pine will take root in Schwerin? Tie the bells back around the necks of the two blacks. Which road are you taking?
NAGELSCHMIDT: The one that leads to Thomas Münzer!
KOHLHAAS: That's good. That's the shortest. The way home.

(The hangman steps before Kohlhaas. Drum roll, then silence. From the distance, the bells of the two black horses can be heard. The sound of voices honoring the Emperor. The scene goes black gradually.)

NAGELSCHMIDT'S VOICE:
Trouble once came on horse's back
Galloping on a gleaming black
To Kohlhaasenbrück
Where a horse dealer
Named Michael Kohlhaas took the attack.

CURTAIN

Sojourn

or

UNUS EST DEUS?

Géza Páskándi

translated by Gabriel John Brogyányi

Béla Ilovszky (MTI)

SOJOURN
[József Katona Theatre, Kecskemét, Hungary]
Directed by Sándor Beke

CHARACTERS:

FRANCIS DÁVID, first Unitarian bishop in Transylvania and the world
MARY, his servant
SOCINO, migrant theologian, his guest
GEORGE BLANDRATA, court physician to the prince of Transylvania
LUKE TRAUZNER, the bishop's son-in-law
CAPTAIN
also soldiers

(Takes place in 1578, in the house of Francis Dávid, in Kolozsvár, Transylvania.)

In 1578, Christopher Báthory, sovereign of the principality of Transylvania, at the suggestion of George Blandrata, invited the Italian Unitarian Fausto Socini to his realm. The guest was quartered in the house of Francis Dávid, with the evident purpose of having the bishop observed. The name Socino used in this play derives from the merging of Fausto Socini. Mary is an invented character. The author observed historical accuracy only regarding the most essential facts. He wished above all to commemorate the humanist and illustrious confessor, Francis Dávid.

ACT ONE

Scene 1

Ringing of a bell. Then curtain rises. Ringing continues, then fades. A staircase and long entrance-hallway to Francis Dávid's house. Candles burning. No one on stage. Sounds of a coach from without, the sound of a key in a lock, a creaking door. Approaching footsteps. Blandrata and Socino come slowly down the hallway. The physician points about. His manner is quiet and professional throughout.

BLANDRATA: Well, here we are at the bishop's house. Here is the side entrance to the rear wing. *(Puts away his key.)*
SOCINO: I seem to have become very important to the sovereign. Why, Doctor Blandrata? *(Puts down traveling bag.)*
BLANDRATA: Your memory is failing you, Socino, and you'll be needing it soon.
SOCINO: You're speaking as if the lot of you were doing me a *favor*.
BLANDRATA: *(Almost amiable.)* The *favor* is mutual. You're our guest.
SOCINO: This is a costly sojourn, my dear compatriot. I don't want to bring shame on our beloved Italy. *(Looks around.)*
BLANDRATA: *(Without smiling.)* Dear *camerata*, you'll be able to stomach what we are asking you to do.
SOCINO: So you think I have a strong stomach — true, you've got a sturdy one too, dear Doctor. You must have cut up a lot of cadavers at the sovereign's court. Blood doesn't bother you — right? But my one God ...
BLANDRATA: *(Interrupts.)* Let's stop dueling. Theological arguments have left a bitter taste in my mouth. Whether God is one or three has nothing to do with the practical matter at hand. Do you know your assignment?
SOCINO: I can guess. But I want to carry out my assignment out of faith. The only

assignment I accept is the one I carry in me. For that I could even kill. But only out of faith.

BLANDRATA: What you must have faith in above all is that the age of innovation is over. We cannot afford to provoke the wrath of the other Churches any more. We have to preserve the Unitarian Church we have become. The age of consolidation is at hand. There's a new prince — after John Sigmund, who was on our side, we now have the Catholic Báthory. At times like these we always have to sacrifice someone. Or more than one. Several men, or merely one man. Even if the victim is a genius, because the lambent flame of genius is apt to snuff out the patient labor of lesser men — the only kind that is secure and lasting. The fire of genius illuminates only itself. Like backlight, it comes from behind, and you can't see what's immediately in front of it, like your face when you hold a candle at the nape of your neck. That is why we have to sacrifice him to the light that shines in our faces. *(Demonstrates with a candle he has seized.)*

SOCINO: Do you have private audiences with God, and does he tell you whom we have to kill? Who elected you to pick out a victim?

BLANDRATA: I'm God's servant, not his elect. But a servant also gives commands to those below him. Do you accept?

SOCINO: I don't in fact know yet what I am supposed to be accepting.

BLANDRATA: You observe the bishop and report what you see and hear. You don't move from his side day or night. The servant girl will carry your reports, or I will come for them myself. Be careful, the bishop is smart! It won't be easy to prove that he is the enemy of our faith and that he has to perish.

SOCINO: So I should kill the smarter one! If we rid the Church of everyone who is smarter than we are, who will remain? Do you want a Church of idiots? If we have all the brave ones beheaded, shall we install cowards as priests and milksops as the congregation? If we exterminate the learned, shall we have a Church of ignoramuses? If we destroy honor, shall we enthrone moral filthiness in our pulpits?

(Brief pause.)

BLANDRATA: I leave it to you. If *you* believe you have something to report, if *you* feel he is guilty of heresy and innovation, that he wants to bring division to the Church, then report it. Only then. If you yourself think so.

SOCINO: And if I don't?

BLANDRATA: Then you will have enjoyed the *free* hospitality of the prince. *(Changes tone.)* But I beg you, always think of the Church's future ... Must division split up what has finally become one? If you think not, then report! Report!

SOCINO: To betray? To denounce? Out of faith — out of faith alone, Doctor!

BLANDRATA: *(Stares at him, speaks almost harshly.)* Well then, act on your faith! You're a guest in this faith also — and don't you ever forget it. *(Exits.)*

(Small pause.)

SOCINO: *(In Blandrata's direction.)* Little doctors dabbling in politics! *(To himself.)* They bring me here to argue with a man—actually to spy on him, on his thoughts. And I have no home, no bed, no wife, no bread ... *(Brief pause.)* Even betrayal would be easy—if I could do it freely.

(Blackout.)

Scene 2

Francis Dávid's workroom and bedroom in one. Bed covered with woolen blanket. Bearskin on floor. Books. Interior stair, at the top a sleeping-nook. The bishop on his bed, turned toward the wall. Loud knocking. Mary quickly comes down steps, opens door. Enter Luke, a sanguine man.

LUKE: Is he in?
MARY: *(Looks at him suspiciously, then lets him in. Shrugs at the bed.)* Where else would he be? Bishop, wake up, your son-in-law is here.
FRANCIS DÁVID: *(Turns, sits up.)* So it's you, Luke? *(He is not pompous and does not act old.)*
LUKE: He has arrived. He's unpacking now, in the other wing. Blandrata brought him. The doctor has his own key, does he?
FRANCIS DÁVID: Could be.
LUKE: He brought him here to eat and sleep in your house, so he can uncover all your secrets.
FRANCIS DÁVID: Only God has secrets, and I'm not God. *(To Mary.)* You hear, Mary, we have a guest. Prepare a good supper.
MARY: I'll do the best I can. *(Exits.)*

(Brief silence.)

LUKE: I don't understand your patience of Job, Francis! The sovereign invites a vagabond Unitarian to come here, whom not a single country in Europe would let in—even kings are afraid of him. They distrust him—whoever's ass he's kissing one day, he'd have impaled through the same orifice the next. Today he flatters you because you're in a position of power; tomorrow—if he's on top—he wouldn't spit in your direction. So this vagabond theologian who lives on his brother's reputation is invited by the sovereign to watch you ... This is the greatest possible affront to you. If at least they had sent someone more worthy of you, another Michael Servetus. Servetus at least had the satisfaction of being destroyed by a man of Calvin's stature. Why don't they send a worthy murderer to you? Don't you merit at least that much courtesy? You too had worthy enemies: That Peter Melius may have had a big, dirty mouth, but at least he went straight for your jugular, and never denied he was out for blood. He never would have struck you from behind, even though he was a Calvinist. But this Blandrata and this Socino, for all their Unitarianism, would gladly deliver you to the Catholic Prince Báthory, that Jesuit mercenary, just so they can be the lords of the Unitarian Church. They are quite ready to compromise. And you ...? What are you doing about it? What are you ...?

FRANCIS DÁVID: Me? I'm a Unitarian.

LUKE: A Unitarian! There are so many Unitarians who serve the cause of the sovereign all the same!

FRANCIS DÁVID: Well, I remain Unitarian in spite of them.

LUKE: It's hard for me to understand you, Francis. Báthory calls in an informer, and isn't even honorable enough to put him up himself. He quarters him in your house.

FRANCIS DÁVID: How do you know it was Báthory who did this?

LUKE: Of course the idea was Blandrata's, but that doesn't matter. What counts is the finishing stroke. He was sent to your house, and you, Francis, are wining, dining, and entertaining him. You are supporting your own informer.

FRANCIS DÁVID: It's God who's keeping him.

LUKE: God? But it's your house, your bread, your wine, and your nerves.

FRANCIS DÁVID: All of us are God's parasites. His ticks, his fleas.

LUKE: But you can't inform on God, or kill him—yet these things *can* be done to you. Be wary as befits a man, Francis!

FRANCIS DÁVID: I'm not suspicious. If I trust in God, I trust everyone. If God kills me, everyone kills me. If everyone kills me, God kills me. *(Not in self-righteous tone.)*

LUKE: Francis, Francis, you are on too high a level—they don't understand you. They sense your profundity precisely because they don't understand you. As long as they have enough to eat and drink and a warm body next to them at night, they couldn't care less whether God is one or three. Or whether Christ was the son of God, or simply a very great man!

FRANCIS DÁVID: If there were only one man on earth who felt the need for a unitary God, that would be a sufficient reason for me to proclaim that God.

LUKE: I understand you. I alone. And that's precisely why I do not want you destroyed—I'd much rather see Blandrata, Socino, or even the sovereign, perish. *(To himself.)* I'll stab this vagabond or drown him in the Szamos river.

FRANCIS DÁVID: Whether me or him, the one more dear to God will perish.

LUKE: Well, you seem to be the one!

FRANCIS DÁVID: That's fine with me, since God wills it so.

LUKE: God, now more than ever, be just. Do not allow a mind, a thought, to perish. Lord, you know that I love all peoples, all men. You see into my heart, you know this is so. Still I say: You've granted long life to so many who killed, who murdered, who thought of nothing but what their eyes, mouths, and shameful parts desired; to so many who each day said nothing but yes, no, my chum, these boots are tight, this sausage is good; to so many, Lord, whose skin never tingled either to the strains of your anthems or to the shadings of your thought; to so many you've granted long life who never gave you a thought, who never thought long and hard about anything—to so many, Lord! Forgive me, I love people, I love the various peoples. Forgive me, Lord.

FRANCIS DÁVID: Were you praying for me?

LUKE: No, I was praying for a thought.

(Small pause.)

FRANCIS DÁVID: *(To himself.)* He may be an informer; still, God is sending him to me.

LUKE: George Blandrata and Christopher Báthory are sending him. He is a *stray* theologian. He goes where the sun shines, and takes along his filth, his spirit. *(Sarcasm.)*

FRANCIS DÁVID: God is sending him, so I can prove the truth of my position ... I believe that Socino won't betray me. He is a good enough theologian to admit that I am right this time. With Blandrata I had no chance, because we have a new prince. *(Sincere trustfulness.)* But Socino comes from a foreign country—he's not prejudiced. It is not a matter of indifference to me who speaks to the prince about my opinions: my old enemy, Blandrata, or this impartial Socino. There's some hope for me! *(Stares into space.)*

LUKE: What a child you are, Bishop. This man is in Báthory's hands. This man has nowhere to go. Either he betrays, or he's sent packing, because he has worn out his welcome everywhere. Not one sovereign can stand him, because he is an instigator, and he peddles his doctrines. Francis, this man has no home, so all he can do is betray you. There is no room for him anywhere, except in betrayal. Betrayal is his home.

FRANCIS DÁVID: I'll have to try even if he betrays me. Even his betrayal may serve a purpose.

LUKE: What purpose, in God's name?!

FRANCIS DÁVID: You will yet know, Luke.

LUKE: You concentrated so much intelligence in one place, Lord, that those who got less want to destroy the best of it out of furious envy. Out of revenge for not being able to pull it down to their level. I can say no more here.

(Exits. Scene darkens.)

FRANCIS DÁVID: My God, everyone else may betray me, just don't you forsake me, ever. *(Blackout.)*

Scene 3

After dinner in Francis Dávid's room. At the table. Mary brings fruit. Two candles adequately illuminate everything. Goblets in front of diners.

FRANCIS DÁVID: *(Looks around.)* Where are the others?
SOCINO: I don't understand. *(A little on edge.)*
FRANCIS DÁVID: The other apostles besides you. Which one are you? *(Clearly thinking of Judas.)*
SOCINO: Perhaps you exaggerate, Bishop.
FRANCIS DÁVID: You are right. This is only the *first* supper... *(Irony.)* I wonder how many till the *last*. *(Brief silence.)* So you were brought here? Soldiers brought you, accompanied you with arms, so you'd be my guest. They would have decapitated you if you refused to be my guest. Am I right? *(Sarcasm.)*
SOCINO: *(Sincerely maintaining his dignity.)* I was quartered here. I couldn't help it.
MARY: *(On her crudely sensuous face there is childish mockery—she twists her slender body.)* That's right, this theology gentleman is the timid kind; when they tell him, come here, he comes. He goes wherever he's told.
FRANCIS DÁVID: Mary!

(The girl, somewhat offended, clears the table.)

SOCINO: What an unpleasant situation I've created—I have upset the tranquility of your house. Believe me it's not comfortable being a guest.
FRANCIS DÁVID: Socino, my dear, you are such a good theologian, I can only profit from your company. You'll have to forgive me if at first I was a bit unfriendly, but there are times when I barely tolerate anything—even my own body.
SOCINO: Being a guest is the hardest thing in this world.
FRANCIS DÁVID: But when you come right down to it, we're all guests. *(Almost intimately.)* My dear Socino, how often do I get a chance to speak to men from foreign lands about the Church, the faith? As for here... *(Shrugs.)* So let me reassure you, I am very glad you are here. Finally, a worthy spirit with whom I can discuss things.
SOCINO: *(Alarmed.)* My dear Bishop, I don't at all insist on talking Church and religion. On the contrary...

(Mary enters. Sudden silence. She notices it and while she clears away the plates she repeatedly brushes against Socino, not innocently. She leaves.)

FRANCIS DÁVID: I know I resemble those who invite guests so they can show off their daughter's harp-playing, or their son's paintings, the cooking, or their furniture, and thus abuse their captive guest. Perhaps I'm no different. But you must understand that I have no one here to talk to.

SOCINO: *(Increasingly anxious.)* Please don't create a difficult situation, let us not talk about the faith! Let me admire Kolozsvár and this magnificent Transylvanian landscape!
FRANCIS DÁVID: *(Touches his chest.)* Let us consider the *inner* landscape, Socino. I desire to speak sincerely with someone after all this time. *(Offers him a goblet.)*
SOCINO: Bishop, I did not come to this house to engage in theological disputations.
FRANCIS DÁVID: *(Disheartened.)* You're suspicious, as if you were afraid of me. But I swear to you there's nothing to be afraid of. Do you think I've got a stake in theological discussions? Do you think I was entrusted with an assignment?
SOCINO: I'd prefer it if you said nothing to me. Do you understand, Bishop? Nothing.
FRANCIS DÁVID: *(Sits down beside Socino with obstinate calm.)* But I am determined to tell you everything.

(In the meantime Mary comes and goes and listens, though not conspicuously.)

SOCINO: I implore you — don't tell me anything.
FRANCIS DÁVID: *(Leans into him confidentially.)* Don't be afraid, I'm not an informer. They did not put you up in my house so that I'd observe and inform on you. But this will remain our secret.
SOCINO: But Bishop!
FRANCIS DÁVID: *(A bit maliciously.)* Of course I can see it must appear suspicious to you that you received lodging in my house of all places.
SOCINO: I do not suspect you.
FRANCIS DÁVID: But we should, in fact, be suspicious! *(Stubborn.)*
SOCINO: I don't suspect you. You can't be watching me. *(Hesitates.)* Who would have told you to?
FRANCIS DÁVID: Let's say God.
SOCINO: Your jokes are not illuminating.
FRANCIS DÁVID: Well, if I'm not watching you, then only one other possibility exists.
SOCINO: Which is?
FRANCIS DÁVID: That you're watching me.
SOCINO: *(Stares at him.)* Since I asked you not to speak about matters of faith, in fact, since I protested against it, I would like to know on what you base your suspicions. *(Pause.)* Fine, let's talk.
FRANCIS DÁVID: Finally! I want to confess.
SOCINO: But only about general things.
FRANCIS DÁVID: What is more general than God? Let's start with Jesus Christ. You would no doubt like to know whether I consider him the son of God, as our Savior or a man. To me he's a man! And he cannot dispense grace in God's place. That's why I am a blasphemer in their eyes — a heretic who stirs up religious strife.

SOCINO: *(Scared.)* No, this does not interest me!
FRANCIS DÁVID: You're afraid I'll influence you, contaminate you. Yet all I'm asking you to do is examine an idea, and if you like it, to embrace it!
SOCINO: I am tired! The journey was long ... not today ...
MARY: *(Enters with a candle.)* Mister Theologian must be getting sleepy ... don't you want to go to bed? I've fixed a bed for you in the bishop's *nice* room. Enough jabbering — time to go beddy-bye.
FRANCIS DÁVID: Mary, don't interfere in grown-up affairs. You're still small. *(Kinder.)*
MARY: *(Seductive, mysterious.)* But Mr. Francis likes me all the same. All grown men like me. This theology gentleman will get to like me too. But now he's still like that priest in Szereda who pushed the servant girl down on the bed and shone a candle between her legs, because that's the only way he could find it! Instead of flashing something else! *(Laughs — not too brashly, lights candle.)*
FRANCIS DÁVID: Mary, don't be distasteful! *(Changes tone.)* We'll sleep *here* ... I will sleep here, and the theologian up there in the nook. *(Points toward stairs.)*
MARY: I'll bring the bed linen. *(Exits.)*
SOCINO: I've heard about women who were able single-handedly to put an entire regiment to shame with their coarseness. And that's no small thing, to make mercenaries blush ... *(Changes tone.)* The spirit, the mind, sometimes gets strangely paralyzed when assailed by raw force ... like a small animal playing dead to protect itself. In the face of naked power, our only nobility is silence.
FRANCIS DÁVID: Then I must be being noble just now.
MARY: *(Enters with blankets.)* Where do I sleep?
FRANCIS DÁVID: In your room, as usual.
MARY: *(Prepares her bed on bearskin.)* I didn't always sleep in my room. It was fine here too, on the floor. *(Mysterious.)* And how!
SOCINO: Bishop, I could really move to another room.
FRANCIS DÁVID: Don't move, son, you are my *intimate* guest.
MARY: Mine too!
FRANCIS DÁVID: Mary, go to bed in your room!
MARY: Don't order me around — you should have done that to your witch of a wife that you left. But her fancy was not tickled by your Bible!
FRANCIS DÁVID: If you don't stop right away ... *(His suppressed threat is fatherly.)*
MARY: What then? I'm sleeping here and that's *that!* My heart is keeping me here. *(Sarcasm.)* I'd so much like for once to sleep in a room where great men sleep!
FRANCIS DÁVID: Mary, come to your senses!
MARY: The bishop keeps saying anyway that I have a small brain ... well, this small mind desires *great* things!
SOCINO: *(Softly.)* You shouldn't be arguing with her ...
MARY: *(Hands a cup to the bishop.)* Here's your medicine! *(Bishop drinks it. The girl starts to undress, the men turn away.)* You can talk in front of me ... I don't understand anything anyway ... Isn't that so, Mr. Francis? I don't understand

a thing. Just don't talk in Latin! Latin makes me think I'm in church. Once, when I was a little girl, I climbed up to the statue of the Virgin, so I could stroke baby Jesus. A young priest caught me, dragged me down, groped me hard, and plopped me in his lap ... good and hard. Latin always reminds me of that. But of course then I was still Catholic ...

FRANCIS DÁVID: *(Blows out one of the candles.)* Let's leave the truth to tomorrow. Good night. *(Turns to the wall.)*

(Socino goes up the stairs. Mary blows out another candle, leaving one burning in the middle of the table. She slips under her cover and watches Francis Dávid, who has fallen asleep.)

MARY: *(Softly.)* That medicine makes him sleep like a log—lately he's kept his clothes on. So, Mr. Theologian, why don't you get undressed? Are you also afraid that they'll take you away? You have to be ready—that's what the bishop says. Always—for anything.

(Socino is silent.)

Men of God, huh? Given up everything. They'll do it with their clothes on, like a teamster in the hay ...

(She suddenly slips out from under the blanket, rushes up the stairs.)

Well, I'll fix you, Mr. Theologian ...

(She throws aside the coat of the trembling Socino.)

SOCINO: *(Almost shuddering.)* Why did you come here?
MARY: *(Whispering.)* Didn't Blandrata tell you? I'll be passing on your reports to him ... The two of us now belong together. Don't we?

(She sprawls on him, erotic tussle. Soon they quiet down, brief silence. Then she speaks, hurt.)

Why don't you speak to me? You embrace me like a cold fish and don't say anything! Blandrata always speaks nicely to me, even though I've never slept with him ...
SOCINO: *(To himself.)* Well, Blandrata, there's no escaping you even in bed!
MARY: *(Attacks him, wants to bite his neck.)* You'll talk, I'll show you! You can't say sweet things? That young priest called my breasts little apples ... you hear? Why can't you say something like that? Say something nice or swear at me, just don't keep quiet, you cold fish, you block of ice!
(Socino winces, then vehemently climbs on top of her.)
(Blackout.)

Scene 4

Side staircase, end of hallway. Socino and Blandrata are approaching each other. They stop. Pause.

BLANDRATA: Your time for reflection is over, Socino. You have to take on the job if you want a home.

SOCINO: What if I don't?

BLANDRATA: The sovereign took you in and is supporting you.

SOCINO: I am being supported by my Church. It is not the benevolence of the prince, but the dead of my faith who have received me and are supporting me here. Our existence can no longer be denied—we are legal, our Church is a power to be reckoned with. We are no longer merely tolerated. What pains them is that we no longer live by their gracious leave, but that we too are in a position to dictate. The time of living off princely charity is over.

BLANDRATA: *(Brusquely.)* We'll send you back to the king of Poland, who is after your hide. And don't think anyone else will take you in—everyone abhors you, you are a troublemaker. When you come right down to it, you don't really believe in anything, only in destroying. So why don't you go ahead and destroy the bishop's principles and the faith of his followers? Then you will have a home.

SOCINO: Why are you bribing me with this land, which isn't even my home? I wasn't born here.

BLANDRATA: Neither was I. Your betrayal will naturalize you. Your sin will make you a real citizen ... our common sin and common victory ... Like a merchant who invests his money in something, then pursues his gains, we invest our new sins in our new country ... and we don't leave, because we're waiting for the interest to accumulate on our new sins. Make no mistake, Socino.

SOCINO: At this price, never!

BLANDRATA: Do you think I found it easy here, as an Italian? My old Italian friends view me with suspicion since I've quit my homeland. And the people here say: fly-by-night vagabond. I fit in neither here nor there. But they have learned to respect me here. No one respects the constitution more than I do. The prince trusts me. And he is afraid of his own doctors—he even suspects them when they prescribe him a laxative. He knows I'd be the last one to poison him, because I'm bound by gratitude. This is how you could describe my home: gratitude and self-justification. And I won't leave. I like this land and these peoples better than many a local nobleman does, even though he lives off this land and these peoples. Tell me, isn't it a matter of complete indifference who provides you with a home? Isn't it all the same where the region in which you live is located, as long as you're doing well? Answer me!

SOCINO: No, it isn't, Blandrata.

(Pause.)

BLANDRATA: Fine, enough of this. Let me just tell you — the servant girl has reported that you and Francis Dávid stop talking whenever she enters the room. Or else you switch to Latin. The prince might be led to think that the two of you are coming to an understanding — that you're conspiring, to put it bluntly. Else why shouldn't a servant girl be privy to your *lofty* thoughts?

(Silence.)

SOCINO: Don't you trust your own stool pigeons any more? You place a betrayer over the betrayer, Doctor? And a servant girl at that? To inform on the informer? *(Furious.)*
BLANDRATA: If you accept the job, the servant's job will be over. What interests us is the truth. Strange as it may seem, it is precisely for the sake of Francis Dávid that you must accept. This is a test of your devotion to him. An *outsider's* word is given more credence. It is precisely his interest that demands our receiving objective, expert reports, as opposed to the jabberings of a servant girl. He does deserve this special consideration since he is, after all, the founder of our Church. *(With dignity.)*

(Small pause.)

SOCINO: In other words, he who *founds* must be killed.
BLANDRATA: We are not getting rid of the founder, but of the man who has turned against his own creation, against that which is already sound. Would you make the fate of a great priest depend on the words of a servant girl? We ask you therefore to save the bishop! *(With deceptive conviction, eyes wide open.)* If he truly deserves to be rescued, and if you know how to rescue him ...

(Tiny pause, Socino would like to believe Blandrata.)

SOCINO: Would you be willing to swear on the sacred name of God, George Blandrata, that my reports will be used in such a way as to benefit the one true God and the Unitarian Church of Transylvania?
BLANDRATA: *(Rapidly, in a dry voice.)* Yes.
SOCINO: Swear!
BLANDRATA: So help me God!
SOCINO: But if you don't keep your oath ... *(Menacing.)*
BLANDRATA: Do not threaten me, I'm not in the mood for laughter.
SOCINO: We will see what we are in the mood for, Doctor ...
BLANDRATA: Well, what should I tell the sovereign?

(They stare into each other's eyes.)

SOCINO: Go and tell him that I accept the assignment. Francis Dávid will tell me the truth, and I will pass it on. I will not add to it, take from it, disguise it, I will not reshape it to fit my own thoughts, so help me God!

(Blandrata bows slowly, exits.)

(Blackout.)

Scene 5

Francis Dávid's room. Mary crosses the room with swaying hips, but gets no attention. Socino sits on the floor, absorbed in a book. The bishop approaches with a book. He taps its cover. They wear rough, big shoes. They are unkempt.

FRANCIS DÁVID: You are not interrogating me enough, Socino! Ask me questions! It is in my interest that the prince find out everything about me. Let us argue, Socino! In the heat of an argument I often let my guard down ... That should be good for you!

SOCINO: Do you want to talk me into betrayal? *(A certain hesitation becomes visible — later this will turn into a stunned attitude, and eventually into a kind of idiocy.)*

FRANCIS DÁVID: Try to understand! It is better for me that you interpret my innovations ... Just don't let Blandrata and his crew appropriate the interpretation of religion. You are my last chance: If you report truthfully to the prince, my seemingly lost cause might yet be cleared up. And Blandrata discredited. I'm suggesting an honest fight, an honorable agreement. I will be sincere, and you, impartial. *(Small pause, he drinks.)* How much time has passed, Socino? What is today's date? *(Small pause. Socino turns pages.)* Socino! How long have we been together here?

SOCINO: *(Does not answer, turns pages feverishly, looking for a passage, mutters.)* Byzantium ruined us, Byzantium ... and Saint Ambrose. And Calvin.

FRANCIS DÁVID: You're playing the Trinity game again. I've told you a hundred times, Socino, that I am not denying the Trinity, but proclaiming the one God. I'm not denying the Trinity!

SOCINO: *(Sits up suddenly.)* So you recognize the Trinity? Then how can you be an anti-Trinitarian?

FRANCIS DÁVID: How can I be against the Trinity when it does not exist? I am not an anti-Trinitarian, but a Unitarian. I believe in the one God, and nothing else.

SOCINO: But by believing in the one God, and by proclaiming him alone, you are denying the divinity of the Son and the Holy Ghost.

FRANCIS DÁVID: I maintain that God is one. *Unus est deus.* I maintain that there is only one God, creator of heaven and earth, judge of good and evil throughout the vastness of time. Time is the whip with which he drives us toward his goals. Christ is needed because of his human form, which makes it easier for them to sway people. To them he is like the pagan Hercules: the fruit of heavenly and earthly nuptials! The child of a divine father and an earthly mother. A kind of *divine half-breed*, who cannot find his place either in heaven or here on earth, because of his doubtful affiliation both here and there. He resembles men—they worship him because they derive comfort from this resemblance, from the possibility that we can become like unto him. But consider how progenitive the pagan gods were—how many of them there were. In the end a person could have a *favorite* god, a kind of domestic idol: God as domestic animal. There could be as many loopholes for lies and lawlessness as there were gods. Well, if God is three, then how do we differ from the pagans, who kept a god in every bush? How does the Father of Creation differ from Zeus, with whose earthly escapades we are all so familiar? Did our God also have this sort of earthly tryst with Mary, who remained immaculate in spite of it?! Pagan stories! God is one and solemn. Or perhaps cheerful, but in his gaiety—infinitely solitary. Hence his benevolence. Because in his solitude he *gives unto us,* and this pleases him.

SOCINO: *(Bitter, complaining.)* I am not trying to convince you of the Trinity, I too am an anti-Trinitarian, after all. I am arguing with you this way in order to recognize every shading of your faith. *(Closes book, puts it down, small pause, different voice.)* Do you want me to take off your shoes for you?

FRANCIS DÁVID: Go ahead. *(Socino does.)* Should I do the same for you?

SOCINO: I'll take them off myself. We are different in bare feet. We are more honest in bare feet. Shoes are constricting. Toes are not visible in shoes. And toes, spread out on the floor, have such truth about them. *(They are in bare feet.)*

FRANCIS DÁVID: Now pay attention. Honesty is important to you now. Your whole being now depends on my remaining honest.

SOCINO: How strange—I am your informer, and you still like me, Francis. Whatever you may say, I feel and I know that you are fond of me. That is because we are equals, because I understand every shading of your thought. You wouldn't open up to just anybody, would you?

FRANCIS DÁVID: No. I'm open toward you because you are good. You betray me, but you are good. Your desire to be good already demonstrates a little goodness.

SOCINO: Then you understand, don't you? You don't take mine to be *that* kind of betrayal?

FRANCIS DÁVID: No. It's better if *you* betray me, not someone crude and mindless. *(Almost affectionately.)* You are a good betrayer, Socino.

SOCINO: That's because I am not after your titles, I don't aspire to replace you as bishop here.

FRANCIS DÁVID: Blandrata and the prince sent another Unitarian to me. Not a

Jesuit or a Calvinist. He wanted us to betray each other within the faith. One brother should keep watch over another and report on him to the Catholic prince. But I trust you, Socino, your betrayal is a mighty fortress to me ...

(Short silence.)

SOCINO: And if you still can't convince me of your truth?
FRANCIS DÁVID: Then I am lost. *(Simply.)*
SOCINO: But if you do convince me?
FRANCIS DÁVID: Then we either win or perish together. But for this I have to open myself completely to you ...
SOCINO: No, I don't want to know all your secrets! Why should I be burdened with them? Keep on carrying them yourself.
FRANCIS DÁVID: They also say about me that I'm an adulterer. They accused me of reforming my faith in order to change wives ... Of shaping the faith to the skirt, rather than the skirt to the faith.
SOCINO: *(Stops up his ears.)* I am not interested! Not interested!

(Small pause, sound of a bell from without. It dies away.)

FRANCIS DÁVID: Have you sent in the report today?
SOCINO: Not yet. *(Brief pause.)* Mary will come. Mary will come soon. Mary will come for my report. I hate the report. I hate Mary.

(Mary enters with two wooden dishes, sweeps everything off the table with her elbow, slams the dishes on the table, takes two forks and spoons out of her cleavage and sticks them into the food.)

MARY: Leave off with the religion talk, and start eating. I don't have time to stand around.

(The two men don't move.)

Let's get a move on, Bishop! You too, Socino!

(They approach the table haltingly, almost fearfully, then sit. Mary leans against the railing of the stair, watches them sternly. She has grown up. Every gesture seems a harsh command.)

SOCINO: *(Quietly.)* Let us pray ... *(Silent prayer.)*
MARY: That's all you're getting. You'll just have to make do with it. And even that's too good for you! *(Quietly raging.)*
FRANCIS DÁVID: Mary, we have a guest!
MARY: *(With hate.)* A guest? This vagabond? *(Socino remains silent.)* You deserve to be strung up, the two of you. *(Stares at them with narrowed eyes.)* Eat! *(They quickly finish eating. Meantime Mary kicks the books on the floor, lifts one.)*

FRANCIS DÁVID: *(Kindly.)* Not that way, you've got it upside down.

MARY: This is how I like it. Don't the letters of the alphabet stand on their heads inside the two of you? You argue about God—whether he's three or one ... As if that'll bring rain for the crops, that's how you argue ... Maybe three would be better. Then there'd be more of them to look after us. And if you really want to know, the reason there are three Gods is that everybody can count to three. Even me. And if I can count to three, why should I just count to one? To look stupid to you? *(With crude sarcasm.)*
FRANCIS DÁVID: Mary, you are a Unitarian.
MARY: What do I know what I am? One thing I know for sure: I've had it up to here with the two of you. All you know how to do is argue and make children.
SOCINO: Stop it! I protest!
MARY: Go ahead and protest! Your voices are as weak as your bodies ... Can't you hear the cannon of the kings and princes thundering somewhere? You can't out-thunder that with the Bible.
SOCINO: Make her keep quiet, Francis!
FRANCIS DÁVID: I have no power over her.
MARY: You did once, both of you. You had power over my groin. Then only my legs opened, but now my eyes have opened too. You swine!
SOCINO: Please make her shut up.
FRANCIS DÁVID: I can't take her words away from her, they belong to her, and I have no use for them.
MARY: How particular the old man is getting! He wasn't always like that. Tell me, do you have to "go"?
FRANCIS DÁVID: Go away!
MARY: *(To Socino.)* You don't have to either?
SOCINO: *(In a challenging manner.)* Have to what? That, or *that?* *(Nods toward door, then towards nook.)*
MARY: You filth!

(Socino reflects. Sits down, writes. After he is finished, he sprinkles ashes on the paper, then folds it.)

MARY: Are you finished?

(Socino steps toward her, looks into her eyes for a moment, then gives her the paper.)

SOCINO: And now go!

(Mary departs quickly, Socino points after her and collapses, acts almost idiotic.)

SOCINO: Francis, she ... she ... she ... doesn't let us sleep with God! She steps right into our souls, Francis. *(Whispers.)* She steps right in.

(Silence.)
(Blackout.)

Scene 6

End of hallway, staircase. Mary leads Blandrata in. Whispers something in his ear. Exits. Socino enters slowly down the stairs. The doctor waits for him. They stare mutely at each other.

SOCINO: What do you want from me?
BLANDRATA: Well, *my brother*, are we informing like a good boy?
SOCINO: I swear, I've reported everything that happened.
BLANDRATA: I cannot believe that a learned minister of our faith such as you, Socino, is unable to determine whether the bishop is guilty or not.
SOCINO: That was not in the agreement! You ought to have entrusted the Catholics with this task, Doctor!
BLANDRATA: It has more credibility when brothers inform on each other.
SOCINO: How much longer are we to do our enemies' dirty work for them?
BLANDRATA: I never suspected we Italians could be so taciturn. *(Points at paper.)*
SOCINO: To each his own, Doctor.
BLANDRATA: The sovereign is dissatisfied with your reports. They are far too brief, and one can't tell from them whether the bishop is guilty or not.
SOCINO: I did not agree to expose the guilt of Francis Dávid, but to report what he says.
BLANDRATA: *(In a different voice.)* If you bear witness, you who are of the faith, then every one of the flock will rest easy, because *we are passing judgment on ourselves.* We will not forfeit to anyone else our right to pass judgment on ourselves! Otherwise we would be betraying to the prince that we are incapable of handling our own affairs... Do you want him to appoint spiritual wardens to govern us? Alien interpreters? Protectors of our attitudes? Acting on our own will bring far greater results. Let us not be too fussy. Our place is at the cutting edge, among the leaders.
SOCINO: *(With sarcasm.)* So people within the faith should be afraid of each other, rather than united against our common enemy! *(Different voice.)* What else do you want from me?
BLANDRATA: I've already told you. Your reports are too brief.
SOCINO: Truth itself is brief. I write only the truth.
BLANDRATA: Too succinctly. The truth changes when we write it out at greater length, Socino.
SOCINO: I am not able to... I'm simply not...
BLANDRATA: But surely you can take a position contrary to the theological formulations of the bishop. After all, you are a theologian—a *famous* theologian. A great debater!
SOCINO: I won't do it! I won't do this! I am only an informer, not an interpreter! Do the interpreting yourselves. After all, that's how you make your living! By distortion!

(Small pause.)

If I were forced to choose between two of my brethren, I would want to choose both of them. We must not dissipate our strength — we are too small for that.
BLANDRATA: The prince wishes your choice to fall on just one in this case, Socino.
SOCINO: I came as a witness, not as a judge!
BLANDRATA: You came as an informer. And you are the prince's guest. You keep forgetting.
SOCINO: I am Francis Dávid's guest. And God's, like everyone on earth.
BLANDRATA: The earth is big, Socino. Other countries can handle their own affairs. Right now this is the land that's providing our purpose and task... This, our immediate homeland...
SOCINO: No, never!

(Silence.)

BLANDRATA: Well, fine. Then we'll rely on Mary's reports.
SOCINO: *(Stunned.)* Mary's? Have you lost all dread? Have you no shame?
BLANDRATA: Her *oral* reports. You know she cannot read or write, and yet she consented to interpret his words.

(Small pause.)

We've no alternative. Francis Dávid's fate will be decided on the basis of the servant girl's reports. *(Very seriously, this is not an idle threat.)*

(Brief silence.)

SOCINO: I will someday draw the limits of this disgrace, Blandrata. Mark my words!
BLANDRATA: Don't threaten me. *(Sullen.)*
SOCINO: You'll see.

(Small pause.)

BLANDRATA: Brother, the intellect must always choose. Either it allows stupidity and ignorance to sit in judgment over the living and the dead, or else it retains the power of judgment for itself. And does not concern itself with whether it soils its hands.
SOCINO: I protest! I alone was to inform! I protest on behalf of the intellect! I protest! I alone was to inform ... no one else ... I alone ... I!

(Blackout.)

ACT TWO

Scene 1

Francis Dávid's room. Disorder. Socino dozing at the table. Mary enters without a word, does not look at them, puts down a small wooden tub with steam rising from it. Exits. The bishop shakes Socino by the shoulders.

FRANCIS DÁVID: Get to work, Socino! Question me! Socino, you're a lazy informer, you want me to say as little as possible. The less for you to report ... *(Tries to provoke Socino, who remains unruffled.)*

(Socino stands up.)

SOCINO: I wrote it already ... I know everything. I have become convinced.
FRANCIS DÁVID: *(A little perplexed.)* Of what?
SOCINO: That you are a religious innovator. Should I wash your feet?
FRANCIS DÁVID: And is that sinful?
SOCINO: Not in my eyes, but in the eyes of my employers it is.
FRANCIS DÁVID: Then why don't you let your own judgment prevail over theirs?
SOCINO: Because by accepting this ... job, I also committed myself to sharing their judgment as to what is culpable.
FRANCIS DÁVID: How can you be so divided? How can someone hold two judgments of the same sin?
SOCINO: The way I do. *(Naturally.)*
FRANCIS DÁVID: And why do they consider religious innovation sinful?
SOCINO: Because Blandrata is glad that he finally has a constituted Church.
FRANCIS DÁVID: And is it your opinion too that having a constituted Church puts

to rest once and for all the need for change and innovation? Every beginning effervesces like acidulous water. Just remember when we followed Luther in the Reformation. How intoxicated we were. As when at harvest time, seeing the boundless wheat-field, the abundance ... And at threshing, how the blessed kernels flow — that was how ideas, one better than the other, abounded, flowed. We were fresh, and we shouted ... And this abundance is still with us! Within us! The soul's ground has not become arid ... I feel it ... the old intoxication is alive in me, the intoxication of change ... Even with white heads we can have lively intellects, no longer unripe like slimy walnuts, but not rocky and parched either. Should there be no more innovation?

SOCINO: I cannot endorse your beliefs, Francis. Never.

FRANCIS DÁVID: Is there no more need for innovation? Is everything perfect now? The dream became incarnate, the Word has been erected?

SOCINO: I also believe that there will forever be a need for innovation. But I am just a ... you know what I am, Francis. I don't even have the satisfaction of an executioner who hangs a criminal. Or at least thinks it's a criminal. I know what you are. But I was sent to you as an informer, Francis. And I now have no home away from here. And a man such as I am owes his allegiance to whoever takes him in. A homeless person does not have a free soul, Bishop. He who belongs to everyone, to the whole world, belongs to no one. *Here* and *now* this is the extent of my freedom. This *strange* job. So here I am with you, trying to do my job without doing violence to my conscience before you, before myself, or before my employers. My freedom consists in this: to describe, not to interpret. My honor consists in this: not to express my own opinion. This is the extent of my freedom here and now. Reticence.

(Mary enters. Looks at them with contempt. They do not even glance at her. She pours salts into the tub, coughs slightly from the fumes, then places her hand on her belly, nauseated. She recovers.)

MARY: Learned men ... wash yourselves ... you look like two dirty vagabonds ... And these fellows preached to us from God's pulpit ... Who needs you, anyway? The *soil* needs you so you'll fertilize it the way the peasants you look down your noses at do. Who needs you? What would you do without us; who'd weave your clothes? You'll drown in your books. You'll be buried in your books, not in the mother earth!

FRANCIS DÁVID: Your words ... I mean just your words ... ought to be burned at the stake!

MARY: Shut up, old-timer, or I'll tell you what you're like ... just keep your trap shut.

FRANCIS DÁVID: Get out of here! Get out!

MARY: I'm going. I have to go to Blandrata anyway, because this *migrant* isn't doing his job well enough. And then he looks down his nose at me ... Even though we're *equals*, Mr. Theologian. Your employers are more ready to believe me ... You're about to be sacked ... So you'd better be on good terms with me, you loafing Italian! *(Exits.)*

FRANCIS DÁVID: *(Suddenly collapses.)* I beg of you, Socino! Do your job! Do what they ask ... don't deliver me into their hands! Don't, otherwise I'll curse you, you hear?! Don't deliver me to that devil Blandrata! *(Brief silence.)*

SOCINO: *(Stares into space.)* Have you ever killed anyone, Francis?

FRANCIS DÁVID: No. *(Stands up.)*

(The bishop puts his feet in the tub.)

SOCINO: Wait, I'll help you. *(Washes.)* Could you kill someone, Francis?

FRANCIS DÁVID: I don't think so.

SOCINO: *(Aggressively.)* Tell me about your sins! You hear? What evil have you done in your life? Because it's impossible that you haven't done evil to someone. Maybe you even committed murder, but you're not aware of it. Or you're denying it even to yourself.

(Socino rubs the bishop's ankles.)

FRANCIS DÁVID: Perhaps. But I did not do it intentionally.

SOCINO: Then why do they hate you so much, Francis? Why don't they hate the sovereign or Blandrata instead? *(Wipes his feet.)*

FRANCIS DÁVID: Because they are afraid of them. They are afraid to hate them. They don't fear me, so they bravely hate me, without running any risk.

(Small pause.)

And those we *dare not* love, we end up hating. They do not dare to love me anymore.

SOCINO: Francis, tell me honestly — what wrong have you done in your life? ... Make it easier for me ... make my difficult betrayal easier for me. *(Throws down the towel, not entirely casually.)*

FRANCIS DÁVID: I was too lazy for sin. For any really great sin. I was afraid, besides. Still, I made them uncomfortable. Wait, I'll wash your feet.

SOCINO: *(Lets him without even noticing.)* What kind of people make them uncomfortable?

FRANCIS DÁVID: People who do not give desired answers, who do not assuage consciences. People who keep asking questions even after everyone has given an answer to every question. These people never kill. These always get killed.

SOCINO: And why do the other Churches hate you more than they hate Blandrata, even though he too is Unitarian?

FRANCIS DÁVID: Because I am more dangerous to them. With my sermons I would have converted the whole Principality of Transylvania to Unitarianism within a few years. And *all* Hungarians. Maybe others, too. But what would have become of the Catholic and Protestant clergy? My innovations are not the real sin ... innovation is just a *code name* to them ... the baby needs a name, now that it has come into the world ... Any name ... My real sin in their eyes is my refusal to put my Church in a museum; I wanted it to grow and develop through the power of my faith.

SOCINO: I never suspected ... *(Stops short.)*
FRANCIS DÁVID: What?
SOCINO: That ... it would be this difficult to betray someone.

(The bishop picks up towel, wipes Socino's feet.)

FRANCIS DÁVID: Calm yourself, Socino, I told you that I wanted you. You by all means. They had tried others on me, but they didn't succeed in wangling anything from me. Because they were clods, they dealt in dogma like merchandise — so I did not open up to anyone. I clung to the last and only freedom left to me: to choose my own betrayer. So do what they ask! You be the one to do this work ... Think of Mary ... of Blandrata ... Beat them to it!
SOCINO: Francis, let us finish this now — once and for all ... *(Looks with suspicion.)* At times I get the feeling that in spite of all appearances you are still hiding something from me. I feel you are saving something for me, some enormous horror, some ingenious horror, which I dread already, and which you will drop on my head only later. Am I right, Francis Dávid?
FRANCIS DÁVID: You may be right. But in that case, I am saving it for the end, truly. Go ahead, write!

(Socino nods, leans over paper, can't write.)

Maybe it'll be easier with me out of the room.

(Exits, Socino writes.)

(Blandrata enters.)

SOCINO: So now you have free access to this place, too?
BLANDRATA: Why not? Is this a sanctuary? After all, we are Protestants.
SOCINO: What do you want?
BLANDRATA: Rewrite it. It's no good. Báthory doesn't like it. Rewrite it. *(Hands him letter. Socino refuses to take it. Small pause.)*
SOCINO: Is this one also ... too short?
BLANDRATA: Yes. *(Brief silence.)*
SOCINO: *(Approaches him, his eyes are wild, he whispers.)* Have you ever killed a person, Blandrata? What kind of taste does that leave in the mouth ... what kind of taste, killing a person?

(Pause.)

BLANDRATA: *(Steps back, shocked.)* Rewrite it. It's too short. Rewrite it.

(Blandrata repeats this while reaching closer with the paper. Puts it down; backs away, practically fleeing from the burning glance of Socino.)

(Blackout.)

Scene 2

Francis Dávid's room at sunset. No one is present. Then the bishop enters with Socino, who, practically beside himself, is tugging at the bishop's coat.

SOCINO: Tell me one of your sins! So I can do it more easily ... *(The bishop keeps silent. Socino is beside himself.)* You are very godly, Francis. As if you weren't even of flesh and blood. Don't rob me of my wits, you may come to regret it! *(Grabs Francis by the shoulders.)* Give me one of your sins, Francis, so I can see you as less godly! So I won't feel so utterly miserable. *(Pause.)*
FRANCIS DÁVID: They're not satisfied with you, Socino? *(Gentle.)*
SOCINO: A sin! Anything—as long as it's a sin! As long as you consider it a sin!

(Pause.)

FRANCIS DÁVID: I believe I have committed many. *(It is getting dark. Lights a candle.)* But there is one you certainly know of. *(Brief silence.)* Like you, I slept with this girl.
SOCINO: *(Nods.)* I have known that for a while now.
FRANCIS DÁVID: That's why she is so bossy with us, why she wields such power over us.
SOCINO: And you consider it a sin that she lay down in your bed?
FRANCIS DÁVID: To whatever height the spirit may lift us, we often lust after the crudest flesh.
SOCINO: Then what do you consider sinful in it?
FRANCIS DÁVID: That I was not younger. That I shamed that young flesh and that I shamed these old bones worn away by my bookish life. *(Dreamy, stares into space. Small pause.)*
SOCINO: You did honor to her young flesh! But to her it's the other way around. Tell me, why does crude flesh demand homage from refined spirit? Why does formless flesh command?! That awkward flesh can't even write, can't even read! *(Virtually shouting.)* Only shout and shove! It shames and humiliates our spirit!

FRANCIS DÁVID: It is within its fleshly rights. The flesh feels the right to rule over you once you have accepted its call. It considers your thoughts, your faith, your entire inner being, a fair exchange for that which is *only* tangible.

SOCINO: *(Almost demented.)* That flesh will be your betrayer. That is what is informing on you. Ignorance. Blind instinct is to be your spy! ... And that monster Blandrata. Not I.

FRANCIS DÁVID: I don't understand. Who could betray me more effectively than I myself? I loudly proclaim all my thoughts. Mary could not inform on me; she doesn't understand one word we say!

SOCINO: But that's enough for the sovereign! They're collecting all types of evidence ... this kind also. A servant girl's opinion is enough for them to strangle a genius ... *(Changes tone.)* Let me hear you tell me once more that you want my betrayal, not theirs! *(Whispering.)* From your own mouth. Say it.

FRANCIS DÁVID: Socino, rest assured; since I have a choice between stammering betrayal and intelligent betrayal, you know very well which of the two I am choosing. The one which aspires to be worthy of the betrayed.

SOCINO: Poor Francis, is this really what your freedom has come down to, the choice between two kinds of betrayal? *(Small pause.)* Is that what it has come down to? *(Brief pause.)* Wouldn't you like to kill? Someone ... anyone ... who gets in your way ...

(Sits down on floor, moves his neck close to the bishop's hands, which are hanging by his side. Touches his neck to them.)

FRANCIS DÁVID: *(Snatches his hands away; quietly.)* Did you send in today's report? *(Points at table.)*

SOCINO: Not yet. What startled your hands? Are Blandrata's hands this jumpy? Or mine? What do you say, do you think I've got brave hands? *(Stands up, places his hands on Francis Dávid's shoulders, close to his neck.)*

FRANCIS DÁVID: *(Unperturbed.)* Have you so much as written it?

SOCINO: No. *(Small pause.)* I used to write nothing but theological tracts and sermons. I never thought this kind of writing possible ... the kind I am forced to do now. There is something incredible about this. This hand, which wrote tracts against the Trinity ... *(Looks at right hand, nods abruptly toward table.)* I use short sentences for the reports, the shorter the better so they can't nab my thoughts. I leave them no space between the words. Informing is like terror: a quick strike, nothing superfluous. *(Small pause.)* There's something incredible about all this. Here I am in your house, a *guest,* and you tolerate my betrayal of you, indeed, every day you remind me of my task as if it were your own, and you ask me whether I've written it yet, whether I've handed in the daily report. But you don't do this in order to torment me, but because you know this is my work, my duty, and you treat it as such. *(Brief pause.)* And

you don't conceal anything, you don't deny anything, even though you know
I report everything. *(Brief pause.)* Or are you merely tormenting me? Is your
gentleness really a fist in the face? Watch out!

FRANCIS DÁVID: My fate was determined the moment Prince Báthory sat on the
throne.

SOCINO: Are they truly after your life? And you don't kill. You tolerate this
without doing anything. *(Almost inciting.)* Can't you find a dagger for Blandrata's heart?

FRANCIS DÁVID: So far I had a life, all I have now is a fate, Socino. Events are
taking their own course.

SOCINO: Of course, you want to incite me against your main enemies! But I've
got other things to do! I refuse to play along! I firmly believe that my reports
will complete the historical record about you: that you are not the enemy
either of the Church or of the sovereign. *(Lights a candle, his hand shakes.)*

FRANCIS DÁVID: The enemy? I have been, and still am, only my own enemy.
Haven't you noticed that every accusation—innovation, heresy, disloyalty to
the sovereign—is just an excuse? They'll welcome anything—just not me.
Everything will be fine—as long as I perish. *(Pause.)* Let's go to sleep. We'll
see whether we will wake up wiser tomorrow. I'll be right back. *(Exits.)*

(Mary enters slowly.)

MARY: Socino, have you written it?

SOCINO: *(With sarcastic loathing; hard to tell which is stronger: hate or irony.)* I'm still
collecting the data. *(To her face, close, confidentially, quietly, in a choked voice.)* You
don't know yet, but I've rewritten the *Our Father* ... and from now on until
the moment of my death, I will always be doing that: rewriting the *Our Father*
... I rewrote it: Give us this day our daily data, now and forever.

MARY: *(Steps back, astonished.)* Sit down and write! I've got to be going, so sit
down and write!

SOCINO: If only I'd gone to the stable, to the animals, to the cows, to the mares,
rather than desire you. *(He pushes the woman down; she seems nauseated; after a
brief tussle they get up.)*

MARY: You hate me because of the two of us you're the guiltier. And since you're
the guiltier, you hate me instead of hating the bishop or Blandrata. Even
though the two of us are birds of a feather. You hate me because I'm weaker!
You hate me because they're smarter. It's riskier hating them than me ...
You're too cowardly to hate them ... But watch it, I can be hated in a different
way now ... I am no longer that stupid girl ... the two of you will see: I've
gotten smart!

SOCINO: Yes, you've gotten smart in our company. The erstwhile stupid girl
became a *scholar*—in our company. Slipping into our beds made you smart,
your whorishness made you smart. Go to that cursed Blandrata—and then

onward to all the clerical leaders. Go, they can all teach you something! Go, you could become a bishop yourself. The bishop of the whores! *(Very brief pause.)* My God!
MARY: You beast! You swine! ... You talk about God, you ... stool pigeon!
FRANCIS DÁVID: *(Steps in just then.)* Leave Socino alone!

(Mary ignores him.)

MARY: *(To Socino.)* Sit down and write! *(Socino rushes out, clutching his forehead. Mary clutches her stomach, goes out the other side. The bishop calmly lies down to sleep. He blows out the candle. A dim light comes from outside. Socino quietly enters, stands in middle of room, glares in the direction of the bishop's bed.)*

(Silence.)

(Blackout.)

Scene 3

Daytime. Francis Dávid's room. Socino alone, arranging books on the floor with great precision.

SOCINO: *(To himself.)* I'm just putting our things in order, Bishop ... Everything should be in its place. You should be ... I should be ... Everyone should be ...
   (Blandrata appears, Socino looks up but registers no surprise.)

BLANDRATA: *(Points to letter.)* Congratulations, Socino! That's the way to go about it. Now *this* has some of the great theologian in it, Socino! But I'm expecting today's report. Just keep working on it calmly — I can come back for it. Once more, congratulations.
SOCINO: Careful ... I may not appreciate your praise ... *(Quietly.)*
BLANDRATA: *(Patting the other's shoulder.)* You seem to be in a bit of an ill humor, my dear compatriot, Italian brother.
SOCINO: I am not your brother. Careful! *(Quiet and irresolute.)*
BLANDRATA: *(Matter-of-factly.)* Necessity will teach you brotherhood. You're a traitor, and you'd better get used to the fact. Francis Dávid has turned his coat on several occasions: he's been a Catholic, a Calvinist, and finally a Unitarian. Of course he knew how to make a moral principle of betrayal — he called it necessary change, development. Aside from that, there is no difference between you. So don't feel sorry for him — he's no great loss. So just take it easy. And if you still can't find a way to settle the matter, take this ... *(Throws a dagger in front of him.)* Learn how and against whom to use it in our cause. Why shouldn't death work in our favor? Death is not just our master, but our servant too. Don't be frightened of death.

(Socino picks up the dagger. Blandrata exits. Brief silence. Socino looks after him in a trance.)

SOCINO: Brother ... *(Nods, hides dagger in his shirt. Again arranges books on floor. Mary enters. He does not look toward her, but knows she is present. Speaks with his back to her. She remains visible in the background. He picks up a book. Nods at another.)* You stepped on this one. Here's your footprint. This is your toe ... your foot's thumb, if your foot had a thumb. This is your foot's index finger, if your foot had an index finger. *(Shrugs.)*

MARY: Where's the bishop?

SOCINO: *(In a somewhat more easygoing tone.)* Mary, did you like those nights? Did those nights please you? I asked you then and I'm asking you now: did you enjoy them? Did you enjoy those nights? *(As if he desired peace between them.)*

MARY: Where's the bishop?

SOCINO: *(As if remembering.)* We would wait until the bishop was asleep, and then you crept—yes, crept, you can't deny that—into my bed ... *(Small pause.)* But I can't deny that at times I lay down next to you on the floor on that bearskin. Sometimes our sweat made it smell like a dog in the rain, but I did not notice it. I smelled it only afterwards. I had no nose beforehand. Only afterwards did I realize I had a nose. *(Small pause.)* Sometimes we did it on the stairs. *(Nods toward the stairs.)* Right there. *(With pointed finger he seems to search for the exact spot.)* Sometimes we even snuck up to the attic ... *(Sits down on stair.)*

MARY: *(Both is and isn't paying attention to him, increasingly obstinate.)* Where's the bishop?

SOCINO: I knew that before my arrival, or after it, you got into bed with the bishop too. After all, you were the only female around. *(Points about.)* We couldn't be choosy. I didn't care. Though I could have. But I loved the bishop. I esteemed the bishop. You don't know men: if I had found the bishop disgusting, if I hadn't admired him, I would have felt humiliated by you. There were a number of women who disgusted me because I despised their husbands.

MARY: Socino, where's the bishop?

SOCINO: *(Lost in thought.)* And I promised to teach you how to read and write. We even started, but you did not learn anything, you are incapable of anything but ... what you're already good at. You couldn't keep your attention focused on anything. Even though they sent you here to observe. *(Small pause.)* And when you got pregnant you were in a quandary: you could not know whether it was by me or by the bishop. But God has always given women brains enough to know when to be domineering. 'As soon as you found that out you took over here; you felt that the two of us were now in your hands. *(Mary is nauseated.)* Now you feel sick to your stomach, and you don't know who caused it.

MARY: I hated the two of you, that's why I went to bed with you, because I can only sleep with someone who has humiliated me ... I hate everyone!

SOCINO: *(Precisely.)* Yes, you hate us *in general* ... like the sutling wench who hates the regiment *in general*, not because she slept with everyone, but because she doesn't know who got her pregnant. So it's really this ignorance she hates ... the fact that the soldiers made her ignorant regarding her own child. *(Small pause.)*

MARY: I hate both of you because you treated me like an idiot ... because you jabbered in Latin ... because I did not know what you were thinking about ... because you thought of me as what I really was ... because you treated me as what I really was. You looked upon me as a lowly servant girl. *(Silence.)*

SOCINO: *(As if remembering.)* Tomorrow is Christmas Eve. *(Nods.)* I am longing for peace. How about you?

MARY: Blandrata says they'll come for the bishop tomorrow.

SOCINO: Who will?

MARY: The prince's soldiers.

SOCINO: And why was this made known?

MARY: Maybe so you can say good-bye to each other. Where's the bishop?

SOCINO: *(Steps next to her.)* Can you understand, do you have the intelligence to grasp the following? The intelligent betrayer hates nothing so much as his emulator, the crude, thoughtless betrayer? And the other way around, the crude and thoughtless informer hates his rival, the intelligent, educated informer. Do you understand this, Mary?

MARY: This is what I both loved and hated in you: you could always speak about something else, never about the topic at hand. But still, you made it appear all right. I don't even know what you're like. *(Repents her momentary lenient tone, now harsh.)* Where's the bishop?

SOCINO: *(A bit to the audience.)* Can anyone grasp the fact that betrayal requires its own kind of conscience? That the intelligent informer is not just an informer for the powers that be, but for truth, for history as well? And that the thoughtless informer is only on the side of power, not on that of truth because he doesn't even know the truth, and if he did, he wouldn't understand it. *(Small pause.)* Does anyone grasp this? Because if not, then I'll have one more reason to ... *(Very quietly.)* do something ...

MARY: Quit stalling, Socino, quit stalling! Where's the bishop? *(Somewhat by way of explanation.)* They told me to look after him. I'm responsible for him. Where is he?

SOCINO: *(Sits down, different voice, less somber.)* I heard somewhere that female guards are the cruelest of them all. With women guards, escape is possible only in dreams. And only the devil and our mute thoughts can set foot in a place women watch over.

MARY: You are the devil! If you don't tell me where the bishop is, I'll report you to Blandrata! *(Starts toward the door.)*

SOCINO: Would you betray the two fathers of your only child?

MARY: *(Comes back, sits down on bed.)* You beast! How can a man of God be so beastly?! Doesn't God ever refine your kind? *(Curtly.)* Will you tell me where the bishop is? *(Silence.)*
SOCINO: *(Stands up.)* I killed him.
MARY: Madman.
SOCINO: *(Gently, reasonably, by way of explanation.)* I killed him because I was sinning against him constantly: watching him, informing on his every move. For this I have been getting nothing but praise from the sovereign. But I would like to repent. So I killed the bishop because that is punishable under law. I wanted to commit a sin against him that is punishable under a written law. Do you grasp that? Because there is no written law against informing; denouncing is supported by those who write the laws, and, as they say, uphold them. *(Slight pause.)* I killed him to punish myself through his death. To make my crime tangible.
MARY: Madman! Is what you're saying true?
SOCINO: Yes. *(Nods for a long time, convincingly.)*
MARY: Madman! I'm going to Blandrata! *(Starts out hurriedly.)*
SOCINO: *(Gently.)* Wait! *(The woman stops in her tracks.)* Wait for me outside ... I have to write today's report for Blandrata—about this, about everything ... he could be here any minute ... this will be my most important report ... the most important one. Wait for me outside ... in the hallway.
MARY: I'll wait for it here.
SOCINO: No. I want to write this report alone. I don't want to be watched while I write it. I don't want to be observed working. It would make me ill at ease. I want to write it alone. It'll be just one sentence. *(Small pause.)* This will be the only sentence in a long time that I write completely alone. *(Small pause.)* Go out there, and wait for me.
MARY: *(Shivers slightly.)* Hurry, it's cold out there in the hallway. And now ... two of us are cold. *(Puts her palm against her belly. Her voice suddenly softens, becomes gentle.)* It's *yours* ... you should know that. Hurry.
SOCINO: *(Reaches for the quill.)* I'll hurry.

(Mary exits. Socino quickly writes a few lines, puts back quill; slowly goes to stairs, his gaze rises as if taking in each step in turn.)

I told you, Blandrata, I will draw the limits of this disgrace ... *I* will hand you this letter. *(Puts letter in shirt, where the dagger is, then slowly, a little hesitantly walks toward door through which Mary left, and exits. Pause. Francis Dávid enters with a book in his hand.)*
FRANCIS DÁVID: I went to the attic for it ... See, I'm not so old ... I'm hardly out of breath ... here it is finally ... I'm covered with dust ... Socino, where are you? Here he sends me for the book, and disappears ... *(Sits on edge of bed, browses in book.)*

SOCINO: *(Enters from where he followed Mary out, stands in middle of room, looks gently at Francis Dávid, says almost cheerfully, almost reassuringly.)* Tomorrow is Christmas Eve.
FRANCIS DÁVID: Impossible! For the first time in my life I did not remember what day Christmas Eve fell on.
SOCINO: Blandrata ... *(Slight pause.)* said that the soldiers will come for you tomorrow.
FRANCIS DÁVID: Did he tell you?
SOCINO: No, he told Mary.
FRANCIS DÁVID: Where is Mary?
SOCINO: What do you think, why did Blandrata bother to let us know? *(Small pause.)* A short while ago he said it was to give you a chance to escape.
FRANCIS DÁVID: Was he here again?
SOCINO: *(Nods.)* I gave him the letter. The *last* letter.
FRANCIS DÁVID: The last one?
SOCINO: *(Nods calmly.)* I finished my job. *(Changes tone.)* So he offered you a chance to escape.
FRANCIS DÁVID: He wants evidence. Someone who tries to escape must be guilty. I escape, therefore I'm guilty. That's what he wants to prove to the sovereign. But I wouldn't get very far. And even if I reached some destination, I still would not have escaped. I have nothing to do in the world outside of my Church and outside of this land.
SOCINO: You'd learn what to do, as I had to. *(Small pause.)* It would be so strange, so good, so truly satisfying for me if you would escape now, if you would leave now, and as an exile come to my homeland, and if my sovereign, my king, would deal with you as an exile, as a homeless wanderer, the way yours has dealt with me ... If he would be just as gracious to you, have such trust in you that he would give you an assignment: to inform on someone. *(Small pause.)* Forgive me. Am I very malicious?
FRANCIS DÁVID: No, Socino, you are not malicious. But you suspected that I was holding a sentence in reserve for you. You guessed correctly. I will now tell you what it is. If I came to your country and your king asked me to do for him what my sovereign asked you to do ... *(Stops short.)*
SOCINO: Would you do it? *(Silence.)*
FRANCIS DÁVID: No. *(Silence.)*
SOCINO: You are the malicious one! *(Suddenly beside himself.)* Why weren't you ever this cruel before? You were cunning because you waited until I weakened, you waited out the very last stroke of the clock. Why weren't you ever as merciless as you are now?
FRANCIS DÁVID: *(Very calmly.)* Because I had no reason to be. I knew the sovereign wanted me out of the way. But you, in your position, could not choose any other role than that of the betrayer. *(Small pause.)* So the least I could do was to make our stay together pleasant and sincere. I wanted to help you keep

them satisfied with you. *(Slightly altered tone.)* I think you had a good time during this sojourn. We got a chance to talk our hearts out. And if it hadn't been for Mary ... *(Hesitation. Suddenly remembering.)* Where is Mary?

SOCINO: You were very cruel, Francis. Why were you deceiving me, why did you say you preferred my kind of betrayal?

FRANCIS DÁVID: You were my guest. I consoled you.

SOCINO: You consoled me?

FRANCIS DÁVID: I consoled you, because I am a minister. I would console even my executioner.

SOCINO: *(Trembling.)* Francis Dávid, what do you want to prove to me at the cost of your life?!

FRANCIS DÁVID: Only this: my God is the stronger one after all, for while you were betraying me, I was consoling you.

SOCINO: Murderer! You killed me! Robber! You robbed me! Because I believed you, I believed it when you said you believed in my good intentions! And I believed in my good intentions!

FRANCIS DÁVID: In the greatest possible good within the greatest evil. *(Pause.)*

SOCINO: You great ones are the monsters of this world! You do good in such a way that you deprive everyone beneath you and behind you of the desire to do good. You love mankind condescendingly. You love people because you see them as so much smaller than you.

FRANCIS DÁVID: Our mothers also loved us most when we were small. And God is forever good to us, because we always remain small in his sight, though he is neither our father nor our mother. And that is why there is no Virgin Mary who could have born a son to the One God. And that is why Jesus is not the son of God, but a mighty man who understood the mind of God. For God has no gender. He begets himself and gives birth to himself. He creates. *(Small pause.)* Tomorrow is Christmas Eve. Maybe that is why this came to mind ... so I could tell you: on Christmas I don't celebrate the birth of the son of *God* ... Only that of a man.

SOCINO: God has no gender? And you are a Unitarian? You deny the male creator, the Father? God has no gender?

FRANCIS DÁVID: How could God have fitted into the little womb of a transitory, mortal woman? How could the infinite be confined in the finite?

SOCINO: You consoled me all right, for good. I'm glad I denounced you.

FRANCIS DÁVID: *(Quietly.)* I intended this, too, for your consolation. Remember, you told me once that you want to be an informer out of faith, out of conviction. Your soul can feel pure now. May this be your consolation forever. And should you ever find that this consolation is insufficient, console others the same way that I consoled you. *(Slight pause, a bell rings.)* Where is Mary? *(Silence.)* Where is Mary?! *(Foreboding.)*

SOCINO: It is my son that died in her! *(Looks at his hands.)* I offered you my neck. *(Bows his head.)* You have yourself to blame. Sometimes we have to kill someone.

FRANCIS DÁVID: Is that what you did? You could do that? My Only God! *(Stunned.)*
SOCINO: *(In tears.)* It was the only way I could reciprocate ... this ... this hospitality.

(The ringing of a bell.)

(Blackout.)

Scene 4

Same scene; a Christmas tree in the middle, no ornaments, just the star of Bethlehem shines on top. Francis Dávid under the tree, Socino sits on the stairs. The bishop is lighting candles.

SOCINO: They'll be here any moment ... What may I do for you?
FRANCIS DÁVID: You've done *everything* for me.
SOCINO: *(Listens.)* I hear footsteps ... *(Footsteps can be heard, but then fade away.)*
FRANCIS DÁVID: I'm sure it's Luke. My dear relative. How often we get bored with good, concerned relatives, while at the same time we open ourselves up to the first stranger ... *(Thoughtful.)*
SOCINO: I think they're coming. *(Nothing can be heard.)*
FRANCIS DÁVID: *(Shouts.)* Luke, is it you? *(Silence.)* It's not he after all.
SOCINO: But there is someone walking ... or maybe several. *(In a whisper.)*
FRANCIS DÁVID: So long as they allow us to finish our psalms.
SOCINO: Let us sing them together.
FRANCIS DÁVID: Let's start.
SOCINO: Let's start.

(Long silence.)

FRANCIS DÁVID: Don't hurry so, Socino. Slower. *(Nods as if he heard it.)* Like that.
SOCINO: Fine. Like that.

(They keep silent.)

SOCINO: Now the eighth. You start it.
FRANCIS DÁVID: Fine. *(Brief silence.)* Like this?
SOCINO: Fine.

(Silence.)

FRANCIS DÁVID: And now let us sing the three hundredth psalm ...

SOCINO: *(Taken aback.)* But ...

FRANCIS DÁVID: You want to say that there are only a hundred and fifty psalms of David. *(Nods.)* And that there is no three hundredth. *(Small pause.)* But tell me — has there ever been a sojourn *like this* for a guest?

(Short silence.)

SOCINO: I have been a guest. I was your guest. Your guest and your betrayer. Still it is with you I prefer to celebrate Christmas. With you, for I have no one on this earth except the one I betrayed. *(Stares in front of him.)* Why do we love the one we've betrayed? *(Pause.)* I was your guest. Your parasite. You were my livelihood. Thanks to you I had a roof over my head. Do not despise me, Bishop, don't abandon me. A tick clings to livestock the way I would dig myself into you, so you couldn't tear me out of yourself. I need you. I will always need you. And perhaps only so I can betray you. Thank you for being my host.

FRANCIS DÁVID: You were a guest in my consciousness. And I was a guest in yours. And both of us were guests in God's. This is our only sojourn. *(Small pause.)* You do not notice, Socino, that you who are awaiting the sovereign's and Blandrata's reward are no happier than I am, who ... is expecting something else.

SOCINO: Nor are you happier than I am, Francis Dávid, in spite of your faith. *(Small pause.)* And now that my stay as your guest is over and we know everything about each other; now that I have informed on you and you have punished me with your consolation, tell me, because I desire to know finally and from you alone: Is God *really* One?

(Noise from without. A captain and soldiers enter, form a semicircle around the Christmas tree. The door stands open. Blandrata's face appears. He and Francis Dávid look at each other for a few moments. The doctor hurries away.)

CAPTAIN: So you did not try to escape, Francis Dávid? It wouldn't have helped, because we've had your house surrounded since yesterday.

FRANCIS DÁVID: I am escaping only from the minds of the unworthy forever.

CAPTAIN: The sovereign commands you to come with us. *(To Socino, who has moved.)* You stay. *(Unfriendly.)*

FRANCIS DÁVID: I'm coming. But first let us finish God's only psalm: silence. *(To Socino.)* Socino, let us sing — the silence! *(They stand mutely. Outside, the bell sounds. The soldiers surround the bishop, he starts out with bowed head. Exit. Silence. Footsteps on the stairway outside, Socino grows tense. Luke enters carrying the corpse of Mary. He places her next to the Christmas tree. Brief silence.)*

SOCINO: Take her away ... take her away ... *(Shuts his eyes. Luke throws a cloth over the body.)*

LUKE: *(Places hand on sword.)* Come, Socino.
SOCINO: *(Whispering.)* Where?
LUKE: Away from here.
SOCINO: Why?
LUKE: *(Hoarsely.)* We'll sing the silence.

(Socino, partly to escape the corpse, starts outward. Luke follows, the bell sounds again.)

SOCINO: *(Almost shrieking after the soldiers.)* Don't kill him! *(Whispers.)* Don't inform on God.

CURTAIN

Cheese Dumplings

István Csurka

translated by Eugene Brogyányi

Imre Rajnógel (MAFILM)

CHEESE DUMPLINGS
[Hungarian Television, Budapest, Hungary]
Directed by János Dömölky

CHARACTERS:

Young Woman
Attendant
Technician
Actor
Sociologist
Psychiatrist
Scholar

Host
Writer
Zamecky
Voice
Young Man
Cook

A small radio studio consisting of two parts: 1. "inside," a control booth separated by a double-plate glass window from 2. the "outside," a carpeted studio containing a round table. A cylindrical microphone hangs above the table. A young woman sits alone in the booth behind the glass, having breakfast. An office attendant in a gray smock enters the studio carrying four chairs, which he places at the table. The young woman presses a button, and her voice can be heard over a loudspeaker. The action takes place alternately in these two locales, which comprise, in a sense, one place. We hear the technicians directly, but the characters in the studio can hear them only when their voices are transmitted over a speaker. Since the mixing equipment in the booth is faulty, it can, when knocked or touched, sometimes transmit the technicians' voices even when they do not intend it to. Furthermore the young woman and the technician can use this flaw to play pranks or take revenge on each other by transmitting embarrassing remarks in this way.

YOUNG WOMAN: What is this, the stockroom of the Domus department store? Why are you bringing those chairs in here?
ATTENDANT: Orders from above.
YOUNG WOMAN: This is a small studio. That microphone can only accommodate four.
ATTENDANT: I'm only doing what I was told. I had a tough enough time just getting these chairs. No one wants to give them up; everyone's afraid he won't get them back.
YOUNG WOMAN: What do they think, I'll take them to my weekend house? I don't have a weekend house, not even a cabana.

ATTENDANT: You put them in the hallway after the taping, and they're gone. These people will take anything they can get their hands on.
YOUNG WOMAN: Here at the station?
ATTENDANT: Sure. Last time we brought two hundred cushions for the chairs, for the seats. I was supposed to start dispensing them upstairs in the literary department. I took thirty of them up and put them in the hallway. I take two into the office at the end, I come out, and twenty-five are left. The editors took three of them. Even though there were enough to go around. First the big shots, then the others. But they can't wait. They want everything right away.
TECHNICIAN: *(Enters, places a slip of paper in front of Young Woman.)* Hi. A peck on your lower left dimple. *Timely Topics* this morning.
YOUNG WOMAN: *(Offers her face.)*
TECHNICIAN: Not that one. The one down there on the left side. *(Kisses her face anyway.)*
YOUNG WOMAN: How do you know I've got one there too?
TECHNICIAN: I know. Girls with firm buns have a little indentation above each cheek. It's an erogenous zone. *(Changes tone.)* That idiot Beke is having a taping here today. The fifth broadcast of *Timely Topics*.
YOUNG WOMAN: Eight participants? Figure that out.
TECHNICIAN: Very significant! Beke no less! A Beke program, you see!
YOUNG WOMAN: What are they doing, punishing us? This is the second time this month we've had that mental giant inflicted on us.
TECHNICIAN: *(While removing his jacket, putting on a smock, and preparing to take his place at the mixing board.)* Isn't it all the same to you who's doing the yakking? There's always someone who's either yakking or has already yakked. Of course old Cornelius here wasn't born yesterday either: I made sure we'd be out of here in time for lunch. I got *Cuisine Today* to use this studio. The cook'll be here by eleven-thirty. You know how pushy she is. "I'm in such a hurry. My dinner'll burn... Let me tape my recipe... Take thirty decagrams of chancre, soften over a low flame..." After that, *Timely Topics* won't be able to go on.
YOUNG WOMAN: That really was a good idea. Of course dear old Marie doesn't talk like that. She's meek and mild...
TECHNICIAN: Have you ever seen a meek sutling wench?
YOUNG WOMAN: Sutling wench? What's that?
TECHNICIAN: She follows an army and provides it with everything. Even herself.
YOUNG WOMAN: You have a one-track mind...
TECHNICIAN: The essential thing is to drive this dumb-ass Beke away.
YOUNG WOMAN: The problem with the cook is the ingredients: "Ingredients." You can never get a single decagram of them.
TECHNICIAN: I think today it's going to be *padlutka*. Have you ever had that?
YOUNG WOMAN: No. And I don't want to.
TECHNICIAN: It's very good. A Transylvanian dish. It's like stuffed cabbage, only spiced differently, and wrapped in mild grape leaves. With sour cream. Nice and juicy.

YOUNG WOMAN: I don't like stuffed cabbage.
TECHNICIAN: You'll learn to like it when you marry some glutton, who'll issue his official morning proclamation: Today we're to have stuffed cabbage with pork flank. You know what that is? Pork flank? Because I'll tear you limb from limb, says the glutton, unless you make it.

(Actor enters the studio. Technician does not see him. Young Woman, as so many times before, has a joke at Technician's expense: She transmits his remarks with one small move and a faint smile. It is clear that Actor outside can hear.)

TECHNICIAN: And you make him the stuffed cabbage, because in the meantime you're cheating on him with a hip young stud, who doesn't need pork flank to get it up, and who likes something stuffed besides cabbage ...
ACTOR: *(Appreciatively, with double-entendre.)* Timely Topics?
YOUNG WOMAN: *Timely Topics*. Fifth program.
ACTOR: *(Looks at his watch.)* They told me nine o'clock. It's five after. I have to be at the film studio by ten-thirty. Who's the reporter or the host, do you know?
TECHNICIAN: Beke.
ACTOR: Comrade Beke? And there are going to be this many of us? *(Indicates chairs.)* All actors?
YOUNG WOMAN: We don't know anything except *Timely Topics* and Beke.
ACTOR: Not even the topic? I swear I never took this blind a leap into anything. They called me, even wrote me, asked me to do it, promised me double the fee, all they said was it'll be a chat with smart people. I have to assume that means they didn't invite actors ... And the topic, I ask, what is the subject of our delightful discourse to be? Veiled in secrecy! So be it! But at nine, I pray you, must it remain so at nine?

(Sociologist and Psychiatrist enter.)

SOCIOLOGIST: *Timely Topics?*
ACTOR: The timeliest.
PSYCHIATRIST: Are you the host?
ACTOR: *(Slightly offended.)* Not at all! I'm Ádám Balogh.
PSYCHIATRIST: Oh, excuse me. Of course ... These days somehow ... all those faces on the screen. I'm Dr. Béla Sipőcz.
ACTOR: Quite all right, Professor. The problem is our host isn't even here yet.
SOCIOLOGIST: *(Holds out his hand.)* I'm Lajos Várhegyi, sociologist. *(Actor smiles.)* I only add my profession for the sake of easier recollection. These days at international conferences one gets a little label with one's name. Here at home when they put a microphone to your face and ask you to comment on something, you're always supposed to state your occupation. I think both are

important, that is to say, both or neither. In a hospital, for example, we become simply "one" or "two," depending on which bed we land in.

PSYCHIATRIST: Mr. Balogh, surely you know why we're here, what the topic of the round-table discussion is to be.

ACTOR: No. As a matter of fact I thought they could pull a thing like this only on a simple clown like me, not letting on about the topic, just promising double the fee. But now I see to my surprise that they're doing it to serious people too.

SOCIOLOGIST: My problem is compounded by the fact that I didn't have a chance to listen to any previous *Timely Topics* programs ... But they didn't promise *me* any double fee ...

YOUNG WOMAN: *(Inside.)* The nerve of that Beke. It's past nine-fifteen.

TECHNICIAN: This tall one's a professor. A psychiatrist. A Kossuth Prize winner. As soon as he sees Beke, he'll take him under his care. You'll see.

YOUNG WOMAN: Why do they let Beke share a mike with people like this? There should be strict rules about who can work with whom.

TECHNICIAN: That's not the problem. The problem is that people like this agree to do it.

YOUNG WOMAN: How should they know what Beke's like? All they know is: they came to *Timely Topics*.

(Scholar enters the studio.)

TECHNICIAN: Who's this now?

SCHOLAR: Excuse me, I don't know whether I'm in the right place. *(Notices Sociologist.)* Hello there, Lajos! *Timely Topics,* you too?

SOCIOLOGIST: *Timely Topics.* Allow me to introduce my esteemed colleague: Bálint Tárkonyos, Professor of Classics and Philology ...

SCHOLAR: Classical Philology.

SOCIOLOGIST: Oh, of course, excuse me, I stand corrected: almighty head of the Department of Classical Philology.

(The hand-shaking in the studio continues, with Scholar going from person to person.)

TECHNICIAN: *(Inside.)* Of course they still haven't repaired the mixer.

YOUNG WOMAN: No.

TECHNICIAN: Let's call a truce. I want to say a thing or two about this jerk Beke.

YOUNG WOMAN: I'll be kicking the mixer.

TECHNICIAN: He almost turned me in last time.

YOUNG WOMAN: Why do you bother with a dimwit like that?

SCHOLAR: *(Shaking hands all around, gets to Actor.)* Oh, Mr. Balogh, so pleased to meet you! I had the good fortune of seeing you in *Pompeius*. It was marvelous. *(To Psychiatrist.)* I think ... I have a feeling we've already met.

PSYCHIATRIST: *(Tactfully.)* I'm Dr. Sipőcz ... presently employed at the insane asylum, Professor ... believe me, we haven't met ...
SCHOLAR: Not even at some private gathering? Where perhaps I wasn't a scholar, and you weren't a psychiatrist, but both of us may have had a few too many?
YOUNG WOMAN: *(Inside.)* They're all men. And all getting on in years.
TECHNICIAN: Even so, your dimples could give them a charge.
YOUNG WOMAN: Cut the dimple bit or I'll turn on the juice.
TECHNICIAN: Oh, I get it, only they're allowed to engage in witty chatter, huh? Do you hear how intelligently they suck up to each other? Chatter, chatter, chatter. They're going at it like a bunch of ducks. Did you ever see ducks slurping with their beaks in the soft mud? They stick their beaks in, and move them fast — so fast you'd think they were driven by an electric motor, 800 revolutions per minute. *(Rolls an r.)*

(Writer enters the studio, and silently, with reserve, shakes hands with everyone.)

TECHNICIAN: That's how a duck slurps. And that's what I have to work with, making sure it's intelligible, stereophonic, clear ... but I'm just a simple technician ... they're the big shots, the brain trusts ... officialdom, position, know-how, power ...
YOUNG WOMAN: Do you really hate everybody? If they're the ones you hate, why take it out on me? Do you think you could amuse yourself with my dimples if *I* were the sound engineer and *you* the tape-machine operator? You've never even seen them ... Well, once you ran into me at the municipal pool when I was in a bikini.
TECHNICIAN: You have no sense of humor.
YOUNG WOMAN: No. You have enough for both of us. Everything is just a big joke to you.
TECHNICIAN: What's eating you?
YOUNG WOMAN: Where's my two hundred forints? You said you'd pay me today. You're avoiding the issue with this dimple number and all the rest. Pay up. I need my money too, you know.
TECHNICIAN: You'll get it today. I don't have it right now. I'll get it. Things have been tough.

(Outside, Scholar sits down facing the window, and places his stuffed briefcase on the table. He is sweating, and wipes himself constantly with a handkerchief.)

YOUNG WOMAN: What does this guy think this is? Tell him.
TECHNICIAN: *(Over loudspeaker.)* Excuse me. There shouldn't be anything on the table. Sound distortion, you know. Perhaps you'd like to use the cloakroom.
SCHOLAR: Of course, of course. *(Stands up.)* Do I have enough time to take it to the cloakroom?

ACTOR: Put it in the corner there. It'll be out of the way... Distortion? What do they mean?

HOST: *(Enters in a dither.)* I beg your pardon, Comrades. Beg your pardon... I'm Bence Beke, your host for the program. I was delayed for reasons beyond my control... Comrade Tornyossy, whom I would have wanted to participate in today's taping of *Timely Topics*... have a seat, Comrades, please sit down, we'll assign places in a moment, though this is a round table, no place is weightier than another... in any case, Comrade Tornyossy called me at ten minutes to nine, and canceled because of an important delegation from Ceylon...

TECHNICIAN: *(Inside.)* Delegation. What did I tell you?... Delegatski.

YOUNG WOMAN: Cut the crap, they can see you. *(Young Woman raises her hand as if to hit the mixer, laughs.)*

TECHNICIAN: Delegatski.

HOST: The concept behind the program is in principle such that it requires the presence of a person of the stature of Comrade Tornyossy. I rushed up to the Director's Office, but they weren't yet... well, they were in conference... and after all, I can't just pluck a person of Comrade Tornyossy's stature off a tree... anyway, the Director's Office began making phone calls... The upshot is that we're getting a person of Comrade Tornyossy's stature. He's on his way now.

ACTOR: From where? That is the question.

SOCIOLOGIST: No doubt from a place commensurate with his stature.

HOST: From home. He's on vacation, but he agreed to do it. I sent a car for him... I beg your indulgence just a little longer, Comrades.

PSYCHIATRIST: In the meantime at least we can find out why we were asked here in such great numbers. What's our topic?

HOST: The concept behind the program calls for revealing the topic only when the tape is running. We're after spontaneous reactions.

SCHOLAR: Excuse me... What if Comrade Tornyossy had come?

HOST: Well, I would have been very pleased...

ACTOR: Clearly. But would his reactions also have been spontaneous?

HOST: I must admit, not in his case.

SCHOLAR: And the one who's replacing him?

HOST: I didn't get a chance to brief him.

SOCIOLOGIST: Is this an experiment or a discussion program?

WRITER: Good question.

HOST: This is the foremost program of the Department of Persuasion.

ACTOR: Who's this "person of stature"? It somehow bothers me when my spontaneous reactions are closely scrutinized by certain persons of "stature."

HOST: He too is only a participant in the round-table discussion. In any case the sixth participant is Comrade Zamecky.

WRITER: Zamecky? I know him. I worked with him in the Democratic Youth

Federation at Veztő thirty years ago ... thirty? Twenty-eight. Whatever. He's a decent fellow ... What's Comrade Zamecky's line these days?
HOST: The state ...
TECHNICIAN: *(Inside.)* You hear, my dear? His line: the state ... He works for the state lines. Must be a choo-choo engineer. *(Zamecky enters, with an attendant, of course.)* But lo, here's Zamecky! *(The female secretary accompanying Zamecky exchanges some whispers with Beke.)*
TECHNICIAN: Stand up, you jerks, you hear?! *(Young Woman suddenly steps to the switch.)* On your feet!

(This last remark goes out over the loudspeaker. A stunned silence follows. The secretary steps out smiling slightly, closes the door behind her.)

HOST: *(Shouts, outraged.)* Having a good time, Cornelius?
TECHNICIAN: *(Over loudspeaker.)* Excuse me ...
HOST: You haven't heard the last of this! *(Pretends to be speechless with rage; he leafs through his notes, prepares to speak.)*
TECHNICIAN: *(Inside.)* What a bitch you are ... What do you want to do me in for? That miserable two hundred forints?
YOUNG WOMAN: I hate the way you always have a comment for everything. What has that man ever done to you? And here you go humiliating him, embarrassing him. Look how uncomfortable the poor man is. You're a coward, an envious coward. Tell them off to their faces, not behind their backs ... You guys just rant and rave ...
TECHNICIAN: What "guys"?
YOUNG WOMAN: You and your kind. Nothing's ever good enough for you. Nothing's true, nothing has any value. If this guy you just embarrassed came in here now, and said he'd hire you at a thousand over your current pay, on the condition that you gave up wanting to stand the world on its ear, you'd go. Without so much as a peep.
TECHNICIAN: At least then I could give you your two hundred.
HOST: *(In the meantime has been trying to start the proceedings outside, but has been too upset.)* Dear Comrade Zamecky, I'm sure I speak in the name of the entire round table, and of the radio station, when I ask you to excuse this unfortunate incident. Its participants will be punished. Allow me now to express to you our heartfelt gratitude, inasmuch as you were gracious enough to step in on such short notice, virtually ad hoc so to speak, in order to replace the unfortunately detained but highly honored Comrade Tornyossy. Truly praiseworthy ... And so perhaps we should begin ... Oh, pardon me, I should introduce the participants ... Comrade Zamecky; Mr. Balogh, the actor, whom perhaps there's no need to introduce; Lajos Várhegyi, sociologist.
SOCIOLOGIST: We've already introduced ourselves.
HOST: That's all right. That was pro forma. This time it's official. *(Continues.)* Dr. Béla Sipőcz.

ZAMECKY: *(Smiling broadly.)* Psychiatrist.

(Psychiatrist nods to Zamecky.)

HOST: *(Also confirms with a smile that Zamecky knows Psychiatrist.)* Quite so ... Bálint Tárkonyos, Professor of Classics and Philology, and last but not least, Comrade Gergely Vad, our most honored and respected Comrade Vad, whose writings have given us so many pleasurable hours.
WRITER: I'm delighted to hear about the pleasure Vad's writing has given, but I'm Lajos Sikvédi. *(To Zamecky.)* Hello, Zami ... remember me?
ZAMECKY: Damn straight, Lajos!
HOST: Comrade Sikvédi, what can I say? Excuse me!
ACTOR: What indeed? ...
TECHNICIAN: *(Inside.)* Now I should keep my mouth shut?! Has there ever been a bigger ass on the face of the earth?! What can he say? "Excuse me!" Our whole rotten life is one big "excuse me!" ... Excuse me for living, excuse me for eating, for not working, for working, for doing a lousy job, excuse me for saying excuse me. Excuse me, excuse me, excuse me.
HOST: Excuse me three times over. Bringing these sessions together makes a person quite... Comrade Tornyossy's sudden withdrawal... Having to replace him ... Anyway, Comrades, excuse me. So then, let's do the sound check. Have you Comrades ever taken part in a sound check? There's nothing to it, really ...
TECHNICIAN: *(Inside.)* Now he's going to jabber on for half an hour about this trifle ...
HOST: It's a necessary evil, this sound-check ritual ... though I could call it a fine old custom... tradition ... Well, according to the tradition of the sound check, the host goes first. *(As if nothing happened.)* Cornelius, may we start?
TECHNICIAN: *(Inside, during the above speech.)* Give me a break. This isn't true. It can't be. Did you hear that? A sound check is a ritual to him. This is, this is ... *(Officially, over the speaker.)* By all means.
HOST: Sound check ... Well now, what can a host say? The traditional thing, I suppose: testing, testing, one, two, three.
TECHNICIAN: Thank you.

(Host points to Scholar.)

SCHOLAR: One, two, three, four! *(Warming up to it.)* Arma virumque cano, Troiae qui primus ab oris ...
TECHNICIAN: Thank you. Please move your chair a little closer to the table.
SCHOLAR: Even when I'm speaking Hungarian?
HOST: That's a good one! Excuse me. Next. *(Points to Actor.)*

ACTOR: *(Prosaically.)*
"Why, I, in this weak piping time of peace,
Have no delight to pass away the time ..."
HOST: *(To the others.)* Interesting that actors always use their own words at sound checks, they never quote from one of their parts ... *(Nods to Sociologist.)*
SOCIOLOGIST: *(Has begun to weary of Host's inanity, with malice.)* Exceptions strengthen the rule. *(Picks up where Actor left off, in an exaggerated scan.)*
"Unless to spy my shadow in the sun,
And descant on mine own deformity..." *(Gets stuck.)*
ACTOR: *(Picks it up, now also scanning.)*
"And therefore, since I cannot prove a lover,
To entertain these fair well-spoken days,
I am determined to prove a villain..."
SOCIOLOGIST:
"And hate the idle pleasures of these days."
YOUNG WOMAN: *(Inside.)* Boy, did he get his! See, you bigmouth? That's how refined people burst a bubblehead.
TECHNICIAN: I just wonder if he caught on.
HOST: *(Smiling, moves on to the next one, taking no note of what just transpired; to Psychiatrist.)* One sentence please.
PSYCHIATRIST: Opportunists are also human.
HOST: *(Moving on to Writer.)* Preferably something of your own.
WRITER: Hickory dickory dock, the mouse ran up the clock.
HOST: Wonderful. Thank you. *(Looks at Zamecky.)*
ZAMECKY: *(Keeps quiet.)*
HOST: Go right ahead, Comrade Zamecky. You're next.
ZAMECKY: *(Keeps quiet.)*
TECHNICIAN: *(Inside.)* Don't tell me you've got nothing to say, bubby. How 'bout a quote from one of *your* classics?!
YOUNG WOMAN: Poor turkey.
ZAMECKY: *(Snaps out of it.)* Now I lay me down to sleep, I pray the Lord my soul to keep ... I mean, that was for the sound check, of course.
HOST: Naturally! Thank you. It's been enchanting. This sound check has reached the highest standard of any in years.
TECHNICIAN: *(Inside.)* Spare me! I can't take any more!
YOUNG WOMAN: Look at the sociologist. He's just about cracking up ...
TECHNICIAN: These poor slobs don't realize what they got themselves into. I wonder what the topic's going to be after this ghastly introduction.

(From here the dialogue runs parallel for a while: Host in the studio, technicians in the control booth.)

HOST: At the risk of sounding immodest, in which case please excuse me, let me say that I feel this topic is very much my own, and I put up quite a struggle for it.

114 Cheese Dumplings

YOUNG WOMAN: Yesterday in the cafeteria I overheard part of a conversation. Amidst peals of laughter, Pozsonyi was telling Mrs. Galeg something about some plan of Beke's to revamp *Timely Topics*. This must be it.
HOST: The topic had its opponents. There'll always be over-anxious types, fault-finders, as you're well aware. But ultimately, I can proudly report, the topic won out against them. *(Takes notes from his pocket.)*
TECHNICIAN: Stupid people are always changing things. Inept people who can't do something the regular way — they'll do it in an irregular way. Obviously, this is going to be an irregular *Timely Topics*. You'll see...
HOST: Surely you've heard the recurrent broadcasts of *Timely Topics*. Undeniably, today's topic will to some extent be an irregular one.

(Technician looks triumphantly at Young Woman, and pats his own shoulder.)

HOST: Because ... because ... well, we'll get to that in due course... Many distinguished thinkers, public figures, women, children ... I mean, not children, it's just that I also work for the Trailblazers, and there I share a round table with children ... Excuse me for digressing ... Ordinary workers, women, young people ... Because, after all, this table is round, the spoken word is of equal weight at every one of its points ... *(Looks at his notes.)*
TECHNICIAN: Will you look at that! He's got this written down ... Unbelievable!
HOST: Now a few words about myself.
TECHNICIAN: Oh no! Please! Spare me!

(Host is sitting with his back at three-quarters to Technician, and so cannot see the latter's grimacing. But those facing the booth, Sociologist and Psychiatrist, can. By now they have caught on, and have become Technician's confederates.)

HOST: I was born in Alpár during the difficult war years, or rather, during the final years of peace ... depending on how you look at it.

(Writer and Scholar look at each other. It is clear that this is too much for them, too.)

ACTOR: Forgive me for interrupting, but I have a ten-thirty shoot at the film studio. And I have to get there first ... This is all very interesting ... but ...
HOST: I'm not saying these things for nothing. They relate to the topic, which is out of the ordinary.
WRITER: Let's dive right in. That's the best way.
ZAMECKY: Though this is costing me vacation time, I'm in favor of laying a good foundation.
TECHNICIAN: *(Inside.)* That's something you can drink to, right pal?
HOST: We have to get to know one another. Comrade Zamecky is right. We have to lay a solid foundation before introducing the topic to the round table. We

mustn't have the slightest suspicion about one another. Doubts, reservations, and mistrust have no place here. So, as I said, I was born in Alpár. I attended secondary school ...

TECHNICIAN: *(Throws switch, over loudspeaker.)* Comrade Beke, I think I should point out that you have the studio only till eleven-thirty.

HOST: *(Correctly interpreting this as a reprimand, again flies into a rage.)* Not till eleven-thirty, but as long as I want it! This is the most important program of the Department of Persuasion!

TECHNICIAN: Tell that to whoever's after you.

HOST: I will! The studio is mine the whole day if necessary. Clear?!

PSYCHIATRIST: I'd like to propose a compromise solution.

HOST: By all means, Professor.

PSYCHIATRIST: Please tell us the topic we were gathered here to discuss, and then together we'll decide, by voice vote, whether our ability to discuss it requires our knowing where you attended secondary school.

YOUNG WOMAN: *(Inside.)* All the more so, since you already know what his grades were like.

TECHNICIAN: Are you kidding? He was at the top of his class. *He* couldn't have failed. Not him. Never. Top grades in everything. He was exempt from gymnastics, of course. And choir. But religion was a breeze for him.

SOCIOLOGIST: Or where *we* attended.

SCHOLAR: I support the proposal.

ACTOR: In my case, I believe everyone right off the bat. Total confidence. Just let's get started already.

HOST: In essence I agree with what has been said, though I wish to mention that when the topic is placed on the table it will immediately become clear why a thorough round of introductions would have been important. In any case, I attended secondary school at Alpár, and finished with honors.

YOUNG WOMAN: *(To Technician.)* Congratulations.

TECHNICIAN: No, no, I was wrong. He's lying. If he'd really finished with honors he'd now be bragging that he flunked out.

HOST: I say that only parenthetically... It's indisputable that we live in a fast-moving age, I acknowledge that. Everyone's time is precious. Please excuse me. So then, let me greet you, Comrades, in the name of the entire *Timely Topics* team. And allow me to extend a special greeting to Comrade Zamecky for having forfeited a part of his vacation, his freedom, so to speak, that treasure most prized by all of us, in order to be here at the round table of *Timely Topics,* filling in for Comrade Tornyossy. Of course, we extend our best wishes to Comrade Tornyossy, who, because of his many obligations connected with the delegation from Ceylon...

SOCIOLOGIST: *(Interrupts.)* It's not Ceylon any more, it's Sri Lanka.

TECHNICIAN: *(Inside.)* It would be if he could pronounce it...

HOST: ... Thank you ... a delegation from ... à la English, right? ... "Sir" Lanka, or Linka...

SOCIOLOGIST: No, no. Sri Lanka ... as its inhabitants would say.
HOST: Oh well, in any case, a delegation from a developing country, at whose reception he had to be present, thereby precluding his scheduled appearance here at our round table.
WRITER: *(Irascibly.)* Look, Comrade Beke, I swallowed the affront of being confused with one of my colleagues, even though in general we writers aren't well-disposed to that sort of thing. But this frittering away of time I find downright insulting. Were we or were we not asked here to discuss some serious question?! We're all engaged in important projects, we don't have time to sit around listening to this... this prattle.
ACTOR: I agree.
SCHOLAR: I suspect that our host is trying to win our good will; unfortunately I must say that it's not working.
ZAMECKY: I'll pass on your greetings to Comrade Tornyossy. Onward!
YOUNG WOMAN: *(Inside.)* It's beginning to take shape.
HOST: Excuse me, Comrades. What can I say? Excuse me three times over. I do regret giving up the preliminaries, but perhaps we can fill in as we go along. I understand that your time is particularly valuable, there can be no doubt about that. Perhaps one more thing, because this is imperative by all means: what we're asking is that you strive to ... to get at it ... the topic ... from the inside ... You were invited here as people whose work, whose lives, whose struggles unavoidably bring you up against it ... face to face with it ... the topic, that is. You are—in our opinion—the most distinguished domestic experts on the topic ... Indeed, even on an international level ... There's much more I could say ... Let this suffice ... And another thing: This program has to be aired tomorrow morning. The Editorial Staff got itself into a situation in which all the topics proposed by the Editorial Staff for discussion on *Timely Topics* were overruled. This one remained. Mine. But that's beside the point. All I want to emphasize is the responsibility. This is the final topic. For the moment. And for the moment the most important one. The most pressing. Of course at other times too. Always! *(In the strident tone of a ringmaster or cabaret announcer.)* Comrades, for the fifth program of *Timely Topics*, the Editorial Staff of *Timely Topics* asks you to discuss the issues surrounding the topic of this program, whose title is "The Role of Stupidity in Our Society!" Best wishes for a productive discussion, Comrades! *(Sits.)*

(Host waves to Technician to start the tape. Technician nods, indicating that he is taping.)

(Outside in the studio, long, stunned silence. The guests look at each other in mute rage, not daring to believe that this is true, that they are not victims of some prank.)

TECHNICIAN: *(Inside.)* And this guy is still on the loose...
YOUNG WOMAN: They're gasping...

TECHNICIAN: In other words, they're now in the forefront of stupidity. Of domestic stupidity ... They're the first among the stupid. They'll be able to get at it from the inside ... And he gets a bonus every quarter...
YOUNG WOMAN: And he was born in Alpár ... and as for secondary school ... Too bad they didn't let him finish his biography.
TECHNICIAN: Didn't I tell you? Now you can see for yourself, this is unbearable without a running commentary. We're just technical personnel. We don't perform intellectual labors. *(Points to the outside.)* They do that. By the way, you know why he wanted to tell them about his secondary-school record? To show them that he's not stupid. Not him!
YOUNG WOMAN: But the others earn their pay too. Why do they agree to it when they don't even know what they're getting into?
TECHNICIAN: *Timely Topics.* That's what got them. I better say something. *(To the studio.)* The tape's running.
PSYCHIATRIST: Turn it off, please. We have to clarify something first.
HOST: That's what I wanted. Go right ahead. *(To Technician.)* Turn it off.
PSYCHIATRIST: To put it very simply, has there been some misunderstanding here?
WRITER: More to the point, are we victims of some prank, some dumb trick?
PSYCHIATRIST: Right.
ACTOR: One question, Comrade Zamecky. Were you not informed of this topic either?
HOST: There wasn't even time for that.
ZAMECKY: No, I'm innocent.
ACTOR: And was Comrade Tornyossy informed of it?
HOST: I must admit that my editor-in-chief did inform Comrade Tornyossy in advance, and he liked the topic very much. He said he'd have a lot to say, and was very curious about what you ... he knows about everyone, and has heartfelt greetings for everyone...
ACTOR: *(Through his teeth.)* For Comrade Gergely Vad, too...
HOST: ...about what you'll bring to the illumination of this topic...
ACTOR: That I can believe.
HOST: I've already mentioned that we're not so much interested in preconceived ideas, as in extemporaneous opinions.
SCHOLAR: I don't see why it wouldn't have been better to prepare for this topic.
HOST: Excuse me. Now the lack of a thorough introduction, a solid foundation, becomes clear, doesn't it? Of course this lack can still be made up for. It's not mere boasting on my part when I say that this topic truly is mine. I thought it up, I fought for it, I got it accepted. This topic came to life in battle. And it won. I struggled hard on its behalf. And I thought a lot about it, did a lot of soul-searching. I have ideas, but I don't want to force them on you. In the course of my analyses I've come to the conclusion that we always come face to face with stupidity unexpectedly. You'll walk in somewhere ... for our

purposes now it makes no difference where ... into an office, a grocery store, whatever ... I'm babbling...

TECHNICIAN: *(Inside.)* You don't say!

HOST: This is just an example ... which depends on the person to whom you turn, who's taking care of you, whom you've entrusted with something ... whatever that may be ... As I said, this doesn't have to be taken as gospel, it's just an example of ... well anyway, and then this person happens not to be a genius ... not only not a genius ... but downright stupid. You're just amazed ... Well, that's why I kept the topic a secret, that's why I didn't give you a chance to prepare. Comrade Tornyossy's a different story ... I think you can understand ... I don't think I have to ... I mean it's clear...

ACTOR: That's not how it is with me. I'm always prepared for stupidity, and then I'm surprised when the person is intelligent.

WRITER: Are you often surprised?

ACTOR: Abroad. Often abroad.

SCHOLAR: I admit, I did prepare by listening to all of the previous *Timely Topics* programs. The topics, coupled with my invitation, led me to believe that we'd be discussing something to do with cultural matters, that sort of thing.

PSYCHIATRIST: My invitation implies a biological approach to the topic. I must say that stupidity is not germane to the study of mental illness. Differences in intellectual and mental capacity do not constitute the subject of medical research. Indeed, not even that of psychology. Of course, it's a different matter when we're dealing with pathological inferiority, mental deficiency, or the many incidents of mental diseases.

SOCIOLOGIST: The tape ought to be turned on. This, for example, is a superb introduction to, and delineation of, the topic. It is possible, after all, to talk about this topic. It's not such a bad topic. Too bad we wasted so much time.

WRITER: Clearly it falls to me to talk about the literary representation of stupidity.

SCHOLAR: The great stupid figures of world literature...

ACTOR: I'm a leading man. I haven't played a small part in years. Stupidity is always portrayed in small parts. It's episodic.

SCHOLAR: Not so. Stupidity has a leading role.

ACTOR: I mean on stage.

WRITER: Well, considering that I've been taken for Gergely Vad ... the point is that, in my case, I'm not an untrained natural talent... I write essays too...

SOCIOLOGIST: Clearly I should chat about the stupidity of the masses, of communities...

HOST: Right ... that's it ... chat...

SOCIOLOGIST: Chat? *(With knit eyebrows, severely.)* Dear Comrade, one can't chat about this. The stupidity of the masses is one of the most dramatic questions of our time. The world over. The masses, you see, are not stupid. Not as a

matter of course. But they can be influenced. They can be maddened. They can be made stupid.
SCHOLAR: Stupidity is a superpower. A formidable superpower.
PSYCHIATRIST: Stupidity manipulates us.
SCHOLAR: Stupidity is intransigent. Stupidity is fundamental.
PSYCHIATRIST: Stupidity is one of life's great bounties.
WRITER: Wouldn't you say rather: one of life's great misfortunes?
ACTOR: Happy are the poor of mind, for theirs shall be the kingdom of heaven.
HOST: The program is taking shape.
PSYCHIATRIST: Stupidity is not conscious of itself. Therefore it is happy. A stupid person who knows he is stupid is no longer stupid. That's quite natural.
SOCIOLOGIST: Yes, but the stupidity that saturates the cells of society is conscious of itself.
SCHOLAR: And it is evil. *(Sighs.)* If I'd known this is what we'd be discussing, I wouldn't have agreed to it.
HOST: Comrades, I ask you to say everything you can in connection with this topic entirely openly, sincerely, without evasiveness. Whatever occurs to you, your experience in confronting stupidity, in having to deal with it, struggle with it, as with the mythological seven-headed eagle. I mean, dragon. That eagle had only two heads, right? I wonder how many stupidity has. Ha ha. This is just a ... a ... I don't want to give you pointers, not for the world. But talk about everything. Boldly. The topic has won its support, as I mentioned. And one more thing. And that's this, though I know it's superfluous to say, after all ... in other words: Comrades, here and now, discuss stupidity — with intelligence!

(Once again, deafening silence in the studio.)

TECHNICIAN: *(Inside.)* Filthy huckster! *(Over loudspeaker.)* Can we roll?
HOST: In any case, that happens to be the subtitle of the program: "About Stupidity, with Intelligence." *(Looks around, no effect, adds.)* Timely Topics, Special Edition. *(Looks around to see whether they are ready.)* Start the tape.
TECHNICIAN: *(Inside.)* Not yet. It'll be half an hour yet, at least.
YOUNG WOMAN: What I don't get is why he didn't let them in on what this would be about.
TECHNICIAN: He would have gotten very concise responses. To the point. They would have told him exactly where he could shove his topic.
SCHOLAR: *(Raises his hand, Host nods at him.)* I must make an announcement.
YOUNG WOMAN: *(Inside.)* I'm starting.
TECHNICIAN: Wait, it'll only have to be erased anyway ... But go ahead ... I don't care ... I'll eat my hat if a program comes of this today.
SCHOLAR: Not for the program ...
HOST: Stop.

TECHNICIAN: *(Impertinently, over the loudspeaker.)* We never even started.
HOST: *(Outraged.)* What's this impertinence again?! If I give the order to start, you start, goddamn it! How can any work get done this way?! Everyone has to do his job! How can an irresponsible worker like you have been assigned to *Timely Topics*?!
WRITER: Nothing's been lost. Maybe he didn't start because he's got experience in these things.
TECHNICIAN: Of the four programs so far, I've done two. The editor-hosts so far had no objections to my work.
HOST: Well I have objections. If there's one more disruptive, uncooperative, insulting, demeaning, or demagogic word out of you, I'll stop the program, and issue a report.
WRITER: Insofar as this is not being recorded, insofar as this in no way lends color to the topic, or serves as an example, I suggest you stop it. It has nothing to do with us.
HOST: *(A little impulsively, because he senses that Writer's contempt is directed at him.)* Mr. Vad, I insulted you but asked you to excuse me. This is an internal affair!
WRITER: That makes three! I'm Sikvédi. Got that? Lajos Sikvédi. I've been Lajos Sikvédi for over five decades, unfortunately.
HOST: Excuse me.
PSYCHIATRIST: We've heard that already. Allow me to make one observation. Never mind that we couldn't prepare, but *you* really ought to have prepared. It would at least have behooved you to know whom you herded here. As far as I'm concerned, I have nothing to say about this thing. Whatever I had to say, I've said. If you want, I'll say it once more, and be on my way.
HOST: Calm yourselves, Comrades. *(To Technician.)* See how you've poisoned the atmosphere with your impudent remarks?!
SOCIOLOGIST: He didn't poison the atmosphere. Not at all. What would he have recorded anyway?
ACTOR: Gentlemen, let's stop this. Let's rattle this off. For that matter, I don't have a lot to say on this subject either. Who's stupid? You or I? We or you? It's a tough question. And I have to tell you that the actors' union might not be too pleased about my adding my observations to this topic.
SOCIOLOGIST: In my opinion, half the program's done. The professor, you, the actor, Professor Tárkonyos also was about to say something...
SCHOLAR: All I wanted to say was that I'm afraid. *(Looks around.)* What about the rest of you?
WRITER: Without a doubt, there's something frightening in all this. One isn't sure whether it's real: what we're doing up to our necks — our ears — in this quagmire. Who shoved us in? Our enemies? Is this a prank or an investigation? Are hidden cameras recording the whole thing?
SCHOLAR: Oh, it's more than that! Much more! Till now, stupidity was not palpable to me. Now it's right here. Standing before me here, like a dark tower

about to topple on me ... I'm powerless. I agreed to this; here I am. Now what should I do? Was I stupid when I agreed to do this, or was I simply duped?
ACTOR: Duped? Program or no program, we're entitled to the double fee.
HOST: Naturally. Every *Timely Topics* participant is entitled to an exceptional honorarium. Guaranteed. What we desire, on the other hand, is that you Comrades furnish something exceptional in keeping with the magnitude of the topic and the program, and of your own standing in society.
WRITER: To furnish something exceptional on the spot about a general, intangible topic?
SCHOLAR: Once more I emphasize: I'm afraid. Maybe my nerves are shattered. Maybe this is simply a scholar's fear, a worker's fear, a professor's fear, a teacher's fear ... Allow me to quote Archimedes: "Noli turbare circulos meos!" I'd like to go.
HOST: No, Professor. Unheard of. What are you afraid of? Me?
SCHOLAR: I can't put my finger on it.
WRITER: I too feel a bit uneasy.
HOST: Luckily the doctor is at hand. Professor, surely you have some sedative with you ...
TECHNICIAN: *(Inside.)* If at least one of them doesn't punch him in the mouth now, I'm going out there and telling him where to get off.
YOUNG WOMAN: Look, the professor's turning red.
SOCIOLOGIST: Things are not that simple! One would expect more tact from a radio host. You must feel some sort of responsibility for herding us here, and then wasting our time. Start the tape for all I care. The topic is ... The topic, if you please, is sheer nonsense! *(Exhales.)* There, I've said it. The devil take it! I tried my best to keep it to myself, but I can't. It's nonsense! But I suppose it's possible to talk about it. In the cabaret. But if it's good enough for *Timely Topics*, well, so be it. Let's get on with it!
HOST: Comrades! There's really no point in our dwelling on who might be responsible for poisoning the atmosphere here. It could be, perhaps, I grant you, that I share in the blame. But Comrades, let me point out one factor. You all agreed to this. You confirmed. Here you sit. I'm not saying the doors are locked. Not at all. You're free to go any time, even without a program having been taped. A *Timely Topics*. After all, I can always round up another half-dozen Hungarian intellectuals ... who'd be willing ... Of course, ethics would require my telling them that such and such persons had nothing to say. Candor is the best policy. If a newspaper reporter these days is not allowed into a firm, he reports as much. And generally that causes more unpleasantness than if he were to print an investigative report.
WRITER: Look, sir, no amount of threatening is going to convince us that this isn't a poorly organized, badly prepared, devil-take-it program.
ACTOR: There're six of us who share that opinion.
HOST: Or perhaps five. Comrade Zamecky, may I infer from your silence that you don't agree with what's being said?

ZAMECKY: I consider the topic an important one. Just as Comrade Tornyossy does. It can and should be discussed, but not now. We're out of time now anyway. The shortcomings in the preparations must be eliminated. That's for sure. Then we'll set a new time. As far as I'm concerned, I don't see why this can't be done ... This can be a very attractive program ... Both sides have a point.

TECHNICIAN: *(Inside.)* Time to call it a day, Comrades. Sound the retreat! *(Imitates a bugle-call of military retreat.)*

YOUNG WOMAN: *(Broadcasts it into the studio.)*

(In the studio, stunned silence followed by laughter. Sociologist, Writer, Psychiatrist, Actor are now laughing delightedly and in full solidarity with Technician.)

TECHNICIAN: *(To Young Woman.)* You viper!

HOST: *(Breaks forth; this was the last straw; bloodthirsty.)* Have you lost your mind, you cretin? Can't you see that you're undermining a program with your idiocy? I'll have you fired!

SOCIOLOGIST: Come now. It wasn't this young fellow who undermined this program.

PSYCHIATRIST: Certainly not! You can't expect anything other than a bad response to such a badly put question.

HOST: Should we rephrase the question? Shall we talk about intelligence?

WRITER: It's all the same to you whether we talk about stupidity or intelligence?! Boggles the mind!

ACTOR: I've been saying all along that it doesn't matter what we talk about, let's just talk.

HOST: As you wish. One moment, Comrades. I'm going to get us a proper technician. I can't work with this ... this hooligan.

WRITER: Don't bother. We hold nothing against this young man. This thing didn't fall apart because of him.

YOUNG WOMAN: *(Inside.)* You don't know human nature. I knew what the effect of this would be.

TECHNICIAN: It's just that he's going to take it out on me.

YOUNG WOMAN: These scholars will defend you.

TECHNICIAN: Sure, as long as they're here. Then they'll forget about me.

HOST: This has been a great lesson for me. I ask you to wait five minutes, Comrades. I just have to make a call.

YOUNG WOMAN: *(Over the loudspeaker.)* What number should I dial? You can use the microphone.

HOST: Call *Timely Topics*, 008.

YOUNG WOMAN: *(Dials, can be heard over the loudspeaker.)* Hello? *Timely Topics?* Comrade Beke from Studio 19, one moment ...

HOST: Hello! Is that you, Comrade Szappanos? Well, I washed out. I have to say it. I washed out ...

VOICE: *(Indifferently.)* What's this about?
HOST: *Timely Topics* Five ... "The Role of Stupidity in Our Society." Subtitle: "About Stupidity, with Intelligence." We've got trouble. Supposedly the topic's bad.

(Scholar is not well; he is sweating profusely; he takes a pill.)

VOICE: *(Disappointed but blasé.)* Oh.
HOST: I washed out ... We've reached the point where even taking civilized leave of one another has become problematic. But the most decisive factor is that I was given a shabby, worthless, four-man studio, with outrageously impudent personnel.
YOUNG WOMAN: *(Inside.)* Are you impudent? *(A click.)*
TECHNICIAN: Did you disconnect?
YOUNG WOMAN: You bet I did.
HOST: *(Does not know, of course, and continues.)* But that's a separate issue. I'm submitting a report about that. The technician's destructive comments completely undermined the participants' disposition, and I must say also that the Comrades are not fully cognizant of their responsibility, of what it means to sit at the round table of *Timely Topics*. Hello ... Be so good as to come down and talk to the Comrades. It seems I don't carry enough weight with them, I'm ... hello? Hello?
TECHNICIAN: *(Over the loudspeaker.)* The line's been disconnected for half an hour.

(Comprehension in the studio, hearty laughter among the guests, then, since Host has just insulted them, they turn grave.)

YOUNG WOMAN: Are we calling again?
HOST: *(Foaming at the mouth.)* I'll let you know soon enough what you're to do!
(Jumps up, dashes out, slams the door behind him.)
ACTOR: Well, as a matter of fact, what *is* the role of stupidity in our society?

(Unanimous laughter.)

PSYCHIATRIST: This defies all reason ... If among my patients ... but no, there aren't any like this among them.
SOCIOLOGIST: Congratulations, young man. We're very grateful. If it hadn't been for you, we'd now be constrained to state our views on stupidity, and I'm afraid we'd have been babbling stupidities.
TECHNICIAN: He'll report me ...
WRITER: We'll all take your side.
TECHNICIAN: Thank you. I'll be needing your testimony, Comrades.
SCHOLAR: You did nothing more than a perky student would have done, and you always chimed in at exactly the right moment.

PSYCHIATRIST: More than that! He knew whom we were up against, so he was helping us out ... To put it bluntly, he was helping us expose him for what he is.

SOCIOLOGIST: Well put.

SCHOLAR: Of course, discipline ... discipline is also necessary ... at a given ... oh, horrible ... what a shame ...

ACTOR: Professor! There's no disaster here! Discipline? In the nut house? *(To Psychiatrist.)* Oh, pardon me.

ZAMECKY: The Comrade is a little on edge.

WRITER: On edge? So what? All's well that ends well. The captain abandoned the sinking ship, so what's keeping the crew?

ACTOR: The dough. If he doesn't sign the vouchers, we won't get paid.

PSYCHIATRIST: We didn't do any work; they just wasted our time.

ACTOR: Not on your life. I agreed to do this in return for double the fee. I need the dough. Case closed.

SOCIOLOGIST: We wanted to leave when he was here, and now that he's gone, we wait? Mr. Balogh, worse things have happened.

ACTOR: My situation is different. This is how I earn my living. By performing. Here and there, this way and that. It's not so much the money as the principle of the thing. I can't set a precedent.

WRITER: I agree. There's strength in unity. It's not as if this measly fee were the issue. The point is, they've got to pay for their folly.

PSYCHIATRIST: All right, gentlemen, I submit to the consensus. But then let's look into the matter at hand. Do any of you know where he rushed off to? *(Looks into the booth.)* Can't you sign them?

TECHNICIAN: No, we can't. But if it comes up for discussion, and it will, we'll testify to your having spent two hours here, and to its not being your fault that no program came of it.

SCHOLAR: Mr. Balogh, if I understood you correctly, you have to be at the film studio by ten-thirty.

ACTOR: Tomorrow. Standard tactic. They have to be prodded. You're not familiar with these sluggards, Professor.

SOCIOLOGIST: He got a thorough lesson today.

(Telephone rings, Young Woman answers.)

YOUNG WOMAN: Studio 19.

HOST: *(Over the phone.)* This is Beke. Are they still there?

YOUNG WOMAN: Yes.

HOST: All of them?

YOUNG WOMAN: All of them.

HOST: Put me on the speaker.

YOUNG WOMAN: *(Does so.)* Go ahead.

HOST: Comrades, this is Bence Beke. Excuse me. Please wait for me. We'll solve everything. I made a mistake, I know. But we can correct it. In the meantime, think. Don't even consider leaving, because they won't let you out the front door unless I sign your slips. Think about the topic. The assignment hasn't changed. There's time. I'll be there shortly with reinforcements.
ACTOR: I was due at the film studio long ago ...
HOST: Who's speaking?
ACTOR: Ádám Balogh, actor.
HOST: Mr. Balogh, of course, you may go. In that case, though, we'll be unable to pay you an honorarium.
WRITER: How long should we wait?
HOST: Please remain calm, Mr. Vad.
WRITER: *(Makes a gesture as if to say, "Not again!")*
HOST: Comrade Zamecky, are you there?
ZAMECKY: Of course I'm here.
HOST: May I ask you to come up to *Timely Topics?* The secretary will come for you.
TECHNICIAN: He doesn't have to think.
HOST: Are you still shooting your mouth off?
SOCIOLOGIST: *(Through his teeth.)* This is an abomination.
ZAMECKY: Where is *Timely Topics?*
HOST: I said the secretary would come for you.
WRITER: *(Sputtering.)* Zamecky doesn't have to think?
HOST: I want to think together with Comrade Zamecky up here. The two of us. And possibly about entirely different things too.
TECHNICIAN: *(To Young Woman.)* He's not as stupid as he seems.
YOUNG WOMAN: He's a slimy character. Till now I thought he was simply an idiot, an oaf. But he's evil too.
ZAMECKY: Comrade Beke, something's very wrong here. *(Looks around, speaks decisively.)* I'm not going! Don't send anyone for me! You come here as soon as possible!
HOST: Of course, of course. I was only ... I mean, I was just thinking that you're sacrificing vacation time, Comrade Zamecky.
PSYCHIATRIST: And the rest of us are sacrificing work time!
HOST: Quite so. We'll speed things up. Think, Comrades! About stupidity, with intelligence. We can do it! *(A click, he hangs up.)*
SCHOLAR: *(After a pause.)* Am I still the only one who's afraid?
ZAMECKY: Afraid? Of what?
WRITER: Of stupidity. I understand what he means.
ZAMECKY: A person tends to be ingenuous. My attitude was, since Comrade Beke's our host, why shouldn't I grant him all due respect? Why shouldn't I give him a chance?
ACTOR: If they hadn't offered double the fee, I'd never have fallen for it.

WRITER: I was attracted by *Timely Topics* ...

SCHOLAR: I was prepared for twenty possible areas of discussion. This wasn't one of them.

SOCIOLOGIST: Today, mass communications make up the most interesting area of our lives. The area most in ferment. The Marconi constellation ... That's why I came ...

(A Young Man steps into the control booth, the men in the studio watch, but do not hear, because Technician has switched off the audio connection.)

YOUNG MAN: *(Shakes hands with Technician.)* Hey pal, they want you up in Personnel. Did you screw something up?

TECHNICIAN: *(To Young Woman.)* He didn't waste any time, did he? *(To Young Man.)* Beke washed out. With a little help from me.

YOUNG WOMAN: Cornelius is innocent.

YOUNG MAN: Go straighten it out. I'm supposed to take over this program ... *(Shows them a slip of paper.)*

TECHNICIAN: *(Resigned.)* Okay, it's all yours. *(To the studio.)* Gentlemen, it's started. I'm being summoned to Personnel. I'm being replaced. From now on my colleague Bérces is the technician in charge. Maybe now there'll be something to say about the topic you came here to discuss.

WRITER: Do you know our names?

TECHNICIAN: I do.

WRITER: Chin up, then. We're behind you all the way. Don't be afraid. They can't do a thing to you. *(Technician exits.)*

SOCIOLOGIST: They can, though. We're leaving; he's staying here.

PSYCHIATRIST: It shouldn't be allowed. This is outrageous ...

SCHOLAR: Is anyone else afraid yet?

YOUNG MAN: *(Inside.)* What happened?

YOUNG WOMAN: Cornelius is always shooting his mouth off. Commenting on the proceedings. Especially regarding Beke.

YOUNG MAN: Beke? You shouldn't pay any attention to him.

YOUNG WOMAN: The mixer's got problems. . . If you bump it, or just touch it, your voice goes out. A few things went out.

YOUNG MAN: Then they'll fire Cornelius. No matter how much of a jerk Beke is, that's crossing the line.

YOUNG WOMAN: These guys will all take his side.

YOUNG MAN: I'll believe it when I see it. The minute they're out of the studio, they'll forget.

(In the studio, Scholar is ill.)

PSYCHIATRIST: *(Takes his pulse.)* Does this happen often?

SCHOLAR: Of course ... angina attack ... it'll pass.
PSYCHIATRIST: You should go home.
SOCIOLOGIST: All of us should go home ... Why are we sitting here like sheep?
SCHOLAR: I told you ... Stupidity has us surrounded. It's got us in a stranglehold. There's no escape. Stupidity is holding the world in its grip. Strangling it ...
SOCIOLOGIST: That's very nice, very poetic, but if we all got up now and went home, then it wouldn't be strangling us. At most it could go for its own throat.
SCHOLAR: I need a few minutes of rest now.
ACTOR: And I need the dough. I'm not going to set a precedent. Please try to understand my position.
WRITER: The power of stupidity has to be met with the heroism of intelligence.
PSYCHIATRIST: Heroism? We were ordered to wait, and we're waiting. We serve and we beg. The facts speak for themselves. Motivations don't count.
SCHOLAR: Five minutes. Don't leave me here!
SOCIOLOGIST: We won't leave you, Bálint. Clearly, stupidity is manipulating us, but ...
SCHOLAR: Stupidity is manipulating the world.
SOCIOLOGIST: We can resist. We have to fight ... Unfortunately intelligence is dispersed. Intelligence has no battle order. We have to join forces.
PSYCHIATRIST: Intelligence is ingenuous, that's true.
WRITER: I shouldn't have agreed to it. They sucked up to me, made promises. It won't be hard, I'll get a lot of money for it ... Frankly, I was attracted by the money too ... I have three children ...
YOUNG MAN: *(Inside.)* What's the problem?
YOUNG WOMAN: Beke wanted them to talk about stupidity, he stormed out, then called, telling them to think and wait for him.
YOUNG MAN: So now they're thinking?

(The Cook steps into the studio.)

COOK: A thousand pardons ... Are you finished? Is this a post-taping chat?
ACTOR: Not yet, Ma'am.
YOUNG WOMAN: *(Inside.)* Cornelius told her to come, to drive Beke away. Just a minute. *(Over the loudspeaker.)* Good day, Ma'am. The Comrades are thinking now anyway. Maybe it'll be all right with them if we tape your recipes ... How many do you have?
COOK: Only two. Last time I read twelve, but these two got left out because they ran out of tape ... I had to come in today because of two recipes. Good day. You don't mind, do you? I'll be done in a flash ... only two recipes ...
YOUNG MAN: *(Over the loudspeaker.)* Have a seat, right there, facing me ... Do you mind, Comrade ...
ZAMECKY: Go right ahead ... *(Gets up from the seat opposite the booth, Cook sits, spreads the recipe in front of her.)*

128 Cheese Dumplings

YOUNG MAN: Total silence, please ... Could you please move as far away from the table as possible? ... Fine. Thank you ... Sound check ...

(Those who have not yet stood up, do so. Scholar is helped to his feet and led to a chair that has been pushed against the wall. They all watch Cook, who alone reigns at the table.)

COOK: I scream, you scream, we all scream for ice cream. *(To the others.)* That's my standard sound check. Do you know it?

YOUNG MAN: We're starting!

COOK: Cheese dumplings are a tasty spring dish. Ingredients: 60 decagrams of fresh cottage cheese, 10 decagrams of wheat meal, 2 tablespoons of flour, 2 eggs, 1 deciliter of heavy cream, 3 decagrams of lard, 3 decagrams of butter, 5 decagrams of breadcrumbs. Strain the cottage cheese, add the whole eggs ...

YOUNG MAN: *(Inside, during the listing of ingredients.)* Very nice, but what makes cheese dumplings a spring dish?

YOUNG WOMAN: I don't know.

YOUNG MAN: Should we stop?

YOUNG WOMAN: Hell with it. What difference does it make?

(In the studio, Scholar is ill; he heaves an uncontrollable sigh of anguish, which can be heard over the recipe.)

YOUNG MAN: *(Over the loudspeaker.)* We're stopping! Could we have silence please!

CURTAIN

Chicken Head

György Spiró

translated by Eugene Brogyányi

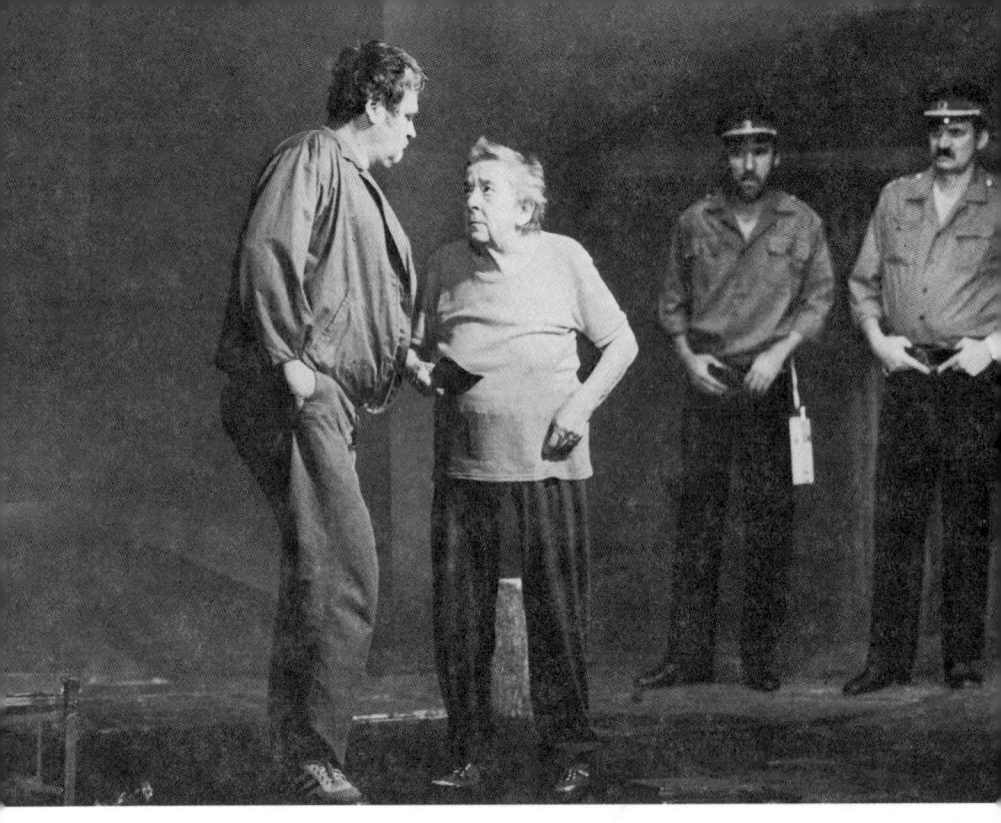

Béla Ilovszky (MTI)

CHICKEN HEAD
[József Katona Theatre, Budapest, Hungary]
Directed by Gábor Zsámbéki

CHARACTERS:

Old Lady	Buddy
Teacher	Sarge
Woman	Cop
Father	Official
Mother	Chick
Kid	Missy

Setting: The interior courtyard of an apartment building in the outlying parts of the city. Facing us to the left, a coachway, at the depths of which is a door. Old Lady's apartment door to the right of the coachway. A garage to the right, Father's apartment door in front. Woman's apartment door to the left, Teacher's apartment door in front on the left. In the center, a carpet-beating stand.

Scene 1

(Afternoon. A hanged cat dangles from the carpet-beating stand. Old Lady enters from depths of coachway, carrying shopping bag dripping with blood.)

OLD LADY: Kitty, kitty, here kitty! Come along now, meow, meow! *(Puts shopping bag on ground in front of door, searches for key.)* Kitty cat, kitty cat, where've you wandered off to? *(Opens door, turns back.)* Come along nicely, I brought the catfood! *(Takes in bag, brief pause, comes out.)* The chicken heads have melted — they weren't frozen through — but they haven't rotted, kitty cat, I smelled them, and they haven't turned green yet — now mama won't have to go for at least ten days — *(Brief pause.)* If you knew what a line there was! — almost wasn't any left by the time my turn came around — but I just made it — I prayed the whole time — they were buying them all up, taking them away in big bags — twenty kilos, even — I thought there wouldn't be any left for me — but there were. We're in luck, kitty cat, you know? Only that long trip — and meanwhile they melted, the blood was dripping — that long trip — even though I put them in two nylon bags — people were staring — the blood was dripping in the tram — now come on, come along, I'll give you some — nice and fresh — then I'll chop up the rest — put it in the freezer — so you can have yummy chicken heads — you've got it good, I'll tell you — you don't even deserve it — kitty, kitty, meow, meow!

(Starts walking around yard looking for cat.)

You didn't even eat this morning — where the hell have you wandered off to? — you must be good and hungry by now — I put it all in the sink — I'll give you some now — then I'll chop it up with the cleaver — because they're frozen on the inside — I'll put them in the freezer — you'll have yummy cat-food — enough for two weeks — twelve days for sure — some life you've got, little furry creature — where can you be, kitty cat?

(Sees cat on carpet-beating stand, pause, lets out an inarticulate scream, stands quaking, steps to it, seizes twine with shaking hands, tugs, tears it off, presses dead cat to lap, runs inside, screams are heard from inside, then silence.)

Scene 2

(Kid and Buddy enter through coachway. Kid goes to Father's door, presses down handle, tugs, door does not open.)

KID: Aw fuck!
BUDDY: Whatsa matter? Ain't here yet?
KID: Goddammit.
BUDDY: Ain't home, huh?

(Kid pounds, pause.)

BUDDY: Ain't nobody here, huh?
KID: Why the fuck ain't he here? Why don't he come home?
BUDDY: It's early.
KID: But why ain't he here? I come home, an' he ain't even here. *(Pounds, kicks door.)*
BUDDY: Why ain't you got no key?
KID: From where? Huh? Jerk.
BUDDY: Why didn't they give you one?
KID: 'Cause they didn't. Shit.
BUDDY: My old man gave me one.
KID: Okay, he fuckin' gave you one. I don't give a shit, dammit.
BUDDY: How come your old man didn't give you one?
KID: Shit. Shut your fuckin' face.
BUDDY: Okay, let's split.
KID: What the hell for?
BUDDY: You wanna fuckin' hang out here, or what?
KID: It's fuckin' botherin' you?
BUDDY: We'll come back.
KID: Shit! I pictured it all. I get home, he's here — I had the whole thing figured

out back there — I come home, an' the old man's here — I seen it just like that a shitload of times, goddammit, an' it was good — so fuckin' good — I seen it all, dig? — we go take in a game, guzzle some beer, the whole bit.
BUDDY: There ain't no fuckin' game today.
KID: I fuckin' pictured it, dig?
BUDDY: Ain't no game noplace today.
KID: I don't give a shit, dammit. I pictured it — a shitload of times — I fuckin' remember it all — all of it — why ain't he home?!
BUDDY: We'll come back.
KID: Sit the fuck down, dammit. Get the hell outa here.
BUDDY: What gives, man? What the hell gives?
KID: Nothin' dammit. Stupid asshole.
BUDDY: Eh, he'll come home.
KID: Shut your face, jerk.

(Brief pause, Buddy sits down.)

KID: The others was fuckin' sleepin' — an' I was picturin' comin' home, an' then I was already here — an' it was all just like I wanted it — it was this — here — this was mine — somethin' only I had — I could always see this here — this yard — they snore — you can't sleep — the duty officer comes in at night to make sure nobody's jerkin' off —

(Buddy laughs.)

KID: Jerkin' off ain't allowed — but we do whatever the fuck we want — a light's always on so the duty officer can see — not everyplace — I got it good now, I'm on a lower bunk — it don't shine in my face —
BUDDY: I'd go for the top bunk.
KID: You can fuckin' have it.
BUDDY: It's better on the top, I think.
KID: Okay, it's fuckin' better. Like you know. Try makin' your bed — they'll kick you right off if you stand on theirs — me too — anybody stands on my bed — kick him right off — try makin' your bed in two minutes — 'cause the fuckin' duty officer's comin', an' if it ain't straight, you get the shit smacked outa you. So go ahead, take the top bunk.

(Brief pause.)

KID: But it ain't up to you anyway, like you fuckin' get to say what you want. They let you have it across the face so fuckin' hard you shit. What the fuck you think? Your fuckin' shoelace breaks, you get one. It's lunchtime, you spill some soup, you get one. An' they knock your fuckin' elbow, you're carryin' your tray, holdin' your spoon — shit yeah — an' ain't no fuckin' good rattin' on 'em — at night they wrap you in a blanket an' kick you till you don't know where your fuckin' kidneys are.

BUDDY: Shit man, fuckin' rough.

KID: They swipe your fuckin' steel file an' grease it — you don't know who — them. Then *you* do the fuckin' greasin' — in two weeks you're greasin' like a motherfucker — an' they puke on your fuckin' duds — then you get dead fuckin' drunk an' puke all over theirs — shit man, ain't like you think.

BUDDY: What do they grease?

KID: Fuckin' file. What d'ya think?! Your prick?!

BUDDY: Your file?

KID: Okay theirs. What a jerk. Theirs.

BUDDY: Oh.

KID: Look, fuck it. You pick out a weaker kid an' fuck with him — that's what you gotta do — then they take you in. Otherwise they fuck you over. 'Cause if you don't show 'em that's what you're like — your ass is grass — I'm fuckin' tellin' ya.

BUDDY: Still, must be good.

KID: What?

BUDDY: Well, back there.

KID: Damn fuckin' straight.

BUDDY: It's somethin' — after all — somethin' — ain't shit here. Back there, you fuckin' got somethin'.

KID: They can do any fuckin' thing they damn well please. We bust ass in the factory, black market stuff, we steal the goods for 'em, do the work, they sell it — that's how it is, we gotta get it out, too — 'cause if not, they fuck us over — the motherfuckers — an' then they feed us this line about we oughta be grateful — about bein' one big family — an' they're our whatsis — our parents, our guardians, all that — an' we oughta be grateful we got a fuckin' ass to bust.

BUDDY: Eh, they shovel that shit everyplace — us too — same thing.

KID: An' then this is what I got — this fuckin' yard — I seen it a shitload of times — like this, only it was bigger — I don't know — but everything was bigger, higher — I wish to hell the old man was here!

BUDDY: Why? What d'ya want from him? Did he write?

KID: Shut your fuckin' face, jerk.

BUDDY: Why? You said he never even wrote — you said so yourself.

KID: How 'bout I fix it so you gotta get your fuckin' face stitched back together.

BUDDY: Why? What d'ya want from your old man? — he don't even know where the hell you are.

(Kid suddenly hits Buddy in mouth. Buddy grabs face and stares uncomprehendingly.)

BUDDY: Why the hell? Why the hell?

KID: Just shut up.

(Brief pause.)

KID: Jerk, be glad that's all you got — what the fuck you mouthin' off for, jerk? Back there you'd fuckin' learn — I even warned you — they don't open their mouth back there — the guardian's a fuckin' boozer — they're stuck with him 'cause there ain't too many — an' you don't know, why he smacks you — he hates every kid — he's only there for the apartment — 'cause they get apartments in there — an' he's a boozer. Shit yeah. — What's that?
BUDDY: What?
KID: *(Points to garage.)* What the hell's that?
BUDDY: A garage. Ain't it? A garage.
KID: What d'ya mean garage?
BUDDY: Garage.
KID: Wasn't no garage here! This thing wasn't here!
BUDDY: I don't know, it's here now.
KID: How come there's a garage here?! In here. How come?

(Brief pause.)

BUDDY: Okay look, we gonna hang out here or what the fuck? Let's split. Let's get the hell outa here. To the square.
KID: Why? What the fuck's there? Huh? What's there?
BUDDY: Nothin' — we can sit — check it out — I sit there an' watch — in case somebody comes — they come — you came, didn't you? I look, I say shit man, this guy's just like him, gets closer, I'm lookin', just like him. Huh? An' I was fuckin' glad, so why the hell you smackin' me? I was fuckin' glad you was comin'. Be some hell-raisin'. Somethin' at last — 'cause ain't ever nothin' — I just sit there an' watch — so why the hell? I never ratted on you, never — huh? — did I?
KID: What d'ya mean?
BUDDY: I remember! I remember everythin'! They fuckin' took you away, an' me here, no buddy, didn't even know how come. So I come around askin', nobody don't know nothin', but I remember!
KID: That was fuckin' long ago. Since then — I been in eight fuckin' institutions since then — fuckin' eight — can't put shit over on me no more — I know the score — ain't nobody puts shit over on me — ain't easy to fuck me over. Not me no more. Right away I know whose ass gotta be kissed — an' they fuckin' kiss mine too, right away, I pick 'em out. There been stupid fuckin' guardians who fuckin' like kids, ooh-an'-ah over you, fuckin' pretend they're concerned, then they pull out an' that's that. I don't fall for none of it — that's where it's at, man — where it's at is where it's at — all their bullshit aside — I can tell, even

136   Chicken Head

the tough guardians are scared, man, an' don't dare pull just any shit on anybody — me neither no more. They can't pull just any shit on me.

(Brief pause.)

BUDDY: Where's the cat, that fuckin' cat?
KID: What?
BUDDY: Fuckin' climbed down! *(Laughs.)* Fuckin' jumped off, huh? The cat! *(Indicates torn twine.)*
KID: Got taken down.
BUDDY: She took it down, huh? *(Laughs.)* Musta had a shitfit, huh? Probably had a shitfit. Too bad we missed it. The fuckin' cat. The way it was writhin', damn near scratched me. *(Laughs.)* Its four feet was goin' at it. Stupid cat. Coulda dug seein' her take it down.

(Kid goes to door, pounds.)

BUDDY: What gives? Your old man get back meantime or what?
KID: Why ain't he here, goddammit? One time I come home, why ain't he here?!
BUDDY: Let's get a fuckin' move on. We'll come back.
KID: Why can just any shit be pulled on me? Christ al-fuckin'-mighty! Why can just any shit be pulled on me?!
BUDDY: Look, let's get a fuckin' move on.

(Woman enters through coachway, bags in both hands.)

KID: Hello.
WOMAN: Hi.

(Woman puts down bags, searches for key, opens both locks, Kid and Buddy watch.)

WOMAN: *(Turns back, to Kid)* What's this? Is it you?

(Brief pause.)

WOMAN: They let you come home?
KID: Yes.
WOMAN: How you've grown.
KID: Guess so.
WOMAN: Your sister didn't come?
KID: I don't know.
WOMAN: Why? Where's she?
KID: I don't know.

WOMAN: Because we haven't seen her for years either.
KID: Me neither.

(Brief pause.)

WOMAN: And now you're here to stay?
KID: No — this is just three days — would you know where my father is?
WOMAN: No.

(Woman picks up bags.)

WOMAN: How you've grown. You must have to fight the girls off, huh? Well, okay.
KID: Good-bye.

(Woman goes in, closes door, brief pause.)

BUDDY: Shit man.
KID: What's up?

(They stare at door.)

BUDDY: Some tits, huh? Shit man.
KID: Eh, that over-the-hill broad?
BUDDY: She's still okay.
KID: Eh, she ain't got it. Her?
BUDDY: She got enough. Why? You wouldn't lay her?
KID: Go ahead an' fuck her. You're even fuckin' chicken to say hello.
BUDDY: Why the fuck should I say hello to her? — I never did before — I don't even know her.
KID: You been hangin' out here for years, what the fuck you mean you don't know her?
BUDDY: Why should I say hello to her? Huh? Why should I? Fuck her.

(Brief pause.)

BUDDY: Let's split. Us here — ain't shit here — we'll come back — or go on in there an' fuck her — c'mon, let's get a fuckin' move on.
KID: Why ain't he here, goddammit? Why ain't nothin' the way it oughta be? Nothin' — ever. Goddammit.
BUDDY: C'mon, let's get a fuckin' move on.

(Both exit.)

138   Chicken Head

Scene 3

(Old Lady comes out, weeps. Goes to Teacher's door, knocks.)

TEACHER: *(In dressing gown and slippers, comes out, stops, looks at her.)* Good day.

(Old Lady sniffles.)

TEACHER: Is something the matter?
OLD LADY: She was still warm! She was still warm! — if I'd gotten home ten minutes sooner — if the tram had come — now how am I going to pass my days?! *(Weeps.)*

(Brief pause.)

TEACHER: Excuse me —
OLD LADY: I come home, sir — from the market — bringing her the chicken heads — I stood in line for a half hour — and the tram didn't come — I thought there wouldn't be any left for me — they were standing in line — and I waited — and the chicken heads thawed — everybody was staring — then I get home, I call to her, she doesn't come — I thought she wandered off — though she didn't have anything to eat this morning — and then I see her — I see her — *(Weeps.)* hanging there — they hanged her — on the carpet-beating stand — what's that thing doing here anyway? — around her thin little neck — around her neck — twine around her neck — sir! — around her thin little neck — *(Weeps.)*
TEACHER: Horrible.

(Brief pause.)

TEACHER: But at least she had a good life.

(Old Lady sobs.)

TEACHER: You did everything you could for her, that's the important thing — yes — it's difficult to say anything at a time like this — she was a beautiful kitty, a healthy, friendly, pretty little animal — I was very fond of her.

(Old Lady sobs.)

TEACHER: I was taking a nap — to rest up for my next lesson — I'm very sorry something like this could happen — I condemn it — but there really isn't anything to be done —

(Old Lady sobs.)

TEACHER: But she had a very good life, that's the important thing, no cat could have had a better life — than she had —
OLD LADY: Murderous lowlifes — all of them —
TEACHER: Please excuse me, but I have to get ready for the next lesson — I had five this morning — with only an hour's break — I'm very sorry —

(Woman appears in her doorway, listens.)

OLD LADY: So much waiting — at the market — at the vet's — so much waiting when she was sick — I prayed for her — when they kept her there, I took her chicken heads — and if there weren't any — you can't always get them — because they grind them up — for feed — when there weren't any, I took her liver — beef liver — because pork liver's forbidden — I got her medicine from the West — when she needed it — because they didn't have any in there — I tended to her every need — her coat was so nice and shiny — I had her vaccinated — and then they grab her — grab that little animal — that innocent little animal — and hang her — with twine around her neck — hang her — she must have been calling for me — when — and I wasn't here — I couldn't help her — what must she have thought then? — what must she have thought? — *(Weeps.)*
TEACHER: Well you couldn't have been here — if you were away — shopping for her —
OLD LADY: Even though in the morning — it occurred to me — there would have been enough for two days — I didn't have to go — I felt it — some voice told me there's enough for two days — not to go today — then she'd be alive now — but I didn't listen — to the voice —
WOMAN: Her cat died?
TEACHER: Yes.
WOMAN: What happened, they hanged it?
TEACHER: So it seems. Excuse my attire —

(Old Lady sobs, hawks up phlegm.)

TEACHER: You'll make yourself ill.
WOMAN: Where did they hang it?
TEACHER: Somewhere — on the carpet-beating stand — excuse me, I'm not yet dressed — *(To Old Lady.)* I'll bring you a sedative — do you hear me?
WOMAN: They hanged it on the carpet-beating stand?
TEACHER: *(To Old Lady.)* Please listen to me — this is bad for you — you'll get out of breath — this'll put a strain on your heart — you mustn't get so worked up —
WOMAN: It was probably the kid.
TEACHER: What kid?
WOMAN: Him — they let him home — I just met him — I was coming home — I was

standing in line for half an hour at the supermarket — I come in loaded down with my bags — and there's this big hulking kid — it's him —
TEACHER: Please calm down a bit — with your permission, I'd like to get you a sedative —
WOMAN: On this carpet-beating stand? Here? Is this the one?
TEACHER: *(To Old Lady.)* Please, listen to me —
OLD LADY: Filthy riffraff — depraved murderers — their whole kind —
TEACHER: Please —
WOMAN: I bet it was him — I come home — I'm loaded down with my bags — all of a sudden I see them loitering around here — him and his buddy — I didn't even recognize him, but then I remembered how long it's been since I've seen him — I don't even know how long — a good long time — he got very big, but it was him — when I opened the door it occurred to me why he must be here when he's supposed to be in the institution — he probably ran away.
TEACHER: All kinds of strangers come and go around here.
WOMAN: I never see anybody loitering here.
TEACHER: All kinds of men come and go here.
WOMAN: I never see anybody.
OLD LADY: A defenseless little animal — a little animal — how could they? — they were born that way — they're not even human —
TEACHER: Please, don't speak that way, one shouldn't indulge such impulses. They're totally out of place.
OLD LADY: Don't you tell me what I should or shouldn't do!
TEACHER: Forgive me, perhaps I didn't —
OLD LADY: Don't you tell me, I don't care if you are an educated man, don't you tell me! You're not going to tell me how I should feel!
TEACHER: Please, it's the furthest thing from my mind to tell you — all I meant to say was that calling everybody a murderer — because of a cat — albeit a very dear animal — is not entirely proper.
OLD LADY: To murder a defenseless little animal — that's proper?! She was the only creature — the only — *(Sobs.)*
WOMAN: Leave her alone. What are you picking on her for?!
TEACHER: I'm not picking on her. I didn't pick on the cat either. It was a very dear animal. And it's most unfortunate that — I'm very sorry, but after all —

(Old Lady sobs.)

WOMAN: Did you see it? Was it hanging? It had been hanged?
TEACHER: No, I didn't see it.

(Old Lady sobs.)

TEACHER: I'm very sorry, but it seems as though there's nothing I can do — If she

needs a sedative, please let me know — I have to get ready for the lesson. *(Goes into apartment, closes door.)*
OLD LADY: Him too — all he can say is that I shouldn't — shouldn't what? Shouldn't! What would he be doing now if she'd been his? What would he be doing?
WOMAN: I don't even dare come home after dark — but how can I afford taxis all the time? — where can I make that much money? — I bring loads of work home, but I still can't make enough — it's terrible what characters hang around here —
OLD LADY: Why doesn't he mind his own business? He's always sticking in his two cents' worth. Because he's had schooling? That doesn't give him the right to stick in his two cents' worth!
WOMAN: All a person can do is be afraid —
OLD LADY: What does he mean sedative? — I stand in line in the market hall — at the open-air market — all that pushing and shoving — I stand there to get her something — I get back, and find her hanging there, and then on top of it all I should take a sedative! There's no compassion in people! None!
WOMAN: It was hanged by the neck? It was hanging there?
OLD LADY: What?
WOMAN: The cat. The kitty. It was hanging?

(Old Lady weeps.)

WOMAN: Where is it now? In there? Inside?

(Old Lady points, weeps.)

WOMAN: Does it look ugly? — the eyes — are they bulging?

(Old Lady sobs.)

WOMAN: You've got to bury it. As soon as possible. It's not a good idea to keep it in there — it'll start rotting — it's got to be buried.
OLD LADY: She was such a good kitty — a person could talk to her — when she was thirsty she climbed into the tub — she didn't even climb in, she just went toward it — toward the tub — and she already knew that I could tell what she wanted — and she always thanked me for her food — even when she was very hungry — she came to me, rubbed up against me — before eating — even when she was very, very hungry — and could she get offended! — she'd sit facing the wall — half the day sometimes — and wouldn't talk to me — and could she be grateful! — grateful — like nobody — we lived together so many years — twelve years — twelve years — and nine of them just the two of us — nine — she'd climb on the bed — at my feet — snuggle in — and sleep — and she was so — so — so

trusting — yes, trusting — when she slept deeply — she'd lie on her back — and cover her eyes with her paw — just like a child — she'd lie there defenseless, because she knew she could trust me — I never hurt her — nobody ever did — a little animal like that — and now — and now — *(Weeps.)*

(Pause.)

WOMAN: Yes — it's a good thing you had a cat — maybe a cat — is a good thing.

(Pause. Father enters through coachway.)

FATHER: Hello.

(Goes to door, searches for key.)

WOMAN: Look what your brat did. Take a good look!
FATHER: What?
WOMAN: She's completely beside herself. Just take a look!

(Father looks at Old Lady, confused.)

WOMAN: Your stupid brat! Yours! That's what I'm talking about.
FATHER: What?
WOMAN: He hanged her cat! Here on the carpet-beating stand! Strung it up! Your son did, yes, your son! Good thing it was just the cat! Good thing!
FATHER: Where's a cat? What d'ya want? Where's my son? Huh? What's goin' on? What is it this time? What the hell is it this time?
WOMAN: Can't you see she's crying?
FATHER: Yeah? She's crying. So what?
WOMAN: Well it's no wonder. None at all. Of course your son turns out like this. A sadistic beast.
FATHER: What d'ya want from me? What the hell d'ya want for chrissake? Where's my son, huh? Well, where? He's in an institution, ain't he? Well, ain't he? What d'ya want? What the hell d'ya want? You're always lyin', the two of you. Up an' down. All the time. But what d'ya want now? Didn't she have him taken away? Huh? Wasn't it her? Wasn't that enough? Ain't I workin'? Am I or ain't I? I got a job. I'm a workin' stiff. What else do you want, huh? What'd I do? To who? What cat? Will you two ever get off my case?! What am I doin'? I ain't doin' nothin'! Goddammit!
WOMAN: Your son killed her cat, you understand? He killed it.
FATHER: Good for him. Damn good. He ain't even here. Well, is he? Not since who the hell knows. Where is he? Here?

(Opens apartment door wide.)

FATHER: Is he here? Is he? Take a look if he's here. Well, where is he? C'mon over. You. C'mon over here, take a look. Huh? Where is he? Let the old lady come over too. Take a look. Where is he? Huh? For chrissake!
TEACHER: *(Steps out his door in shirt and jacket, but still without tie, still in slippers.)* Please, if possible, don't shout. Please.
FATHER: Why shouldn't I? They're always fuckin' with me! Always fuckin' with me! How come? Huh? You got education for chrissake, tell me, what'd I do?
TEACHER: Please, be so kind as not to shout. I can't do my work.

(Teacher goes back, closes door.)

FATHER: 'Cause he got education? That's why I'm always the one? What'd I do to him? He's a jerk. An asshole. All his education. He lives here too. The prick.

(Father goes in, slams door.)

WOMAN: If I ever get the money, I'm getting the hell out of here. What am I doing here?

(Old Lady weeps quietly.)

WOMAN: Please stop. Please go inside — please bury it somewhere — all right? Please go on in. That's right. Please be careful. And please bury it — as soon as possible — it's got to be buried.

(Old Lady goes in. Woman closes door, goes to garage door, examines lock, returns to apartment, closes door.)

Scene 4

(Two policemen enter through coachway, stop, look around.)

SARGE: Damn long driveway.
COP: Yeah.
SARGE: This is one of them old what-d'ya-call-its. When carriages used to drive in. A coachway.
COP: Yeah.

(Pause.)

SARGE: They can come into these kind. At night. 'Cause it's dark. So they come in.
COP: Yeah.

(Brief pause.)

SARGE: Nothin' goes on daytime, 'cause it's daytime. Only at night. 'Cause there ain't no lights usually. Damn dark.
COP: Yeah.

(Brief pause.)

SARGE: If you come in at night — come in with your back against the wall — ya dig?
COP: Which one?
SARGE: What?
COP: Which wall?
SARGE: Which wall?
COP: 'Cause there's a wall here — and there.
SARGE: It don't make no fuckin' difference, one of 'em. What does it matter? One of 'em, that's all. So they can't come at you from behind. Ya dig? That's how you go. Slow.
COP: Yeah.
SARGE: But you don't have to come in. You see it's too damn dark, so the hell with it.
COP: Yeah.
SARGE: You go to the saloon — you go in — the two of you — there's always two of you — you go in — you don't do nothin'. They're fuckin' scared of you anyway. You're inside, then you split. Ya dig? Don't take no booze — they always offer — on some excuse — they try to suck up to you — 'cause they're afraid. Ya dig? You don't show 'em you got a fuckin' load in your pants. 'Cause they're afraid. If you're checkin' Personal I.D., check the others. Ya dig? Not the regulars.
COP: How do I know?
SARGE: What?
COP: Well, that they're not.
SARGE: Not what?
COP: Not regulars. How do I know?
SARGE: 'Cause you're there all the time, an' you see who's there all the time, an' who ain't.
COP: Oh yeah.

(Pause.)

COP: What're we doin' here?
SARGE: We're here, dammit. We don't gotta be doin' nothin'.
COP: Yeah.
SARGE: We look around, 'cause this is our beat, so we let 'em see us, then we split.
COP: Nobody sees us.
SARGE: 'Cause they ain't here. Or they're inside. We look around, an' we split.

(Pause.)

COP: An' what're we doin' now?
SARGE: We're here. This is our fuckin' job.

(Pause.)

COP: Hey, a carpet-beating stand.
SARGE: Yeah.
COP: We had one like that.
SARGE: Oh yeah?
COP: Yeah. Just like that.
SARGE: Well, it's a carpet-beating stand.

(Pause.)

COP: I don't even know what happened to it.
SARGE: To what?
COP: The carpet-beating stand. At our place. At my what-d'ya-call-it's. My stepmother's. The first one. We had one just like that. Then it wasn't there no more. I don't even know when — I didn't pay no attention — they just took it away — but when was that?

(Pause. Father comes out.)

FATHER: Hi guys.
SARGE: Hi.
FATHER: I'm bein' fucked with again, dammit. Always somethin'.
SARGE: Why? What's up?
FATHER: I'm comin' home — I had a shitty day at work — nothin's workin' out — I'm runnin' between two machines — my vise ain't worth shit — then I'm comin' on the bus — it's crowded as all hell — an' then I'm comin' home an' they come at me — they're yellin' — I don't know what the hell their problem is — they're always fuckin' with me — that's how it always is — goddam them.
SARGE: Yeah.
FATHER: He ain't even here — since who the hell knows — 'cause both of 'em got

taken away — him an' his sister — an' then they fuckin' accuse me — I don't know which way is up no more. How 'bout a drink?
SARGE: Can't now.
FATHER: A short one, how 'bout it?
SARGE: Can't.
FATHER: Okay, but even so, how 'bout it?
SARGE: Not now.
FATHER: I'm tellin' you, man — this can't go on — how the hell am I supposed to put up with this? — Shit — I come home and then this. You really won't have a drink? Homemade.
SARGE: No thanks.
FATHER: Dig, I'm comin' home — all fucked out — an' then this. Ain't enough shit all the time — this too.

(Old Lady comes out, black kerchief on head, carrying dead cat, stops center, they stare at her.)

OLD LADY: I don't know — she's got to be buried.

(Pause. Old Lady stands still.)

SARGE: Cat. Dead.
COP: Yeah.
OLD LADY: I don't know — I didn't even — she was still warm — and now I've got to bury her — I don't know —

(Pause. Old Lady puts cat down, stands, then goes back into apartment.)

FATHER: This is what she's pinnin' on me. Her fuckin' cat.
SARGE: What?
FATHER: That my kid — when he ain't even home — since who the hell knows. Old bitch.

(Old Lady comes out with shovel.)

OLD LADY: Got to be buried. *(Looks around.)*
FATHER: Not here. This is a garden — we ain't gonna have carcasses rotting here — not here.

(Old Lady looks at him. Pause.)

FATHER: No way — carcasses here — then the flies'll come.

OLD LADY: They said she's got to be buried — where? —

(Pause.)

SARGE: In my opinion I don't know, but it's okay.
FATHER: Let 'er — for all I care — but not here — this is my garden.
SARGE: What d'ya mean? It ain't just yours — it's a common courtyard.
FATHER: I don't care — let 'er get a permit — from the Council — what do I know.

(Old Lady stands and weeps.)

SARGE: Go on, dig it for her.
COP: C'mon, Granny, gimme it, I'll do it.
OLD LADY: No! Get away from here! Get away from here!

(Cop shrugs. Pause. Old Lady begins digging. Woman appears in doorway, watches. Old Lady digs, they watch. Old Lady seizes cat, embraces it, strokes it, kisses it, places it in ditch.)

COP: No coffin? *(Laughs.)*

(Old Lady looks at him, then sweeps dirt into ditch. They watch her. Old Lady kneeling, smooths dirt with hands, kneels, pause.)

COP: *(More quietly.)* She prayin'?
SARGE: Shut up.

(Old Lady kneels, perhaps prays, stands up, goes into apartment.)

FATHER: Nuts — huh? — completely off her rocker — mournin' a lousy cat — stupid —
SARGE: *(To Cop.)* No point mouthin' off. She's fuckin' mourning. Happens.
COP: Okay, I just —
SARGE: Your job is dealin' with the fuckin' public, the shittiest job there is. That's how come you get more dough — so you know when you gotta keep your mouth shut.

(Old Lady comes out, carrying bag dripping with blood.)

OLD LADY: What do I do with this? What do I do with this now?

(Goes to grave, stops.)

OLD LADY: Two weeks' worth—two weeks'—I stood in line—I carried it home—the tram wouldn't come—now what do I do with it? Her dish is inside—in the kitchen—in front of the sink—her little dish—

(Old Lady rushes in.)

COP: What's this?
SARGE: Must be catfood or somethin'.

(Old Lady comes out carrying plastic dish.)

OLD LADY: This was her dish—what do I do with it now?

(Pause.)

OLD LADY: I look around—in the kitchen—I see her dish—and I cry. I just can't look at it—I can't—her dish—I can't leave it there. For twelve years—she ate out of it—this was her dish. It was always there—under the sink—she'd tug the food out of it—pull it across the floor—I always had to wipe up after her—for twelve years—every day—how I scolded her!

(Stands, tries to break dish, cannot, puts it on ground, goes into apartment.)

FATHER: She's out of her mind. I mean it—too much—an' then they listen to her—not me, only her—she reports me—an' then they believe her, her! This the Council don't see! Why ain't the Council here now?!

(Old Lady comes out, cleaver in hand. Goes to dish, hits it with cleaver repeatedly, until it breaks to pieces. Hits bag full of chicken heads also, the others watch.)

OLD LADY: There—there's your catfood—there—it's yours—all yours—

(Teacher appears in doorway, by now in shoes, but still without tie, watches.)

OLD LADY: *(Grinds debris into ground with feet and shovel.)* There was never room for my food—in the freezer—now there'll be room—my food'll be in there—in the freezer—I dragged you to the vet's—when your paw got infected—I bought medicine—medicine from the West—never again for anybody—never again—I've had enough—*(Stamps ground.)* There—there—*(Pants, looks around spitefully, throws down shovel next to cleaver, rushes into apartment, slams door. Pause.)*
FATHER: Out of her mind—oughta be locked up—huh?—completely off her rocker—an' she reports me—they come out here—nose around—say things ain't in order—I ain't feeding him—even though they didn't give me no

apartment — they gave me nothin' — an' then they come out here — 'cause the old lady — this moron — says she'll take 'em in — she will — who asked her to? — what business is it of hers? — an' then they come — me with egg on my face — what do I do with 'em by myself? — I was on disability, wasn't I? You tell 'em, Teach, wasn't I? — an' then they come — nose around — at my place — for chrissake — they act important — when a person like this oughta be locked up — off her rocker —

(Teacher goes in, closes door. Pause. Woman goes in, closes door. Pause.)

SARGE: Right. So we'll be movin' along — we'll be back.
FATHER: Well, ain't she off her rocker? — an' then they take away both my kids — 'cause of her, goddammit — 'cause what the hell did I do?
SARGE: Let's go.
COP: This carpet-beating stand — we had one like that — but what happened to it? I don't even know. Too bad I can't go back there — to find out — when —
SARGE: Okay, good-bye.
FATHER: See ya 'round.
COP: See ya.

(Sarge and Cop start to leave.)

FATHER: She's off her rocker — I'm tellin' ya — buries her cat — I'm tellin' ya —

(Sarge and Cop disappear through coachway.)

FATHER: See you guys around! *(Brief pause.)* Buries her cat — I'm tellin' ya — *(Goes into apartment, closes door.)*

Scene 5

(Old Lady comes out, stops, stands still, then starts toward Woman's apartment, stops, goes to Teacher's apartment, stops, knocks. Teacher opens door, still without tie, book in hand.)

TEACHER: Hello.
OLD LADY: Excuse me, sir — this must be — for bothering you —
TEACHER: Not at all, it's just that I'm preparing for a lesson.
OLD LADY: Excuse me, sir — but somehow now —
TEACHER: Yes, of course. *(Sighs.)* I was just now preparing for a lesson, but — come in, please.
OLD LADY: No, I don't — but the thing is that I have to — don't be afraid, I've calmed down — I'm not going to — I got over my — my — I'm no longer so upset — the way I was before when I — I was pretty muddled, wasn't I?

TEACHER: No, not at all —

OLD LADY: But I've — believe me, I've calmed down — really — and that's not the reason I'm now — it's just that it can be so painful — but don't you worry, sir — I won't cry — not any more — it's just that it can be so painful —

TEACHER: Yes, of course.

(Brief pause.)

OLD LADY: Because I'd thought about it — I was always afraid — of what would become of me if — if — *(Her voice cracks, brief pause.)* I won't cry, sir — don't worry — because I was worried about what would become of me, and I thought that if I died first — if she outlived me — it wasn't very nice of me — I know — because then what would have become of her? — who would have fed her? — I just wanted to be spared — so I wouldn't have to mourn her — so she'd have to mourn me — it wasn't very nice of me.

TEACHER: Yes, well — we all tend to think that way — sometimes —

OLD LADY: Because I imagined — if it's to be her — then what — if she goes first — if — and I cried, too — in advance — so that — how can I say it? — you understand? — as if she'd already gone, even though she was alive — but I cried, so that — how can I say it? — to have mourned in advance — you understand — but it can't be done like that — no — all I wanted to do was cry then — and it was good to think about this — really — because then I could cry — a person has to cry every once in a while — has to — but this is different now — completely different from the way it was then — I can't say just how, but it's completely different — please tell me, sir — don't be angry with me, but — because this is so wicked now — is there a God?

(Brief pause.)

TEACHER: Why do you ask?

(Brief pause.)

OLD LADY: Because if there isn't — I don't know, but if there isn't — then I — I don't understand anything at all. Not a thing, sir. But if there is — if there is, then — you understand? — because if there is, then maybe after all, it's him — you understand? — him — who's punishing me — and then this — then this — makes sense. Because if it's him, then I deserve it — even this — I deserve. Even this, believe me.

(Brief pause.)

OLD LADY: There must be a God, sir. And I'm — I'm getting what's coming to me — because I've sinned so much. Yes. And then this — this — how can I say it? — then what's happened — has to be — then it had to happen this way — and I have to bear it — this too — because I deserve it. Yes. I never went to church, sir — except when I was very little — but not since — I didn't think about these things — only later — but not then either — not really about these things — not this way — only when I sat in the waiting room — at the vet's — there were a lot of people — with parrots, cats, dogs, hamsters — with guinea pigs, white mice — there were lowlifes there too — who caught stray dogs — and took them in — for a twenty — to be experimented on — they were wicked people — I could tell — it shows — and the dogs — poor things — didn't suspect — they're stupid — but the others were decent people — there were children — and old ladies — old gentlemen — I looked at them — and prayed: my God, don't let me become like them — even though I had only a cat — but that's what I prayed for even so — they were all decent people — and I was wondering why fate is so rough on them. That's what I was wondering. Once — when was that? — once there was a nice old lady — she must have been eighty, ninety years old — her face was all furrowy — full of furrows — she was bringing a little kitty — that was all that was left to her — a kitty — the kitty's sister had already died, not long before — and now this one was sick — the one that was left — and the old lady was very afraid — well, she was telling me that they had a mynah bird — it was a very smart bird — and when her husband died — the old lady's husband — the mynah bird knew exactly what happened — and didn't eat — and starved to death. It was a very smart bird, the lady told me. A very smart bird.

(Pause.)

OLD LADY: I was there a lot — she was sick often — and also it was good there — we talked a lot — they were constantly complaining — always them — they never listened to me — not me — but still it was good — I sat there and wondered — what makes people so unfortunate — not all — just those who don't have a family — but an awful lot of people don't have a family, sir — an awful lot of people don't — for example — not you either anymore, sir, right? — don't be angry with me for bringing it up — I wondered what the reason for that could be. And a person gets old — and is left all alone — and it's terrible — there's nothing worse — and there's nobody left to mourn you — what could the reason be? But I didn't really think about these things then — the way I should have — because I had my cat —

TEACHER: Yes —

OLD LADY: I don't want to hold you up, sir — but this — now — while you're young, you think there must be possibilities — in spite of everything — all the hopelessness — when my little girl died during the siege — she was still so very little — but that's how it was then — a lot of people died then — and I thought something could happen — but no — my marriage was no good, sir — still I thought there've got to be possibilities — but there weren't — and when my husband's leg went bad — you didn't live here yet, sir —

TEACHER: No, I didn't.

OLD LADY: He was diabetic, and his toes began to rot — then the rot moved on up — they amputated his leg at the knee — he walked on crutches — I tended him for a long time — even though I didn't like him much — but I tended him faithfully, because if I couldn't love him, at least I should tend him — then they cut off the whole leg — and I tended him and gave him a decent burial — I didn't think about this then either, really — because I had things to do — because I had hope, I definitely had hope in possibilities — I thought it just can't be that there aren't any. And it was a bad thing when I had to retire, very bad, but then I had my cat — and I took in work here at home — that was good — not much pay, and I got fed up — and I still didn't have to think about these things — sir, there has to be a God — who's punishing me for my sins!

TEACHER: Well, yes.

OLD LADY: Do you know why God is punishing me for my sins? Because I wasn't good. That's why all this has happened. I didn't love my husband. I have to say it outright, sir. I couldn't love him — I didn't give it a thought for a long time — only when he'd say I loved the cat more than him, he no longer had his leg when he said that, that's when I realized that I really did love the cat more than him — and I lied and told him he's an idiot, but he wasn't — he knew it too — but I could see he was pleased I said it — that's why I did — it's true I loved my cat more, and I didn't love him. I took care of him — cooked for him — but I didn't love him. That was a sin. Don't say anything — I know. And it doesn't make up for it, my visiting his grave — I even pay extra — they still don't take proper care of it. — And I had even bigger sins — in the Nazi times — right before the siege — they came to me to hide them — and I was afraid — and I told them to go away from here, because I was afraid — everybody was afraid — and they got caught, I found out later — and they didn't come back. I wouldn't help them — because I was afraid, everybody was afraid — my little girl was alive then — but they died because of me, sir, that's what happened — I never told this to anybody, but that's what happened, sir —

TEACHER: You can't be sure that was the reason —

OLD LADY: I know it was because of me, sir — I know it — though I forgot about it right away then, and I didn't think about it later, but it was definitely a great sin, sir. And if God is punishing me this much — this much — then it had to have been a great sin. And there were other great sins too — sins I committed — there were a bunch —

TEACHER: Look —

OLD LADY: And in forty-six I had an abortion — because I was starving — everybody in the city was starving — but why couldn't I get any food? Tell me, sir, why? I could have, even if the whole world was starving! And then I would have had a child again, and abortion was illegal then, and they aborted it even so, because my husband and I decided it had to be that way — his pay was low — and I thought so too — because the world was a bad place then — but now I know that was a sin too — a great sin — because the world's always bad — it's always bad — I know — and also I didn't want a child by him —

TEACHER: Look, people commit many sins of this sort, everybody does, and yet God doesn't punish everybody the same way. I think that everyone has his own God, you see. Everyone has his own. Because he's inside, you see. And there are those who are never aware of this. In them there is no God. But in spite of that they're still human, only different — a little — and we mustn't look down on them, because they're human beings too. We mustn't, precisely because we have God in us. We have someone inside of us. And for this reason we are capable of suffering. Feeling and suffering deeply. And this is our wealth, our immeasurable wealth. And this is good. It is a gift from the Lord. He makes an exception of us, because we suffer. We are favored by him.

OLD LADY: And I don't know — but he must be watching us if he punishes us this much. And not the smallest offense escapes him — it must be like that — because if not, then — then we'd be suffering for nothing — so terribly — but this way maybe all this must be a kind of — a kind of — you know —

TEACHER: Moral lesson.

OLD LADY: That's it! Moral lesson! About the persons we've become! Don't you think so, sir? Excuse me for holding you up —

TEACHER: Oh no, not at all.

OLD LADY: I'm thinking now that — it's about time — I became good — What do you say to that, sir?

TEACHER: Well — I think you've been good all along, and that those sins you mentioned weren't such serious sins —

OLD LADY: But if they weren't so serious, why is God punishing me so harshly?!

(Brief pause.)

TEACHER: Yes — perhaps they were sins after all — true sins — major sins —

OLD LADY: You see? — and now I have to — I have to — do penance — that's it! — because of them — that's what I have to do now — but if I'm good — I can still be good for a while — then maybe I can change something for the better — and it might even turn out better for me, too.

TEACHER: Of course. There's nothing that can't be made better.

OLD LADY: The way it is now, I don't know — I get up in the morning — and what do I do, sir? I wouldn't go to the market just for myself — even though it's cheaper over there — and now I don't have to buy anything for the cat either — I get up in the morning — and then what? But if I'm good now — then there can still be something — do you understand, sir? There're still possibilities.

TEACHER: Of course.
OLD LADY: What can I do that's good, sir?

(Brief pause.)

TEACHER: I can't say, suddenly like this —
OLD LADY: It should be something that lasts a long time. Something that's — somehow — difficult.
TEACHER: Yes. I understand.
OLD LADY: I don't know — I could clean house for you, sir — every day — for free —
TEACHER: Thank you very much, but I like to do my own cleaning.
OLD LADY: But I'd do it for free —
TEACHER: That's not the point, it's just that I enjoy doing it myself.
OLD LADY: I understand — I don't know — maybe these people here — the wife's always going away anyway —
TEACHER: For them? He's always taking his wife back — instead of finally putting his foot down — he deserves what he gets. It would be wasted on them, but we'll think of something. We'll definitely figure it out. I'm here, trust me, we'll figure it out. Right now I have to get ready for a lesson, but then we'll figure it out. And please be reassured, the intention is in itself already a sign of goodness.
OLD LADY: What do you mean?
TEACHER: Good intentions count. And we'll figure it out. I have to go — good-bye, good-bye.

(Teacher goes in, closes door. Old Lady stands, then knocks at Woman's door. Woman opens it.)

OLD LADY: Excuse me for bothering you —
WOMAN: Not at all —
OLD LADY: I'd like to do your housecleaning — for free, for free — every day — I'll do your marketing — I have time — I have an awful lot of time — and that's good — marketing — on the way — and standing in line — there's always something — there're faces — a person can watch —
WOMAN: Thank you, but I get along just fine the way I am —
OLD LADY: But tell me, what should I do?! Tell me! Tell me!
WOMAN: Oh dear.
OLD LADY: To live alone like this — you're pretty — young — and you live here alone — you need a man — I'll get you one — you know what, I'll get you one.
WOMAN: Please don't. I can handle it. I'm loaded with guys.
OLD LADY: Oh come now — your guys! — they leave you after a single night — you think I don't see it happening?
WOMAN: Because that's what they're like. What does it matter? This is how I like it.

OLD LADY: It can't be that there's no decent man for you — it just can't be —
WOMAN: Oh no?
OLD LADY: No. It can't be allowed — I should know — it already ruined me. Have a baby — by anybody — don't be taking those stupid pills — you need a family — I'll help —
WOMAN: Where do you intend to look?
OLD LADY: For what?
WOMAN: Well, the guy. I have twenty a year. Minimum. At least fifteen. Where are you going to find me this guy?
OLD LADY: I'll look into the matter — I have time — I will — I'll find one eventually — for instance, here's the teacher —
WOMAN: The teacher! He'd like to be ten years older than he is — he purposely walks stooped — when he knows he's being watched — the teacher indeed! — I don't need help — why don't you get a new cat?
OLD LADY: Not that! — never again — I'm not cheating on her — not even if — not even if she's — dead — no — every time I cheated on my husband — it always turned out bad — even though I didn't love him — it was bad even so —
WOMAN: Well sure, if there's someone to cheat on!

(Brief pause.)

WOMAN: Please calm down, you're all worked up now, but it'll pass, and then everything'll be all right.
OLD LADY: Don't you understand? — You don't. It's not that — that she died — that's not it — you don't understand. Neither does the teacher — in spite of his schooling — he still doesn't understand —
WOMAN: He doesn't understand anything — not a thing. Well fine, then please come in, I have a little cognac, I got it at work, from one of the guys, he wants to get me into bed, but I hold out until I get cognac, so come on in, it'll do you good —
OLD LADY: I don't know — isn't there a place — where a person can get along — as long as we're around — where a person can still be useful — isn't there?
WOMAN: Why, me too — I come home — I bring work, I draw, I measure, it's no fun — but if I don't bring work home — then what? Where can I go? I can go up to my girlfriend's and we get plastered. But I can't go there every day. She comes over here, we cry, and get plastered, but she can't come here every day — we couldn't stand it — I go to my mother's — every Saturday afternoon — and then the Saturday afternoon visits get to be a chore — at my class reunion — last year — they were showing their kids' photos — a bunch of them are already divorced! — I sit here at night — alone — it's better that way — because they probably stink — have athlete's foot — herpes — a bunch of strangers — I sit and put on a record — I drink — without that I probably couldn't even sleep —

OLD LADY: I don't know — this whole thing — when I'm feeling on edge — I don't know — I chop wood — even though they've come up with so many smart things — all sorts of things — but how you ought to live your life, especially once you're not so young any more —

WOMAN: Even if you're still young —

OLD LADY: If my brother hadn't been killed in the war — he probably would've had a bunch of buddies — then I would've had suitors — a bunch of them — but — listen — I have a little money — it's hidden in the wall — so I'd have it — I saved it up — back when I was taking in work — to have it — and if I borrowed from it, I always replaced it — even out of my pension — I'd eat only soup if I had to — so I've got it — because I thought, what'll happen if she has some serious problem — and it costs a lot — even though it couldn't possibly cost a lot — couldn't possibly — or if we go away on some trip — that was foolish, because she wouldn't let herself be taken — I bought one of those baskets — I buckled it closed — but it still had to be held closed, because she pushed — she was very strong — and did she cry! — in the basket — even so I thought we'd go somewhere some day — I had no idea where — now what do I do with it?

WOMAN: It'll come in handy, don't worry, the way prices are going up.

OLD LADY: But I don't need it — what do I need it for? — I'll give it to somebody — there must be somebody who needs it a lot —

WOMAN: Not me — I have money, see? I make ends meet, I even own a garage — a few years ago I wouldn't have dreamed — that I'd have an apartment, and a garage — well I do — *that* I have. *(Weeps.)*

OLD LADY: But there's no problem —

WOMAN: Now I should buy myself a cat? To go chasing after? And if it dies? Should I buy a dog? It's still early for that — *(Weeps.)*

OLD LADY: Oh, my dear God.

WOMAN: How can it be — that I come home — and rush about in the room — my room — my mother — I waited it out — I can't help it that the old fellow died — I took care of him — he stank — nobody would even give him the time of day.

OLD LADY: Why, I bought him apples —

WOMAN: Nobody — but me — I had to take the stench — but I can't help it if it was good for me that he died — why, did I kill him? I took care of him as if I'd been his daughter — and I even mourned for him — and then I could have had his room — but I stayed in the small one — and I wake up with a start at night — the floor creaks — even though I had it repaired — I threw out a bunch of money — my expenses weren't all covered — the floor still creaks — the wardrobe creaks too — even though I threw his out — bought a new one — but he's in there too — almost every night — as if I poisoned him — or else he's just taking revenge on me for still being alive — I take tranquilizers by the fistful — I bring up guys so I won't have to listen to it alone — only with sleeping pills — even though I'm too young for that — why aren't there convents any more? — so nice and cool — ah, this whole thing — please excuse me. Excuse me.

OLD LADY: Why — I sit in the kitchen — I heat the place with the electric stove — the kitchen isn't so large, after all —
WOMAN: Excuse me — I'm moving away anyway — I'm going to trade this in — garage and all — that way I'll get two whole rooms — in exchange for the one and a half with the garage — I'll throw in the car, too — and I'll furnish my room — and I'll furnish another one completely — so if he comes, it'll be there for him — as long as it's far away from here — that can only be an improvement, and things'll work out. Please excuse me. And believe me when I say I loved that cat. Really. So that — please believe me — whatever I can do — really.
OLD LADY: If you like — I can sleep here at night — at your place — and then it won't creak —
WOMAN: No! No! I can't stand being in a room with anybody! I can't stand anybody's smell! This is my apartment, mine!
OLD LADY: All right — I didn't — I didn't — or maybe you could sleep at my place — there surely isn't an old fellow there —
WOMAN: No chance — I furnished this apartment — every stick of furniture — and I painted it — no chance — I come home, I close the door, and everyone can go to hell — I could have had a telephone — a guy tried to make it with me by telling me he'd get me one — that's all I need — to have everybody coming here to use it — from all over the neighborhood — that's all I need —
OLD LADY: Okay, I didn't mean to —
WOMAN: Because they're envious — incredible how envious people are — because I succeeded — what the hell did I ever succeed in? — but I worked at it — and nobody ever gave me a hand — ever — so let them work at it too. What do they think? Nobody's gonna settle in on me — no way —
OLD LADY: Why? — is that what I want? Is it? — my dear girl, do I want to oust you? You can rot in your apartment for all I care — in your garage — drop dead in your apartment, dear girl!

(Runs into apartment, slams door.)

WOMAN: Everybody can go to hell! Leave me alone! I've had it!

(Runs inside, slams door behind her, sound of chain latch can be heard. Teacher appears in doorway, looks about, mutters, goes back, closes door.)

Scene 6

(Chick and Missy enter, stop in front of Teacher's door.)

CHICK: Laca's goin' with Mara now, but they're just makin' out, Ildi said they're just makin' out, Ildi's all upset 'cause she's still got eyes for Laca, but Laca doesn't give a damn for her, even though he's only makin' out with Mara, an' Ildi says he hasn't even felt her up yet. Laca's sure got big hands, huh?
MISSY: *(Leafing through her notebook.)* Uh-huh.
CHICK: Cut that out now. What's the point?
MISSY: Wait, just a minute. *(Reads.)* "An authentic expression of Symbolism must be ambiguous if it is to get at the essence of things, because things are unambiguous only on the surface." *(Looks up.)* Things are unambiguous only on the surface. Things are unambiguous only on the surface. *(Reads.)* "While Symbolism rejects as simplistic and naive Positist ... Pos-i-ti-vist causality ..." *(Looks up.)* Positivist causality ...
CHICK: Laca's hands are unbelievably big, huh? Just think how big his cock must be.
MISSY: Yeah. *(Reads.)* "... rejects as simplistic and naive Positivist causality, it does accept existence as an attribute, thereby positing a world, devoid of causes and precedents, that is enigmatic yet predetermined ..." *(Looks up.)* Enigmatic yet predetermined, enigmatic yet predetermined ...
CHICK: If you were Mara, would you let him lay you?
MISSY: Leave me alone now, okay? *(Leafs through notebook, reads.)* "Para ... paradoxically it is through a motif of partic ... particularity — the personal image of God created for the I — that antipar ... antipartic-u-larity, the need for species identity, has found expression."
CHICK: What?
MISSY: *(Shrugs, reads.)* "As a sense of responsibility toward all mankind, this genitally subsumed characteristic..." *(Looks up.)* Genitally subsumed characteristic, genically subsumed characteristic ... *(Reads.)* "... explains the union of the image of God with motifs so typical of species identity..." *(Looks up.)* What does genitally subsumed characteristic mean?
CHICK: What?
MISSY: Genitally subsumed characteristic: what's that?
CHICK: The hell if I know. You're a woman and Laca's a man, no?

(Brief pause.)

MISSY: *(Reads.)* "... motifs so typical of species identity as historical time." *(Looks up, pause.)*
CHICK: Mara doesn't even have tits. Does she?
MISSY: Leave me alone.

CHICK: She doesn't even have tits. D'you think they'll grow out? They're not going to, that's what I think. I'm gonna get me a guy, he'll have a car, a Mazda — or a Honda — he'll have long hair — you'll see —
MISSY: *(Reads.)* "... motifs so typical of species identity as historical time ..." *(Brief pause, weeps.)*
CHICK: What's the matter now? Idiot.
MISSY: *(Wiping her tears, sniffling.)* I don't even know why I wrote all this out ... I wrote out a bunch of stuff ... *(Reads.)* "... All of the symbols, directly or by implication, refer to the central figure, the I. The redup ... reduplication or amassing of substantives and verbs, moreover, demonstrates that neither by themselves nor as a group can they give full expression to the subject ..."
CHICK: Let's see. *(Takes notebook, leafs.)* A shitload of stuff you wrote out here. This all from the textbook?
MISSY: Not just. Another book too. A real thick one.
CHICK: *(Reads.)* "The natural and spiritual aspects of man have become isolated from each other ..." *(Looks up, sighs, reads.)* "... Man's spiritual aspect glistens in godlike splendor compared to the other aspect, which is trapped in a biological prison, in death and in sex." *(Giggles, looks up.)* You're an idiot. *(Reads.)* "Respect for mankind has become expressed in terms of the love of God, in other words, our love of ourselves: Pro-meth ... Promethean humanism." *(Looks up, sighs, reads.)* "A deeply worldly feeling, an-thro-po-logical optimism, has gained expression through this love, in religious — albeit twistedly religious — terms."

(Pause, Chick reads it over again silently, knits her brow.)

CHICK: Big deal. All it means is man exists and he's miserable, and then there's this happier being, who's only in the mind, and that's God. *(Reads on silently, giggles.)* Hey, get this. *(Reads.)* "A major feature of man as historical-social being, and as spiritual being, has attracted increasing attention: his earthly nature, his immortality as an earthly being, his communality, his species identity. The poet's attention to this aspect of man is demonstrated, in grammatical terms, by the waxing comparative." *(Stops, cries out.)* Waxing comparative! That's a good one! *(Reads on, shouting.)* "...the waxing comparative. In *Love of Ourselves* there are 47.8 comparatives per 100 poems. In the later poems the number jumps to 56.6. As so often in lyric poetry, such tendencies are indications of the essential thrust of the work." *(Looks up, grinning.)* You believe this?! Waxing comparative! Is that really what it says in the book?
MISSY: Yeah, sure.
CHICK: Waxing comparative! Sublime!
MISSY: Let's go in.
CHICK: What's the big rush, idiot?

MISSY: I have to, so I'll get accepted! I have to! I can't take it any more — I have to get away — an' I'm going to — because I can get accepted outside the capital — understand? — for you there's no problem — they kiss your ass — but I can't take it — understand? — my stupid rotten father — my stupid rotten mother — I can't take it!
CHICK: Don't go getting hysterical on me, stupid idiot.

(Pause.)

CHICK: Breaking your sweet ass won't help if you're stupid —

(Pause.)

CHICK: Waxing comparative! *(Burst of laughter, knocks at Teacher's door.)*

(Teacher comes out in suit and tie.)

CHICK, MISSY: Good day, sir.
TEACHER: Good day, ladies. Come in, please.

(Girls go in, Teacher follows, closes door.)

Scene 7

(Old Lady comes out holding sheet of paper. Hesitates, then steps to Woman's door, knocks. Woman opens door to extent chain permits.)

WOMAN: Hello.
OLD LADY: This is — if you don't mind —
WOMAN: Please don't be angry — I'm sorry about before —
OLD LADY: What?
WOMAN: Don't be angry about before —
OLD LADY: Oh, that doesn't matter —
WOMAN: I didn't mean it — I was so upset —
OLD LADY: Read this — what do you think — is it all right this way?
WOMAN: What's this?
OLD LADY: Last will and testament.
WOMAN: Last will and testament?
OLD LADY: Take a look at it, please — is it all right?

(Woman undoes chain, opens door, comes out, takes paper, reads.)

OLD LADY: It even says so on top: Last Will and Testament.
WOMAN: Uh-huh. *(Reads.)*
OLD LADY: I was sitting inside — crying again — then I had to kneel down — in the kitchen — strange, it happened in the kitchen — I was kneeling — and then I prayed — and then I cried — and then all of a sudden — I don't know — as if a voice — really — I don't even understand — but it was as if — as if I was being spoken to — being told what I've got to do — and for who —
WOMAN: Wardrobe with mirror — couch — and the bed —
OLD LADY: Double bed — with box springs — we had it made — it's more than forty years old — it's a very sturdy double bed — hardwood frame — they don't make those any more.
WOMAN: And who're you leaving all this to? All this?
OLD LADY: Well, him — he's such a nice little boy — poor thing — he was so fond of me — the way he tended his father — that stupid oaf — and he was so glad to be able to come into my place and warm up — he never came inside the room — just stood by the door — he was all blue — but this'll be good now — because as I was kneeling there — that's when it happened — as if somebody — whispered to me — I heard it — I don't even know, it was a kind of — voice — and everything became clear — I calmed down — and I knew what I had to do. So then I sat down — wrote everything down — everything I have — I itemized it all — I didn't leave out a thing — I walked all around the apartment — nothing was left out —
WOMAN: Right — so what am I supposed to do?
OLD LADY: Well, tell me if it's all right like this, or if it needs anything else — because this really is a good thing I'm doing — it's good — so this has to be in order.
WOMAN: Well, it seems to be okay — it's just, I don't know — I think it was the kid who — who hanged the —
OLD LADY: I wrote Last Will and Testament as the title — see? — it's right there.
WOMAN: It's there. But I think — him of all people — I think —
OLD LADY: I even put the date at the end — today's — and where I wrote it up — and I signed it — I don't know, but shouldn't there be some kind of seal on it? —
WOMAN: I don't know — I don't think so —
OLD LADY: And is this one copy enough? —
WOMAN: Must be, since it's in your own handwriting —
OLD LADY: Well then, sign it.
WOMAN: Me?
OLD LADY: Because I need two witnesses — I know — I heard there have to be two witnesses — everything needs witnesses —
WOMAN: Okay, I could sign it, of course, and then what? Let's say he inherits everything when you die — of course, let's hope that won't happen for a long time —

OLD LADY: Well, a few more years maybe.
WOMAN: And then he gets it afterwards.
OLD LADY: Afterwards, of course. I need it till then, what I have, because I use it.
WOMAN: Right — okay, I could sign it — but how urgent is it, after all? There's plenty of time, you could have second thoughts again and again.
OLD LADY: Never. This is how it's going to be. I knelt there — on the kitchen floor — and all of a sudden — I knew this is how it's got to be. And that's that.
WOMAN: Right — I don't know — I never witnessed anything like this. If I sign it now, and somebody contests it — and my signature's on it —
OLD LADY: What do you mean contests it?
WOMAN: Okay, never mind, I was just wondering —
OLD LADY: Why don't you sign it already?
WOMAN: I'll sign it — but it needs two witnesses anyway —
OLD LADY: If it needs two, I'll get two.
WOMAN: Maybe the teacher could be the other. *(Knocks at Teacher's door, brief pause, knocks again.)*
TEACHER: *(Opens door.)* Yes?
WOMAN: Sir, there's a problem here.
TEACHER: I've got a lesson now. Afterwards I'm at your service.
WOMAN: Yes, but if you'd just tell us if this needs a witness.
TEACHER: Please, I'm working now. Afterwards I'll be happy to oblige you.

(Teacher closes door.)

WOMAN: Let's not bother the teacher. In the meantime you can think it over — and if you still think so — then —
OLD LADY: I don't understand! Nothing's ever simple! Never — when it ought to be! Why is that?
WOMAN: Look, it'll keep.
OLD LADY: No, it won't! There were so many things I wanted to do and later nothing came of them! I don't have enough time! I don't have any time!
WOMAN: Oh dear, now why are you carrying on? —
OLD LADY: You don't understand — neither did I for a long time — as long as there's time, you can't know what it's like — not to have time —
WOMAN: But you're in very good health.
OLD LADY: Well, that's just it — there's nothing wrong with me — still I've got to pass on — *(Weeps.)*
WOMAN: Oh my God. Please don't. What is it now? —
OLD LADY: Nothing ever came of anything — and a person — couldn't even understand any of it — life was long and boring — still somehow — there was a minute or two — when I dream — then I can see it — it was so much like now — I dream about it often — I'm running in the yard — long ago — my mother's there — my

father — and then I think — in the dream still — that anything's still possible — only meantime I'm afraid, afraid they'll die — my mother — my father — and I watch to see if my mother's sick yet — because I know she will be — but she isn't sick yet — but I'm very afraid she will be — and my father's very young — and I don't understand — he hasn't been killed in the war yet — how can I remember this — I must have been how old? — four — but I already know in advance — things a person's not supposed to know in advance — then I don't know — when I wake up — whether I ought to be happy because I saw them — or whether the whole thing's horrible —

(Old Lady sobs, Woman fidgets.)

WOMAN: I don't know — why don't you come in? — I've got some cognac —
OLD LADY: *(Angrily.)* Why don't you sign it?! Is that too much to ask? — to scribble your name there — even that?
WOMAN: That's not the point —
OLD LADY: A person never does anything bad — all her life — she just helps — helps others — and then this is what she gets — when she's the one who needs something!
WOMAN: But that's not how it is —
OLD LADY: Why, will it wear you out? Strain your hand?
WOMAN: You need two witnesses anyway —
OLD LADY: The teacher's an educated man — even so, if it comes to helping, he won't — not even him!

(Throws herself at Teacher's door, pounds. Teacher angrily opens door.)

TEACHER: Don't bother me! The nerve!
OLD LADY: That's right! The nerve! A person begs for some help, and then — and then —

(Woman signals to Teacher.)

OLD LADY: Because it's all the same to you if a person drops dead right beside you! Even though it would take only a single word — but nobody could care less! That's the truth!

(Chick and Missy appear in doorway, giggle.)

OLD LADY: I suffered through it all — fine — through all of it — fine — but this is too much! When did I ever get anything — in my life — When? Tell me! When? And then a person writes it down — late — but finally — she does it — something good — and then not even that — not even that — they won't even give you a signature — even that's too much for them — *(Weeps. The girls giggle quietly.)*

WOMAN: She wrote her will, it's got to be signed — two witnesses —
TEACHER: Give it here, please.

(Takes it from Old Lady, reads it, brief pause.)

TEACHER: You're leaving all this to him? All of it to him?

(Old Lady nods, sniffles, blows nose.)

TEACHER: Fine, I find nothing reproachable in this. We'll sign it nicely, and then everything will be in order. *(Searches pocket for pen.)*
MISSY: *(Hands him a pen.)* Here, sir.
TEACHER: Thank you. *(Signs paper, hands it to Woman.)*
WOMAN: I don't know — this sort of thing requires your personal-identity number, too.
TEACHER: Very well, then. *(Takes back paper, writes.)*
WOMAN: I don't know mine by heart. Just a minute. *(Goes into apartment, brief pause.)*
TEACHER: There now, you see? Everything has a solution. Everything can be brought to a felicitous conclusion. And it really isn't necessary to pound the door.
OLD LADY: I knelt there — on the floor — and prayed — in the kitchen — for God to help me — and you see, he did. He suggested this to me. I'm sure it was him.
TEACHER: Yes. So then everything turned out all right.
OLD LADY: Thank you very much, sir.
TEACHER: Not at all.
OLD LADY: It's good there are good people. I always knew you were a good person, sir.
TEACHER: Yes. Now please excuse me, I have a lesson.

(Teacher ushers girls in, follows, closes door.)

OLD LADY: In spite of everything — it's good there are good people — *(Waits, knocks at Woman's door, brief pause.)*
WOMAN: *(Opens door, remains motionless.)* I don't know where I put it —
OLD LADY: Doesn't matter. When it turns up, you'll add it.

(Brief pause.)

WOMAN: Okay.
OLD LADY: Here. *(Holds paper out toward her.)*

(Pause.)

WOMAN: It might be better — if you gave it some more thought — him of all people — what good is that? —
OLD LADY: What?
WOMAN: They'll take it away from him anyway — they'll drink it up — they're always shouting — they won't even wait — till you're — that's what they're like — and I can't take it. It'd be better if you stayed out of it. I've had dealings with the court — God forbid I should ever have to again — a proceeding, and all the complications — it'd be much better if you didn't. I'm telling you. Or go to the what-d'ya-call-it — go to the — the notary public, that's it, you could do that, go to the notary public, and get an official seal stamped on it — that's the best thing to do, and then I won't have to get mixed up in anything. Otherwise anything I can — any time — please believe me —

(Brief pause. Woman slams door. Sound of chain. Pause.)

OLD LADY: *(Tears up paper, throws it in front of Woman's door.)* There, you worm — there — there — clean it up!

(Runs into apartment, slams door.)

(If necessary, intermission comes here.)

Scene 8

(Kid and Buddy enter through coachway.)

KID: But they don't give you no dough — except in place of some dumb worker who's jerkin' off in the john meantime — once what happened was a guy gave me a fifty — there's one of them leather things — y'know — hangs around the neck — one of them leather sack things —
BUDDY: Change purse?
KID: Yeah. So I changed it for a bunch of singles — so it'd be full — 'cause I wanted it to be full — an' then it was —
BUDDY: Fuckin' good move.
KID: 'Cause soon as we get somethin' — we drink it up — heavy drinkin', man — there's this fuckin' millionaire — this private-sector guy — got two fuckin' Mercedes — two — but he's okay — 'cause if we want, he's open till eleven — even later — two fuckin' Mercedes — beats a rusty fuck —
BUDDY: Shit man, that's a good one. *(Laughs.)* That's a good one. Beats a rusty fuck! That's a good one!
KID: It's a good place — we fuckin' go there — an' they buzz off — even though it's a tough place — an' then the Bad-ass comes on with a song — top of his

lungs — an' us along with him — an' nobody gives us no fuckin' lip — 'cause we're the wolves — I even go there alone sometimes — I start singin' some number — an' they don't dare say nothin' — even when I'm alone —
BUDDY: That's good. That's good.
KID: You can get out at night — I did it a shitload of times — I tied a bunch of sheets together — an' climbed down — from the fourth floor —
BUDDY: Like on TV?
KID: Shit yeah — even now I came out — up an' walked right out — fuckin' guard starin' drop-jawed — not everybody'd dare — an' then the chicks waitin' downstairs — two, three of 'em — an' then you go to it — all night — then when you're done, back up the sheets, man —
BUDDY: Wow —
KID: They blow you — then you smack 'em one — an' that's it —
BUDDY: Shit man —
KID: 'Cause they dig me, man. They really groove on me — just me.

(Pause.)

KID: We got everything there — there's this secret tunnel — everybody knows about it — there's a bunch of machine guns down there — only we ain't found it yet — but we will — an' when we do — shit man —

Scene 9

(Old Lady comes out carrying broken crutch.)

BUDDY: *(Quietly.)* Watch it, man — the old bitch —

(Pause, Old Lady sticks crutch into freshly dug earth, pushes it as far as it will go.)

KID: Hello —

(Old Lady looks at him, does not see him.)

KID: Hello — don't you recognize me?
OLD LADY: What?
KID: It's me — don't you recognize me?
OLD LADY: Who?

(Pause.)

OLD LADY: What?

(Pause.)

OLD LADY: You — it's you?
KID: Well, of course —
OLD LADY: God in heaven — it's not true — this can't be true —

(Pause.)

KID: Will you fuckin' say hello —
BUDDY: Hello.
OLD LADY: You're bigger than — your father — dear God —
KID: I'm strong too — I work out — there's this way of workin' out — you push against a wall — it don't move, but I get strong that way —
OLD LADY: To grow so much — in such a short time —
KID: Not so short —
OLD LADY: This is something — I thought — you had such a thin little neck — you were such a skinny little boy — with such sad, intelligent eyes — such a frightened little face — how can this be? — how? —
KID: Well, I don't know — but it's good, 'cause they can't beat me up no more — I can't be pushed around no more —

(Brief pause.)

OLD LADY: I don't know — do you remember? — you came into my place when they locked you out — you came in to warm up — remember?
KID: Well, yes.
OLD LADY: I gave you food—but you didn't want to eat, you were just cold — remember?
KID: I did eat though — it was some kinda what-d'ya-call-it — noodles — with something —
OLD LADY: Noodles?
KID: Yeah, that was good.
OLD LADY: Cheese dumplings?
KID: Coulda been — some kinda noodles —
OLD LADY: What could it have been — noodles and cheese? When did I ever make noodles and cheese?
KID: It had a little — sort of — paprika in it. It was good.
OLD LADY: Then that was noodles and potato!
KID: I don't know —
OLD LADY: Sure, that's what that was! Don't you remember?
KID: Yeah — yeah —
OLD LADY: Well, of course! And how you liked it — of course it was noodles and potato!

(Pause.)

OLD LADY: *(To Buddy.)* The way he ate, poor thing — the way he wolfed it down — though he said he wasn't hungry —
BUDDY: That's funny. *(Laughs.)*
OLD LADY: Because sometimes his father didn't feed him for three days — and him wasting away —
KID: No, it's just that — he didn't have no money then — that's why —
OLD LADY: Oh go on, he had money!
KID: No, he didn't — really — he didn't.
OLD LADY: He sent you to steal food, didn't he? And he just lay there — supposedly pining after his wife — who went a-whoring!
KID: No! He was sick! He was on sick leave!
OLD LADY: Sick! As soon as you were taken to the institution he was up and about — because there wasn't anyone to feed him! Him sick — ha!
BUDDY: *(Laughs.)*
KID: Shut your face, jerk!

(Pause.)

KID: That's not how it was — no matter what you say — it's not — he had fever — he was on regular sick leave — who wouldn't have taken care of him — who?
OLD LADY: What are you defending him for now? — he didn't even heat the place — you were frozen — you were blue from cold — don't you remember?
KID: Well, 'cause it was cold —
OLD LADY: But he did heat the place — while you were at school — and how! — it only got cold by the afternoon — so you'd feel sorry for him — I saw it — so you'd feel sorry for him —
KID: No! — no! —
OLD LADY: What do you mean no? I saw it!
KID: No!
OLD LADY: You didn't even have a cap — I knitted one for you — I lent my pot — and then I had to beg to get it back — and they didn't even clean it — I had to scrub the filth out — even your mother, when she was here —

(Pause.)

OLD LADY: So now you're here — it's good — that you came back just now — but I knew it — I asked for it — and the Lord granted it — I don't know — if you're hungry, I could cook something for you now. This is like — what do they call this sort of thing — it's an act of grace — from the Lord —
KID: Did you happen to see my father?
OLD LADY: So now you're here — *(To Buddy.)* He was such a nice, smart little

boy — well then I'll go in now and write another one — so it'll be all right for him, you know?
BUDDY: Uh-huh —
OLD LADY: I don't know — he won't fit in the bed — but I'll buy a long one — I didn't think of that — and will you be growing any more?
KID: Will I what?
BUDDY: *(Laughs.)* Will you be gettin' any fuckin' bigger?
KID: Shut your fuckin' face!
OLD LADY: What's this language? Don't use language like that!

(Pause.)

KID: I didn't —
OLD LADY: I'm going to tell you now — that I sensed this — and a long time ago at that — I bought everything — baby things too — and children's things — such nice things — because I saw them in the shop windows, and they appealed to me — they were so good to touch — the material — and I bought all sorts of things — and I hid them — so my husband wouldn't find out — they're down in the cellar — in mothballs — I don't know — I guess by now you've outgrown them — you were so much smaller — when I bought them — but they'll come in handy when you get married — for your child — so I'll add those too — I'm going in now to write it up again — my God — just when a person seems to be at the end of the line — then all of a sudden — *(Smiles, goes in, closes door.)*

Scene 10

(Pause.)

BUDDY: She's completely nuts, the old bitch —
KID: It ain't true — I only went in 'cause it was cold — it ain't true I ate — the fuckin' old bitch is lyin' — what the hell could my old man do about the heat? — he didn't have nothin' to heat with — not a fuckin' thing!
BUDDY: She didn't notice the cat —
KID: Shut the fuck up before I break your face!
BUDDY: Now what gives?
KID: Why ain't nobody here? — goddammit —
BUDDY: Maybe he came back meantime —
KID: Shut your fuckin' face — shut it —
BUDDY: Okay, I didn't —

(Pause. Kid pulls himself together, knocks, silence. Pause. Kid knocks louder, then kicks door. Father opens it.)

FATHER: *(Shouting.)* Goddammit! —

(Pause.)

KID: Dad —

(Pause.)

FATHER: What's up? —
KID: Dad —
FATHER: Is it you?

(Pause.)

BUDDY: Hello.

(Pause.)

FATHER: God you're big.

(Pause.)

FATHER: You run away? You run away or what?
KID: I didn't run away! I didn't run away! They let me out!
FATHER: They did?
KID: For three days!
FATHER: What? For three days?
KID: For three days! They let me out!

(Pause.)

FATHER: So they let you out. *(Pause.)* Well — hi. — They let you out, huh? — and is there a document? — 'cause they'll come nosin' around — an' I'm the one they'll pin it on — dig?
KID: Sure I got one — why don't you believe me — why? —
FATHER: Okay, I believe you — just y'know — so then they let you out?

(Pause.)

FATHER: For how many days — what'd you say?
KID: Three days.
FATHER: That's good, three days, that's good. What is this — vacation or what?

(Brief pause.)

FATHER: You coulda wrote—to let me know—you coulda wrote you're comin'. You shoulda wrote—to let me know when—next time write first—when you're comin'. Huh? Say somethin'.
KID: I didn't know.
FATHER: What?
KID: That I'd be gettin' out—
FATHER: Why didn't you know—they didn't tell you or what?
KID: No.

(Pause.)

FATHER: Okay—no problem—if they didn't tell you, they didn't tell you—okay—then you couldn't know—when you'd be comin'—ya see—no problem—I'm home—good thing—I'm home. *(Brief pause.)* You been here already—when I wasn't—you been here already? Today?
KID: Yeah.
FATHER: Look here—tell me—did you touch that cat? Huh? The old lady's cat—an' don't lie to me!
KID: No.
FATHER: No?
KID: No.
BUDDY: We didn't even see no cat.
FATHER: It died on her, an' she's blamin' me—you sure?
KID: Sure.
BUDDY: Sure.
FATHER: You can tell me—the stupid old bitch—she had it comin'—huh? So tell me—nobody'll hear—did you touch it?
KID: No.
BUDDY: No.
FATHER: No? Okay then—that's good—then it's okay.

(Pause.)

FATHER: So then you came home—for three days—have a good time—huh?

(Pause, they stand still.)

BUDDY: Okay, I'll be goin' now—I'll drop by later on.
KID: I don't know—I'll go too—
FATHER: Where you goin' now?! Why can't you stay put a while?! You ain't goin' noplace!
BUDDY: You stay here—I'll drop by later on—see ya—goodbye.

(Runs out, pause.)

FATHER: You can go with him — if that's all this is to you — bein' able to come home at last — after all that time — an' then you can't stand bein' with your old man — just you go ahead —

(Pause.)

FATHER: If you'da wrote — then I woulda had eats waitin' for you — somethin' — anythin' — woulda been better — next time try lettin' me know —

KID: But I couldn't — they didn't want me to — 'cause then they need that fuckin' thing — that what-d'ya-call-it — from the Council — that document thing — but the Council guy — the custody supervisor — he won't issue one — if the parent don't ask for it — an' you didn't — you didn't ask for it — an' without that it's no go — but then the assistant director — he couldn't take it no more — me always botherin' him — he's a decent guy — he let me out — even without that Council document — an' he ain't even supposed to —

FATHER: Yeah? Well, I don't know — they didn't say nothin' to me —

KID: I wrote to you — long time ago — to invite me home — an' then the Council guy'll inspect —

FATHER: Here? Nobody's inspectin' here — I had enough of that — they can go fuck themselves — *(Brief pause.)* What d'ya mean? — you didn't write — I never got nothin' — really — what d'ya mean, when?

KID: Long time ago — I don't know any more — year an' a half — I don't know —

FATHER: I didn't get it — didn't get nothin' — probably got lost — mailman don't even come here — I didn't get nothin' —

(Pause, they stand still.)

FATHER: So then — how is it down there? —
KID: It's good.
FATHER: It's good?
KID: Yeah — good.
FATHER: What'd you say? Where is it?
KID: The place I'm at now?
FATHER: Yeah.
KID: You know — where the factory is. We live next to a farm.
FATHER: But they didn't take you there right off —
KID: No — I was here — in one of them transit detention centers — an' then all over the place—I don't know—they shuffle you from one place to another—
FATHER: How's the food? Shitty, huh?
KID: No, it ain't bad — it's okay.

FATHER: It's okay?
KID: It's okay. There was places it was bad — but not too many. You can have seconds an' everything.
FATHER: Cut the shit — I bet they starve you — the bastards — they steal the food right outa your mouths —
KID: No — really — they do steal — but not food — an' if they do, there's still enough —

(Pause.)

FATHER: An' what d'you guys do?
KID: I don't know. Whatever needs doin' — we hang out —
FATHER: And?
KID: Nothin'.
FATHER: An' what's up — you learnin' a trade?
KID: Yeah. But there ain't that much of it — we do grindin' — we hang out — like that —

(Pause.)

FATHER: That stupid sister of yours — she's probably makin' money already —
KID: I don't know — 'cause they don't keep brothers an' sisters together — so I don't know what's up with her —
FATHER: Ah, she's probably makin' money already — never wrote once — probably became a whore, huh?
KID: I don't know.

(Pause.)

KID: Once there was one hell of a fuss — they stuck a frog in the guardian's bed —
FATHER: What? A frog?
KID: Yeah — but they didn't know who —
FATHER: Who was it?
KID: The dimwit — we had one — a real jerk — he'd raise hell all night — they made us get up — we stood there at attention — but nobody ratted — hell of a fuss —

(Pause.)

KID: There was lotsa frogs — there's lotsa frogs over there — we made 'em smoke cigarettes — you gotta stick it in its mouth — it smokes an' smokes — gets all puffed up — an' blows up —
FATHER: The frog?
KID: Yeah.

(Pause.)

FATHER: Don't you do no smokin' — ya hear? Don't smoke —
KID: Eh.
FATHER: You smokin'?
KID: No.

(Pause.)

FATHER: Well there ain't nothin' around here — Feró went away —
KID: Feró?
FATHER: Yeah — he had that shitsure lotto system — y'know —
KID: Feró?
FATHER: Yeah — he went private sector — came back once — says he's makin' five times as much — probably lyin' — but he is makin' money — he was wearin' a suit — good thing he wasn't wearin' them what-d'ya-call-it gloves — gloves — he don't even go to the game no more — somethin', huh?

(Pause.)

KID: Once I dreamt — it was real bad — I dreamt you got your leg cut off — the machine did it — I don't know — an' you was runnin' at me — on one leg somehow — an' blood was pourin' outa the other one — which was missin' — an' I was runnin' away from you — an' you on one leg —
FATHER: My leg was cut off?
KID: An' you was runnin' —
FATHER: Which one was cut off?
KID: I don't know — I can't say — was there anythin'? — with your leg —
FATHER: Nah — my leg?

(Brief pause.)

KID: An' then — this happened too — I was scared slivers was gonna go in my eye — an' they'll take out my eye — an' they took it out — the whole eye — I could see outa the one they took it outa — I could see what they took out — but nothin' ever goes in.

(Brief pause.)

KID: *(Points at garage.)* What's this — this wasn't here — what's this?!
FATHER: A garage — belongs to that stupid broad — she's got a car — it's inside — 'cause she don't know how to drive the fuckin' thing — flunked five fuckin' times — funny, huh?

(Laughs.)

KID: But why a garage — how come it's in here?
FATHER: Well — it's a garage.

(Brief pause.)

KID: The shed used to be there —
FATHER: Yeah.
KID: It was like — the shed — you could always go there — the shed —
FATHER: It was crumblin' away — from rot — what's up? —

(Brief pause.)

FATHER: How'd you get so fuckin' big?

(Brief pause.)

KID: *(Takes paper bag from pocket, opens it.)* Dad — look —
FATHER: What's this?
KID: I made it — outa metal plate — with a saw — they're animals — look — I didn't use no outline —
FATHER: *(Picks up one or two little figures, looks at them.)* What's this?
KID: Which one? That's a cow.
FATHER: This?
KID: You got it upside down — it's a cow —
FATHER: Yeah, a cow.
KID: All kinds of animals — I just kinda start, and it gets to be an animal — first I used to give 'em to the chicks — 'cause they dug 'em — then I got a ten-spot for each — not bad, huh?
FATHER: Pretty good.
KID: I'm a damn good grinder — get this — I didn't know I could do it — they said it's hard as hell — I can use a tiny little boring bit too — even the chief tool-maker has me doin' it — how 'bout that? —
FATHER: That's good.

(Brief pause.)

FATHER: I was relaxin' before — I was readin' —

(Brief pause.)

KID: Dad — I'm already a wolf.

FATHER: What are you?
KID: A wolf — 'cause while the guardian's there — or the workin' stiffs — they lie low — but then they go away — an' at night the wolves take over — they're strong as hell — whoever don't kiss their ass, gets the living shit beat out of him —
FATHER: What d'ya mean wolves?
KID: The gang — you can't sneak away — they'll beat you up — when I was little I thought I could raise hell — once I even landed in the hospital — 'cause of that — my two teeth here, they knocked 'em out. *(Shows him.)*
FATHER: Motherfuckers.
KID: But now I'm a wolf too — it don't matter if it's a new place — I know right away — how to be a wolf — by the time I was in eighth grade — right off I pick out the gang leader — you can tell who it is — an' I tell him it's okay — I don't wanna fuck him over — even though he ain't even always the biggest guy — but you can tell —
FATHER: That's okay then —

(Pause.)

FATHER: Me, I'm in my prime — the best age — not even forty — huh? — any woman sixteen to forty-five suits me — but not just anybody — I got pretty picky — your fuckin' old lady took away my best years — she wrung me out — like a dishrag — but never again — I learned my lesson about what I'll take an' what I won't — these little chicks come up to me — at work too — there're these little chicks — all they've got on is their smock — not even a slip — nothin' — they're makin' eyes at me, smilin' like hell — but I watch out for myself — I learned my lesson — what I'll take an' what I won't —

(Pause.)

KID: And Dad — you okay?
FATHER: Me? I'm okay. Why — what else would I be? — nothin' special — I bust my ass — I work days — morning shift — but we'll figure it all out — what to do these three days — I don't know — we'll go someplace — here an' there — everything —
KID: And — I don't know — somebody takin' care of you?
FATHER: Me? I don't need nobody — what do I gotta be taken care of? —
KID: I don't know — like me — back then —
FATHER: Eh — what for? — that was then —

(Pause.)

FATHER: You were a decent kid — really — when I was laid up — you were real decent—an' they took you away just then—just when I was laid up—the bastards—your stupid sister didn't even spit in my direction—only you—an' then they grabbed you an' took you away—

(Pause.)

FATHER: Okay, so then—it's a mess inside—so what, huh? Not everything's where it used to be—but we'll fix it up—
KID: I'll clean up.
FATHER: Eh—what for?—it'll be okay—

(Brief pause.)

FATHER: Hey—I was thinkin'—what a shit-brained thing—you learnin' some stupid trade—why don't you go to work?—make money.
KID: I don't know—everybody's doin' it this way—
FATHER: It's shit-brained. Take me—if I wanted—I could make more than them fuckin' senior skilled workers—if I wanted—only what the hell for?—hey—what if—let's say you got out—came back—an' went to work—a big guy like you—I don't even know what the hell you need a trade for—you could be makin' money—I could be makin' money—together, I'm talkin' heavy dough, dig?—if they'd let you out—'cause this way what d'ya get?—years you're workin' for them—they don't give you nothin'—only when you get out—an' by then—I don't know—c'mon home—we'll talk 'em into it—okay, so they'll come nosin' around again—the motherfuckers—but we'll talk 'em into it—we can shovel the shit, dammit—the two of us, huh? *(Laughs.)*
KID: Dad—I wanna stay here—Dad— *(Breaks into tears.)*

(Brief pause.)

FATHER: Don't cry—why—what I been sayin'?—hey—
KID: It's so bad—so fuckin' bad— *(Weeps.)*
FATHER: Hey—I'm sayin' we'll take care of it—
KID: I don't wanna go back!
FATHER: You don't wanna, you don't wanna—okay—that's what I say too—we'll fix it—you're here now—what'd you say, for how long? How long you stayin'?
KID: I don't wanna go—
FATHER: When you leavin'?—tomorrow?
KID: Day after.
FATHER: Okay—so it's three days—huh?—that's good—stop cryin'—before, you said it's good over there—didn't you?—the food—the wolves—why, what'd

I say? — I said you'll come home — an' we'll make a shitload of money — but for now you'll go back — 'cause they'll get you for runnin' away — they'll come after me — an' lay it all on me — I know — an' then the whole deal's blown — don't you get it?

(Pause.)

FATHER: Okay, so this is for three days — so what d'ya wanna do? — What we gonna do?
KID: *(Whimpering.)* I don't know.
FATHER: What d'ya mean you don't know? — am I supposed to know? — at your age I knew — I was chasin' chicks — goin' to the movies — stuff like that — we didn't have no TV in them days — we played soccer — with the buddies — you guys down there — you play soccer?
KID: Ain't no field —
FATHER: How come? — that's how come we never win the championships — I always say — 'cause there ain't no facilities — the paper says so too — even so there ain't — how come there ain't no field?
KID: I don't know — was a ping-pong table — they took it away — a guardian — he got it —
FATHER: The ping-pong table? An' it ain't even his, huh? — belongs to you guys — an' he took it — huh?
KID: I never even seen it — they told me about it —
FATHER: You guys oughta take a stand — make him bring it back — why don't you guys take a stand? — don't let him — that's how they get everything — 'cause you let 'em — so it's no fuckin' wonder they take it — tell 'em I said so —

(Pause.)

FATHER: Okay — let's say we go now — okay? — we'll go around — or you go to the movies — I don't know what's playin' — I'll give you some money — I'll give you a twenty — okay? — meantime I'll do some readin' 'cause I usually read — after work — I'll give you a twenty —

(Pause.)

FATHER: An' then meantime I'll straighten up — I didn't have no time — but now 'cause you're here — it's a good thing after all — you comin' home — I'll straighten up —

(Pause.)

Scene 11

(Female Official enters through coachway, in both hands shopping bags containing food, drink, briefcase.)

OFFICIAL: Good day. Is this forty-four?
FATHER: It is.
OFFICIAL: I don't understand. There's no house number. I've been wandering around here for half an hour. No street sign, no house number ...
FATHER: 'Cause it fell off — an' then I made one — put it out — it was up — 'cause the old one was all — y'know — all faded — then the Council came — they said y'know — it ain't standard — they took it down — said they'll take care of it — been nothin' since then.
OFFICIAL: I don't understand, at the neighboring lot, on that wooden fence, it says twenty-eight ... I asked around, nobody knew anything.
FATHER: The mailman too — he don't come in — 'cause he says he don't gotta — if there ain't no number — an old lady lives here — she goes out there — when she's expectin' her pension — 'cause the mailman don't come in — we don't even exist. *(Laughs.)*
OFFICIAL: *(Puts down shopping bags, takes a plan from briefcase, opens it, studies it.)* I don't understand ... this isn't what's here.
FATHER: What're you lookin' for?
OFFICIAL: I'm from the Council.
FATHER: The Council?
OFFICIAL: Yes.
FATHER: Say, if I could just — this here's my son — they took him away an' put him in the state's custody — but it's bad for him there. Could you get him out?
OFFICIAL: That's a custody case. *(Studies drawing.)*
FATHER: They took him away — for no good reason — his sister too — why don't you come in? — everything's in order here — it's clean — I got a job — an' then they take my kids away!
OFFICIAL: I told you that's a custody case. There're officials who deal with custody cases. Go to them. *(Looks around.)* I don't understand.
FATHER: Let him out — and appoint me his y'know — make him my — my — what-d'ya-call-it — my y'know —
OFFICIAL: Your ward.
FATHER: That's it! 'Cause it can be done — I know it —
OFFICIAL: Custody case. *(Points at garage.)* What's that?
FATHER: A garage.
OFFICIAL: There's no such thing.
FATHER: Belongs to that woman — who lives in there —
OFFICIAL: It's not a dwelling?
FATHER: That? I'm tellin' ya — it's a garage — belongs to that woman —

KID: Used to be a shed — a shed — mine.
FATHER: I'll get her out here — don't you bother — *(Knocks at Woman's door, silence, knocks again.)*
WOMAN: *(Opens door, but only a crack, as far as chain allows.)* What is it?
FATHER: Come out here — the Council's here because of the garage.
WOMAN: What do you mean the Council? I got the permit, it's mine.
FATHER: The Council says it's a dwelling.

(Woman undoes chain, comes out, goes to Official.)

WOMAN: Are you from the Council, Comrade?
OFFICIAL: I am.
WOMAN: This is my garage. I got a permit for it — it's inside, I can bring it out. There wasn't anything here. Just a broken-down shed. I had this built.
OFFICIAL: It's not indicated on this drawing.
WOMAN: What do you mean it's not indicated? I was at the Council a year and a half ago...
OFFICIAL: And when did the Council inspect the premises?
WOMAN: I don't know ... *(To Father.)* Did they inspect?
FATHER: When they took my kids away — my son — for no good reason — 'cause the old lady denounced me — even though she's nuts — she just buried her cat — tell her, didn't she just bury her cat? Didn't she?
WOMAN: She did.
OFFICIAL: What is this, a garden? Because according to this, it's a garden.
FATHER: It's a garden.
OFFICIAL: Not an interior courtyard?

(Brief pause.)

FATHER: This a garden?
WOMAN: I don't know. Why, is there a difference?

(Brief pause.)

WOMAN: The teacher probably knows — and he can tell you this is a garage — *(Goes to Teacher's door, knocks, pause, knocks again, Teacher opens.)*
TEACHER: Please, will you let me work!
WOMAN: Excuse me, but this Comrade's from the Council — could you tell her — is this a garden or a courtyard? And tell her that's my garage. Please tell her.
TEACHER: Please — I've asked you a hundred times not to bother me while I'm teaching —
WOMAN: But this Comrade's from the Council!
OFFICIAL: *(To Teacher.)* Is this number forty-four?

TEACHER: It is.
OFFICIAL: Nothing here corresponds to this. I'll have to check it all out because of the gas lines, but the neighboring lot's number twenty-eight, and there's no number on it. This garage isn't here at all.
TEACHER: Just a moment. What gas lines?
OFFICIAL: Well, you're going to be tied in to the gas lines.
TEACHER: Now?
OFFICIAL: Within the next three months.
TEACHER: Excuse me, but the way I understood it, they're going to tear this whole thing down.
OFFICIAL: Of course.
TEACHER: If they're going to tear it down, then why tie in the gas? It might have been a good idea some time ago, but if they're going to do away with everything here, then why tie in now?
OFFICIAL: It was in the plan to have gas here, but there wasn't enough capacity. Now there is.
TEACHER: This is going to cost the Council a great deal of money.
OFFICIAL: That's right. So be grateful you're getting it.
TEACHER: If they tie us into the gas lines now, we'll use it for a few months, a half a year, a year maybe, then the bulldozer will clear everything away. The public utility lines will be moved. Tremendous expense. They'll build one of those ten-story apartment blocks of the kind that're already around here. They'll lay new pipes...
OFFICIAL: That's right.
TEACHER: Wouldn't it be simpler not to tie us in now?
OFFICIAL: That isn't your concern. It's been approved.
WOMAN: Don't make a fuss, sir. If there's gas, then they'll have to give us better apartments in exchange for these.
TEACHER: It's still a waste. The state is squandering a great deal of money.

(Chick and Missy listen with interest at Teacher's doorway.)

OFFICIAL: That's how it is. Are you sure this is forty-four?
TEACHER: This is forty-four.
OFFICIAL: Even the dimensions look wrong.
TEACHER: If you please, as long as they're determined to tie in the gas, fine, so be it. But then perhaps they needn't tear it down. This isn't in such bad shape, neither are the other buildings in the neighborhood — they've renovated many of them, not so long ago. One of those tall buildings hardly accommodates more people than all the ones they'd be tearing down to make room for it. And there are lovely gardens around here, fruit gardens, all of which will have to be destroyed. It would be a shame.
OFFICIAL: There's been a Resolution. Just be glad you're getting everything for free.

TEACHER: These buildings are brick. They've got cellars; they're in good shape; they can easily take another forty, fifty years. More than a prefabricated housing development.

OFFICIAL: Please leave me alone. I'm just doing my job. You can always go to the complaints office. Extended office hours are on Mondays.

FATHER: Gimme a document that says everything's okay here, I don't drink, I got a job, he's makin' money too, look at the size of this kid.

OFFICIAL: Explain to him that that's a custody case.

FATHER: You're from the Council—an' now I'm appealing to the Council—about how it was when my wife left me—I was left here—wrung out like a dishrag—an' my son took care of me—'cause I wasn't even able to get up—that's right—an' he brought me food—everything—he cleaned the house—did the wash—'cause his sister strayed off too—except for him I'd have croaked right then an' there—he was still just a little kid—but he could take care of everything—an' then they denounced me—an' the Council took him away from me. Ain't that the truth? Tell her! Ain't it?!

WOMAN: That's how it was, because the old lady wanted to help, to take him in with her, and that's when there was an inspection, and that's when the state took note of what was going on here—but he couldn't be turned over to the old lady, because they would have been feuding all the time—so they took him away—

OFFICIAL: *(Sighs, looks at Kid.)* And?

FATHER: He wants to come back—'cause it's no good for him there—why can't he come back?!

KID: Let me stay here—I don't know—back there I always dreamt about coming back—an' then me an' Dad—here—even though he didn't even write—but I'd like to be back here—with him. *(Weeps.)*

OFFICIAL: You'll have to go to the Custody Division.

FATHER: *(Opens his apartment door.)* Please come in—it's neat in here—clean—see for yourself—this is where he belongs—

(Teacher goes back, ushers in girls, closes door.)

OFFICIAL: The official in charge of custody cases will come out, all right? *(Puts drawing back into briefcase, picks up shopping bags.)*

WOMAN: Excuse me, I have a permit for this garage—I can show you—it's inside—with this garage—I'm entitled to a two-room apartment with full conveniences—in return—go ahead, assess it—

OFFICIAL: They'll be out.

(Old Lady comes out of apartment, wearing a clean dress somewhat unsuited to her years, in makeup, carrying sheet of paper.)

OLD LADY: *(Shouting.)* You get away from there!
OFFICIAL: *(Jumps away in fright.)*
OLD LADY: You're trampling the grave! The grave! Get away from there!
WOMAN: Just a minute — it's only a cat — they hanged it —

(Official starts to leave, Father rushes after her, grabs her by the arm.)

FATHER: This rotten old lady — I'm denouncing her now — 'cause she had my son taken away — she's the one —
OFFICIAL: Let go of me!
FATHER: She had no right! She had no right! She's crazy — she buries her cat here — crazy — an' the Council believes her!
WOMAN: *(To Old Lady.)* She's from the Council —
OLD LADY: *(To Official)* Please sign this for me — it's my last will and testament — because only the teacher's willing — nobody else — please sign it for me —
OFFICIAL: Let go of me!
OLD LADY: I'm leaving everything to him — to this boy here — everything — the furniture — everything — my money too — ten thousand forints — that too — I wrote it up all over again — please sign it —
OFFICIAL: I'm not signing anything — let me go — you're all mad — I'm here to get you gas —
FATHER: She had my son taken away — 'cause she wanted him for her ward — it was a trick — to get the money — if he's her ward — then she gets paid —
OLD LADY: Don't you understand, you blockhead, I'm leaving everything to your son?! Don't you understand?!
FATHER: What?
OLD LADY: This is a will — I'm leaving everything to him — my money — ten thousand forints — and I'm going to take him in — I'll write a petition —
FATHER: You got money, huh? The money you stole outa my pocket — I figured it all out — 'cause the subsidy for a ward is at least four hundred a month — I know that — I'm no fool — you think I don't know? Up to now you stole 9,600 forints outa my pocket — 9,600 — I figured it out!
OLD LADY: What are you talking about? I stole — from you?
FATHER: 'Cause if I'd been the kid's what-d'ya-call-it — his guardian — the kid's — this one here, I ain't even figurin' in my daughter — then in this much time that's what it comes to! — It's all figured out! — That's how much you owe me!
OLD LADY: Well I never —
FATHER: You denounced me — you said I just lie around — *(To Official.)* This one denounced me — she said I just lie around — 'cause I was laid up — 'cause this one here — she wanted to get the money — the support for the kid — she figured it out! But she didn't get it after all — 'cause the custody official came — an' saw what the story was — but I didn't get it either — goddammit — neither did I! *(To Old Lady.)* 'Cause if you hadn't been such a rotten lowlife — then I woulda got it!

WOMAN: The way that happened was that the official who came out could see that all hell would break loose if the lady — even though she meant well — she really did —
FATHER: Well I woulda wrung her neck — that's for sure —
WOMAN: The poor boy was such a decent kid — he took care of his father — he cut school, went to work — so there'd be money — they threw him out of school for stealing money —
KID: An' I didn't even steal! Only from my sister! I didn't even steal!
WOMAN: His father was just lying there — he was certified as sick — the boy even cooked for him, cleaned house, everything — it's too bad the Council had to come out just then — I know the Council meant well —
OFFICIAL: *(Frees herself).* Go to the Custody Division! *(Runs out coachway.)*
OLD LADY: *(Shouts after Official.)* At least sign it — I need two witnesses — sign it!

(Official disappears.)

FATHER: *(Shouts after Official.)* I never even spanked him — never! Everybody beats their kid — not me, ever! *(Brief silence, to Kid.)* Did I — ever?
KID: No.
FATHER: There you go! A few whacks, but beat you — never! Kids oughta be taken away from where they're beaten half dead — but no — only from me — when they're big — when they're makin' money — that's how come too — 'cause if they ain't here — then I don't get a bigger apartment — that's what it comes down to — I know it! 'Cause the Council too — how come they gotta meddle in a person's life — how come? — when it's so damn hard as it is — then how come they gotta meddle — how come?!
WOMAN: They meant well — believe me they did — that was a very decent custody official.
FATHER: Then what was he doin' meddlin' — in a person's life — what was he doin' that for? *(To Old Lady.)* Filthy squealer.
OLD LADY: We have nothing to talk about. I'm leaving everything to your son, do you understand? But you and I have nothing to talk about. *(To Woman.)* Neither do we — you cowardly bitch — can't even sign a thing like this — but that's all right — because the Lord doesn't want evil to rule in the world — *(To Kid.)* You'll see —
WOMAN: Me a bitch! Here I am defending you — and then you — you — but that's just like you — always — you drove away the only one — the engineer — the oarsman —
OLD LADY: I did what? To who?
WOMAN: He was the only guy — you wouldn't leave him alone — he had to go in for coffee — you were here whenever he came — and he couldn't take it — he was the only guy — who —
OLD LADY: You've lost your mind.

WOMAN: I have? Oh yeah? What did you use to tell the old fellow? — about me — all the time — I know all about it — he told me — that all I was interested in was the apartment — all the time that's what you said — because I'm young and attractive — you were mean — jealous — I know all about it —

OLD LADY: What? Me? He was an old geezer!

WOMAN: He was younger than you!

OLD LADY: A feeble old geezer! I felt sorry for him — because you just did the bare minimum for him — and he was left to rot here by himself all day — so I asked him in — I bought him apples — and you were afraid I was after his apartment — because there's only meanness in your head — nothing else —

WOMAN: You're always spying — whenever I talk to the teacher you come rushing right out — so nothing should happen between —

OLD LADY: Well I never —

WOMAN: Oh yes!

FATHER: *(Laughs, to Kid.)* How 'bout this? They're at each other's throats — pretty good, huh? *(Laughs.)*

WOMAN: You shut up — all you can do is stand around gawking!

FATHER: Dumb bitch — you go to bed with anybody — you think I can't tell? — anybody — your tits are always hangin' out so I can see 'em — filthy bitch —

WOMAN: All of you can — can just —

(Woman runs inside, slams door behind her, sound of chain.)

OLD LADY: Because she wanted my cat — she wanted to lure her away from me — and that stupid animal — it even rubbed up against her —

FATHER: Your cat! *(Laughs.)* Your stupid cat! Your cat croaked, my dear! The kitty kicked off! "Kitty cat, kitty cat, meow, meow, here kitty!" *(Laughs, begins hopping around crutch, emits Indian cries, summons Kid.)*

KID: *(Laughs.)* Dad — Dad — *(Joins him in Indian dance.)*

OLD LADY: *(Watches, straightens up, stands motionless.)* Dear God — thanks be to you, Lord, for reminding me — reminding me once more — Lord —

(Father and Kid dance, occasionally hitting their mouths while howling.)

OLD LADY: You know, Lord, why this is necessary — you know, my God —

(Father and Kid stop, panting, Father throws arm around shoulder of Kid who is taller than he.)

OLD LADY: *(Wipes her tears, smearing her rouge.)* That's all right, Lord — it's all right even so — even so — *(Goes into house, closes door.)*

FATHER: *(Panting.)* Shit man — huh? *(Laughs, pants.)* I'm tellin' you man — shit man —

KID: *(Laughs.)* Dad — shit man —

(Mother enters through coachway carrying shopping bags, stops.)

FATHER: *(Clears throat.)* Oughta get more exercise, huh? Soccer — or somethin' — *(Takes deep breaths.)*

(Kid notices Mother, steps to her, looks at her, becomes ill, sits down in front of garage, stares at her, pause.)

MOTHER: What's up?

(Pause.)

FATHER: Nothin' dammit — nothin' — your kid's here — can't you see?

(Mother looks at Kid, says nothing.)

FATHER: Go on in — straighten up for chrissake — I can't even give him nothin' to eat — where the fuck you been — when he's here — an' straighten up, goddammit — take your bed to the kitchen — 'cause he's sleepin' inside — with me — you fuckin' got that? — what're you starin' at? — get goin' — an' put your shit away —

(Mother goes into apartment, pause.)

FATHER: Your mother's here now — came back long time ago — she's here now — she came back — an' now she's here — at least she cooks, huh? — no point kickin' her out now — so what gives? — at least while she's here — she cooks, huh? — What gives? What the fuck gives now? Why don't you say nothin' to her? — She's your mother for chrissake.

(Pause.)

FATHER: Ain't even nothing' — between us — she could come back — what am I supposed to do? — Where's she supposed to go? — she's always gettin' herself thrown out — so where's she supposed to go? — let her cook — I don't care — let her do what she wants — let her get married — if she can find some loser — but she's always comin' back — she can't get it together. *(Laughs.)* Who needs an over-the-hill broad like her? — She's got ideas — but it ain't so simple — so I don't say nothin' — for a man this ain't old — this age — I ain't even forty — whatever I want — I'm in my prime — any broad sixteen to forty-five suits me — but I watch out for myself — I learned my lesson — what I'll take an' what I won't —

(Pause.)

FATHER: What're you sittin' there for? — your mother's cookin' — I'll go on in. *(Brief pause.)* You c'mon in too — probably hungry, huh? — see ya inside. *(Goes into apartment, closes door.)*

(Pause. Kid sits in front of garage door, keeps still.)

Scene 12

(Buddy enters through coachway, stops.)

BUDDY: What's up?

(Pause. Buddy sits next to Kid in front of garage.)

BUDDY: I was sittin' out there — waitin' for somebody to come by — nobody came.

(Pause.)

BUDDY: What's up?
KID: Fuckin' bitch —
BUDDY: What's up?
KID: *(Gets up, seizes cleaver.)* I'll smash in her head — I'll smash it in —

(Buddy keeps still.)

KID: I'll smash in her head! *(Attacks lock on garage door, breaks it off, shouts.)*
BUDDY: We takin' the car?
KID: *(Panting, throws down cleaver.)* Fuckin' bitch —
WOMAN: *(Comes out.)* Jesus! What are you doing?! Why?! *(Runs back inside, leaves door open a crack, latches chain, looks out in terror.)*

(Buddy opens garage door, looks in.)

BUDDY: It's a Polski.
WOMAN: Please — don't!
BUDDY: She's scared to come out — *(Laughs.)*
WOMAN: Don't do it — please — don't!
BUDDY: We takin' it?
KID: Sit the fuck down.
BUDDY: Can't you drive?

188   Chicken Head

KID: No. Sit the fuck down!

(Buddy sits down, pause.)

WOMAN: Please, please — don't —

(Pause.)

BUDDY: The broad's havin' a shitfit — *(Laughs.)*
KID: Shut up.

(Pause. Woman stares terrified.)

Scene 13

(Teacher comes out with Chick and Missy.)

TEACHER: So then till next week.
CHICK: Yes, sir. *(Takes out money.)*
WOMAN: Sir!
TEACHER: *(Looks at her.)* Yes?
WOMAN: Nothing — only — excuse me for bothering you — during your lesson —
TEACHER: No problem — no problem — *(Pause.)* I'd just like to add that this prayer, this brilliant, deeply human prayer is a prayer of desperation. It is perhaps the greatest Hungarian poem, not only of this century, but in general, because, as I've pointed out, like the greatest writers of the age, Dostoevsky and Nietzsche for example, the poet here grapples with experience that remains, as they say, relevant to this day, insofar as the world is in exactly the same predicament, the entire world, if you please. But that's not the main reason. Rather it is because this brilliant, desperate, deeply felt, profoundly human prayer, this self-torturing outcry, is the ultimate expression of the spirit that believes in spite of itself. And, I dare say, that in this, the poem surpasses even the greatest of them. Because in this poem it is not repentance that drives the poet to the Lord, nor even belief in the Lord's existence. This is not a weak man seeking solace here, but a mature, serious man, one who is weighing the consequences of renouncing this nevermore-to-be-resurrected God, if you please.

(Meanwhile Chick and Buddy are exchanging glances.)

TEACHER: And by coming to terms with his weakness, to which he owns up, he is no longer weak, as is clearly demonstrated when he writes:

> "Give we up ourselves in faith to him
> Who despite all is the best Phantom,
> Since naught remains to believe in,
> Believe we the is-or-isn't Lord."

Note, if you will, that till now he's been referring to him as God, and now all of a sudden he calls him Phantom, with a capital letter naturally. A Phantom can just as well be a sinister spirit. So what the poet is saying here is that whether or not there is a God, whether he is good or bad, in any case he must exist, even if, indeed especially if, "naught remains to believe in." This is an incomparably deep thought emanating from solemn, desperate man. The poet is saying here that no matter what that certain spiritual entity may be, that spiritual aspect hovering above man, be it even ruinous, be it hostile toward man, it is still better that it exist, than not exist. And this is what we find in the last stanza, in the most beautiful four lines of Hungarian poetry, which I ask you to memorize:

> "Despite all he is the best Phantom.
> And since it's dreadful, it cannot be
> That Life belong to no one,
> Or that Life belong to man."

(Missy slips money into Chick's hand.)

TEACHER: Note, if you will, that good or bad, Phantom is designated "the best Phantom" here. In other words it matters not what his nature is, so long as he exists. And the explanation is that it is horrifying and impossible first of all that life be nobody's — note, if you will, the paradox wherein the adjective that is independent of the poet, "dreadful," commingles with the outcry that arises from the depths of the poet's desperation, "it cannot be." And only then comes the truly profound, truly great thought, which life has since confirmed, the most terrible prophecy ever uttered by a poet, the weightiest Cassandrian augury, which has come to pass:

> "And since it's dreadful, it cannot be
> That Life belong to no one,
> Or that Life belong to man."

Because man is unworthy of life, because when man gains mastery over life, he wreaks havoc upon it.

(Brief pause.)

TEACHER: So please memorize not only the last stanza, but the last two. *(Brief pause.)* And when you realize these things for yourselves, then these eight lines will come to mind, even if you don't fully appreciate them now.
MISSY: But we do appreciate them, sir.
TEACHER: And if they come to mind, then no matter how strange it may seem, you will be comforted. You'll be comforted because you'll feel that you too are part of something grand, something horrifying in which souls as magnificent as Endre Ady have already suffered. And then you will become aware of the beauteous, great community to which humanity belongs — those who are capable only of wreaking havoc upon Life — but if you sense this, then that Spirit, that Phantom, about which Endre Ady talks, will make his presence felt in you — the Lord will make his presence felt in you.

(Teacher wipes tears from eyes, pause. The girls stand still. Pause.)

TEACHER: *(Clears throat.)* So please memorize the last eight lines — I have to go now.
CHICK: Thank you, sir. *(Hands him money.)*
TEACHER: Yes — *(Takes it.)* Thank you. So then, till next week.

(Teacher quickly goes into apartment, leaves door open. Chick and Missy titter.)

CHICK: Ssh!
MISSY: Ssh!

(Teacher comes out carrying shopping bag.)

TEACHER: I forgot to do my shopping — when I came home after school, I didn't have my bag with me — I've got to hurry — good-bye. *(To Woman.)* Good-bye.
CHICK, MISSY: Good-bye, sir!

(Teacher hurries out coachway.)

BUDDY: Get a fuckin' loada that —
MISSY: Okay, c'mon.
CHICK: What's the rush?
MISSY: C'mon, will you?!
CHICK: What a cute guy.
MISSY: C'mon.
BUDDY: Get a fuckin' loada that —
KID: Leave me alone.
BUDDY: They're starin' at us. Huh? They're starin' at us.
MISSY: *(To Woman.)* Hello.

WOMAN: *(Quietly.)* Hi. Hello.
MISSY: Okay, c'mon.

(Buddy stands up, goes a little closer to girls.)

CHICK: Cute guy — the one who's sitting. Huh?

(Buddy stops.)

CHICK: Looks like he can't stand up.

(Buddy bursts out laughing.)

MISSY: Don't — what for? —
CHICK: He's sitting there like a bump on a log.
MISSY: *(Laughs, then stops.)* Not with them.

(Chick and Missy start toward coachway, Woman keeps still, watches.)

CHICK: *(Looks back.)* He can't budge.
BUDDY: *(To Kid.)* What the fuck you waitin' for?
KID: Filthy sluts.
CHICK: *(Angrily.)* C'mon.

(Chick and Missy exit through coachway.)

BUDDY: Now what the fuck was that for — huh? — couldn't you tell they was cock-happy — couldn't you fuckin' tell?!
KID: Will you shut your motherfuckin' face!

(Woman listens in terror.)

BUDDY: *(Goes back to Kid, sits down.)* What gives now — huh?

(Pause.)

BUDDY: Good lookin' chicks — why the hell —

(Pause.)

BUDDY: What gives — your old man split or what?

(Pause.)

BUDDY: 'Cause you ain't got no fuckin' key — I told you to get one — I got one —

(Pause.)

BUDDY: Dig this — she's starin' — the broad — she's starin —
KID: Shut your face, you stupid asshole jerk —

(Pause.)

KID: She took my old man's money — ten thousand forints — the rotten old bitch —
BUDDY: What?
KID: Rotten old bitch — everything's her fault —
BUDDY: What? — that old bitch — the one with the cat? —
KID: *(To Woman.)* What're you starin' at?! What the hell you starin' at?! What?!
WOMAN: Don't — please —
KID: You took away the shed — it was mine — why'd you take it away?! *(Weeps, pause.)*
BUDDY: Don't — hey —
WOMAN: I didn't know — I'm sorry — I didn't know —
BUDDY: What gives now? —
WOMAN: What can I give you? — if you want something — I'll gladly —
KID: Go to hell! — stop starin'! — I'll smash your car to smithereens if you keep starin'!
WOMAN: Don't — not that — I won't stare — but not that —
KID: Go to hell!

(Woman withdraws, but leaves door ajar.)

BUDDY: We trashin' it — her car — huh?
KID: Stupid asshole jerk —
BUDDY: Now what —

(Pause. Teacher returns carrying bag containing bread, milk, wine, cold cuts. Woman, hearing footsteps, appears in doorway.)

WOMAN: Good day, sir.
TEACHER: I didn't take my bag this morning — forgot — so I had to go shopping now — I had five lessons, I forgot. So I had to go after teaching — right away in the afternoon — otherwise one can't get East German earplugs — and those are the best — they're in short supply. They're the best. *(Toward the boys.)* Hello fellows. *(To Woman.)* The constant sound of TV, you know — I even have to use sleeping pills —

WOMAN: Yes, you've mentioned it before.
TEACHER: But I try to limit my use of sleeping pills — Géza Csáth smoked opium — have you read him? I'll tell you about him sometime — he wrote beautiful stories — well, good-bye.
WOMAN: Good-bye, sir.

(Teacher goes into apartment, sound of lock. Pause.)

BUDDY: Dig — she's starin'.

(Kid takes cleaver, studies it. Woman closes door, sounds of chain and locks. Pause.)

KID: She ripped off my old man — took his money —
BUDDY: The old bitch? — At least we wasted her cat — huh?

(Kid puts down cleaver, pause.)

BUDDY: No point shittin' bricks — no big deal — we go in an' she fuckin' gives it back —

(Pause.)

BUDDY: Damn straight she'll fuckin' give it back — she won't dare squawk — we go in an' she gives it back —

(Pause.)

BUDDY: *(Picks up cleaver.)* She'll see this — shit in her fuckin' pants — then she'll fork over the money, man.

(Pause.)

KID: Four hundred's mine.
BUDDY: What?
KID: 'Cause she stole nine thousand six hundred — an' she's got ten thousand. So four hundred's mine.
BUDDY: Why — I'm goin' too — ain't I?
KID: I didn't ask you to.
BUDDY: Like she'll give it to you alone — jerk.

(Pause.)

KID: Then two hundred's yours.

BUDDY: Why two hundred? Five thousand.
KID: In a pig's cunt. Nine thousand six hundred's Dad's.

(Pause.)

BUDDY: Aw c'mon — your fuckin' old man —
KID: Watch your face — I'll fuckin' let you have it again —

(Pause.)

BUDDY: I don't know — we oughta have y'know — stockings — over our heads —
KID: What the hell for? Shit.
BUDDY: Well that's how they do it — ain't it?
KID: Shit.

(Pause.)

Scene 14

(Cop and Sarge enter through coachway. Kid and Buddy stand up, Buddy holding cleaver.)

BUDDY: Hello.
SARGE: Hi. — Who's this?
BUDDY: It's what-d'ya-call-him — y'know, it's him.
SARGE: Personal I.D.

(Kid takes out booklet, hands it over, Sarge looks at it.)

SARGE: Oh, is it you? I didn't recognize you. *(To Cop.)* His son.
COP: Yeah!
SARGE: But you're in an institution — right?
KID: Yes.
BUDDY: He ran away! He told me! He ran away!

(Pause, Kid looks at Buddy, takes out a document, hands it over, Sarge looks at it, hands it to Cop.)

SARGE: Is it a regulation leave permit?

(Cop studies document.)

KID: It's regulation.

SARGE: I didn't ask you.

(Brief pause.)

COP: Well — it's a permit.
SARGE: Is it stamped and dated?
COP: Stamped. Dated.
SARGE: Letterhead?

(Cop nods.)

SARGE: *(Takes it back.)* This is a regulation leave permit. For how many days?
KID: Three.
SARGE: I didn't ask you.

(Cop looks at document.)

COP: Three.
SARGE: This is a regulation leave permit for three days. *(Hands document back to Kid.)* Nothing's allowed to be kept in the Personal I.D. book.
KID: There ain't nothin' in it.
SARGE: I didn't say there was something in it, I said nothing's allowed to be kept in it. Isn't that what I said?

(Pause.)

SARGE: Isn't that what I said?
KID: It is.
SARGE: The Personal I.D. always has to be kept on one's person.
KID: I had it on my person — didn't I have it on my person?
SARGE: I didn't say you didn't have it on your person. Did I say you didn't have it on your person? *(To Cop.)* Is that what I said?
COP: No.
SARGE: *(To Kid.)* Is that what I said?
KID: No.
SARGE: The Personal I.D. must not be mutilated.

(Pause.)

SARGE: This one is not mutilated. Its loss must immediately be reported to the appropriate police authorities.

(Pause.)

SARGE: There. Here ya go.

(Kid takes booklet, puts it away.)

SARGE: Have you seen your father yet?
KID: Yes.

(Woman opens door a crack, listens.)

SARGE: Well, okay then. Carry on.

(Pause.)

SARGE: What's up? What've you guys been up to so far?
BUDDY: Just shootin' the breeze.
SARGE: Okay. Carry on.
WOMAN: Good day.
SARGE: Good day.

(Pause. Woman withdraws, sounds of chain, locks. Kid starts toward Old Lady's door, Buddy follows after brief hesitation. Kid opens door, both go in. Pause.)

COP: That was a woman —
SARGE: Yeah.
COP: A whore, huh? — probably a whore — oughta be kicked in the cunt — how come she fucks all the time? — *(Laughs.)*
SARGE: Was that supposed to be a fuckin' joke? That's just stupid!

(Brief pause.)

COP: Not me — I don't — really — I sleep in uniform — I mean — only at daytime — when they stare —

(Pause.)

SARGE: Okay. — Young guys like that, sometimes they forge another date on — they scratch out the old one — or they use ink remover — you gotta watch for that — an' they tell you they had it but lost it — on the train —
COP: Yeah.
SARGE: But this one's a decent kid — when his father was laid up — he took care of him — even though his father was laid up — this was when his wife left him second time around — she was still a good looker then — an' his sister was a tramp — she went hookin' — so this kid's a decent kid.

(Pause, Cop leans against wall.)

SARGE: Beat, huh?
COP: Nah, just y'know —
SARGE: I never said this was easy — walkin' around all day — all over — fuckin' pain in the ass — huh?
COP: No — just in my back —
SARGE: Well that's how it goes — in the cold — the heat — you're breathin' dust — smoke — to keep the peace — that's how it goes.

(Pause.)

SARGE: You'll get used to it — an' havin' to watch out for yourself — keep your eyes open — you'll get used to it.

(Pause. Suddenly screaming, collapsing are heard, then silence. Cop jumps away from wall, looks around startled.)

SARGE: *(Impatiently.)* Whatsa matter — you shit in your pants?
COP: What was that?!

(Pause.)

SARGE: Nothin', dammit — probably the TV — some crime show —

(Pause, they listen.)

SARGE: So okay — we been here too — so now let's go —

(Kid and Buddy emerge from Old Lady's apartment, pale, their hands and shirts bloody, they stop.)

BUDDY: Why'd you have to — why? —
KID: Her brains — her brains —

(Both are nauseated. Sarge and Cop stare, then leap at once, throwing themselves on Kid and Buddy, prostrate them. Kid and Buddy do not resist. The boys are handcuffed together.)

SARGE: *(To Cop, kneeling on Kid and Buddy.)* Take a look —

(Cop hesitantly goes in. Pause. Cop comes out, ill, then slowly, breathing deeply, recovers.)

COP: Caught in the act! Caught in the act!

(Sarge and Cop pull Kid and Buddy to their feet, take them at a running pace out through coachway, disappear.)

Scene 15

(Woman opens door, removes chain, comes out, sniffles, goes to garage door carrying new lock, puts it on, picks up old lock, starts back, stops, goes to Teacher's door, knocks, waits, then goes in own door, locks it.)

Scene 16

(Pause. Father and Mother come out.)

FATHER: Where's that kid? —
MOTHER: What's-his-ass came in today — the jerks — an' all day — 'xcept me — all day they was runnin' around — an' me — no time to take a leak even — an' that y'know — died, huh? — sounds fishy to me — I heard it on the radio — real fishy — at ten — but I couldn't go out — the rest of 'em — for me they couldn't give a shit — Liz especially — I got a headache — but they're all gonna croak too — an' then I'm comin' home — by the church — in his heart, huh? — for real? — with that thing — that what-d'ya-call-it thing — it's wood — y'know — it's got a hook-like — at the end — metal — huh? — I don't get it — it's y'know — terrible — an' them hangin' out there — all the time — I ain't even got the time to take a leak — an' them with their big mouths —
FATHER: Okay — not now —
MOTHER: 'Cause — I've had it — they're comin' — Liz too — the dumb bitch — she comes over to me — shootin' her mouth off — an' there I am — but I told her — why not? — if the big shots can — huh? — you'll see —
FATHER: Shut the fuck up!

(Pause. Sound of Leonard Cohen song, "Who by Fire," can be heard coming from Woman's apartment. Father pricks up ears.)

FATHER: She's got company already — hear that? — company already!

(Pause, song is heard.)

FATHER: Okay. The kid's here — straighten up the fuckin' place — 'cause it's bad for him — if he sees we messed with the room — you'll go out to the kitchen — while he's here —

MOTHER: Why should I — where? — an' the radio said — that the — the — y'know —
FATHER: 'Cause you're goin' the fuck out — that's why — an' then he fuckin' comes home an' that's how it's gonna be then too —
MOTHER: What d'ya mean he comes home?
FATHER: He's comin' home — an' then I'll get appointed — he'll be my what-d'ya-call-it — my — he'll be my — he'll be my ward — that's the word — an' that's at least four hundred a month — dig — 'cause I'm gonna get appointed — 'cause now it's can-do — he's a strong kid — good an' strong — he'll go to work — the hell with that learnin'-a-trade bullshit — right away he'll be earnin' four big ones — five — fuckin' strong kid — dig — how much does it cost to feed a kid like that? — let's say he eats a thousand-worth — he gets let's say one for himself — that leaves two — maybe three — dig — so get the fuckin' lead out — straighten the place up —
MOTHER: I'll straighten it up — I'll throw out the stupid books —
FATHER: Just you try, bitch — just you try —
MOTHER: I'll throw 'em all out — tales — seventy-seven Hungarian folk tales — an old bastard like this — readin' tales —
FATHER: 'Cause they're fuckin' nice — an' none of your business — what I do — you be glad you ain't out on your ass — so now get the hell inside — an' it's gonna be like I say around here!

(Mother goes in. Pause.)

FATHER: Okay — 'cause it's gonna be like I want.

(Starts into apartment.)

FATHER: What the hell's on TV?

(Goes in, slams door.)

END

Kozma
a tragedy

Mihály Kornis

translated by Eugene Brogyányi

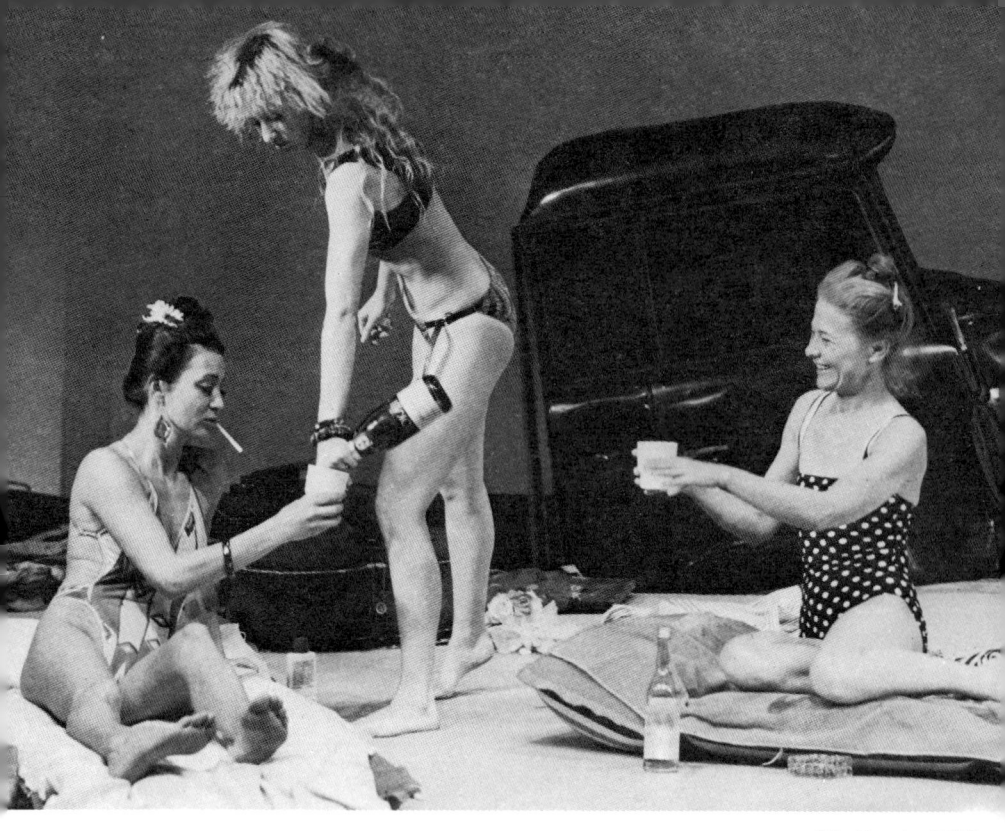

Béla Ilovszky (MTI)

KOZMA
[Pesti Theatre, Budapest, Hungary]
Directed by István Horvai

CHARACTERS:

KOZMA, a 33-year-old man, if true

furthermore

BETTY, 46 years old, widowed Comrade, if true
CRYSTAL, 24 years old, her mother's daughter, if true
HEDI, 32 years old, recent widow, if true

furthermore

The Victims of the Tragedy

(Takes place around 1980 in Hungary.)

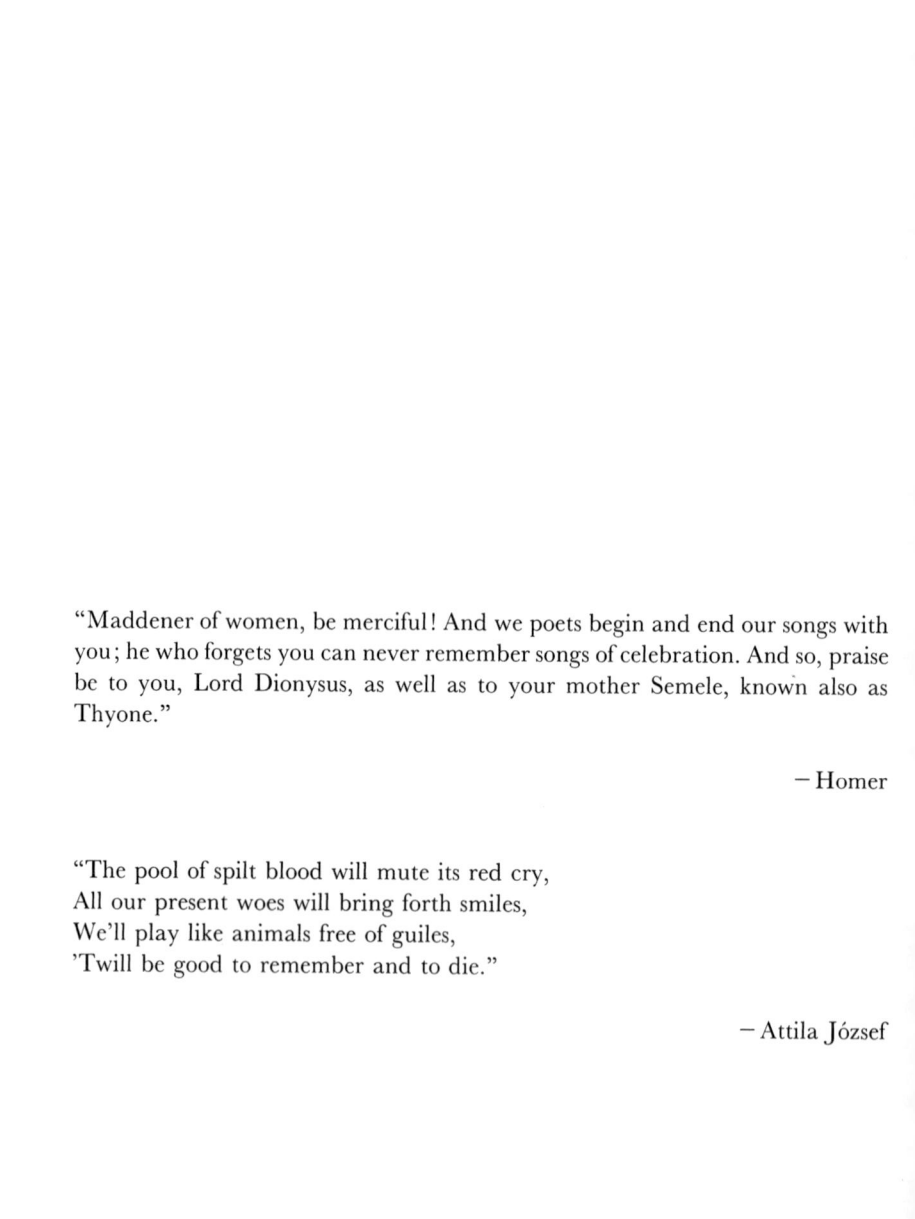

"Maddener of women, be merciful! And we poets begin and end our songs with you; he who forgets you can never remember songs of celebration. And so, praise be to you, Lord Dionysus, as well as to your mother Semele, known also as Thyone."

— Homer

"The pool of spilt blood will mute its red cry,
All our present woes will bring forth smiles,
We'll play like animals free of guiles,
'Twill be good to remember and to die."

— Attila József

Setting: The enclosed beach area of a resort on Lake Balaton. The sun-drenched shore of gray sand rises toward a brick wall, two or three meters in height, that covers the horizon. Fleecy clouds adorn the blue sky. The wall is surmounted by a barbed-wire fence. In the center, toward the back, a rickety, open-bed military truck, suitable for personnel transport, is stuck in the dirt. The vehicle's rapidly rotating wheels are not advancing it so much as a centimeter. Fifteen to twenty people are seated on metal benches in the truck bed. Their winter, summer, even nighttime dress, representing a selection from the last forty years of Hungarian fashion, consists of such varied attire as work-clothes, pajamas, negligees, and overcoats. Apparently these people were placed here as they happened to be found, without having had time enough to change their clothes. The helplessly struggling truck is making a dreadful racket.

In the foreground, three women are sunbathing, naked, on rubber mattresses fashioned into chaises longues. Their eyes are closed, one of them is wearing a small leaf on her nose. Each woman is a pearl of her age-group, though the youngest wears thick eyeglasses. Beside them, under an umbrella stuck in the sand, are ice-buckets and insulated carrying cases full of savory drinks, from the cheap to the very expensive; cut-glass crystalware and bathroom tumblers; tubes, creams, and all sorts of women's toiletries testifying to garish taste ... To the women, the hellish vehicular noise seems to be the natural background of their relaxation; it is as though they were hearing the sound of the wind. Not at all perturbed, they are lounging with their limbs scattered casually about.

The image is exceedingly unlikely. The space is completely enclosed; a truck could not have gotten into it. Only a narrow gravel path leads offstage, up left. The heat is oppressive.

Kozma, the driver, turns off the motor. Silence. He swings open the door of the driver's compartment, jumps down, looks around, spits out his butt and slams his newspaper-wrapped victuals on the hood, which is in the shade. He casually saunters to the back and unhooks the three sides of the truck bed. They bang resoundingly against the chassis. He then perches on the hood, spits a thin stream and, before dispassionately unwrapping his breakfast, pulls a newspaper out of his jacket. He reads without apparent interest, eats, and seems bored with the whole affair from the start.

INTERMEDIARY: *(Fishes an official document out of his pocket.)* My name is Madarász. I am the intermediary between the social committee, which has been delegated to examine the tragedy, and the Organ. Attention please!
DIE CASTER: And the what?
MRS. DIE CASTER: Them!
DIE CASTER: Oh! *(Still no comprehension.)* Uh-huh, uh-huh. Of course, I might have known ...
INTERMEDIARY: *(Calling them to order.)* Excuse me?!
MRS. DIE CASTER: It's nothing, just my husband. But everything's okay now. We're paying attention!
BUTCHER: What kind of tragedy?
INTERMEDIARY: Fall in!
HEAD BOOKKEEPER: *(In a nightshirt, half-asleep, barefoot.)* This won't do at all. I'm dragged out of bed, shaken up out of the sweetest of dreams, only to find myself without slippers; I couldn't even put in my dentures; I left the bedside lamp on; and then ... *(Yawning, sways from side to side on his heels.)* What's going on here?!
NON-SOLOIST: *(In an overcoat, with stuffed shopping bags.)* I'm late. *(Dazed, speaking to himself.)* I'll never make it to the day-care center on time. The nurserymaid will have my head. We'll miss our bus, even the express! And the child will be hungry. He'll be wailing the whole way home, driving me crazy. Then at home they'll all jump down my throat: "Where've you been?", "What've you been up to?" I'll be in trouble all week. My mother-in-law will finally have a perfect excuse to ... *(Looks down.)* The milk leaked all over everything.
ANNIE MENOPAUSE: *(In heavy makeup and a rabbit-fur coat.)* The last time they rounded up people in the street was toward the end of the war, but not women even then. In my opinion this is simply ...
INTERMEDIARY: You are the social committee! You have been delegated! *(Corrects himself.)* WE have!
(Silence.)
If you'll allow me, I'll quickly identify everyone by name, occupation, et cetera.
BEGGAR: Identify away, sonny, identify! That's the ticket!
INTERMEDIARY: *(Reads.)* One minor, occupationless, male child: Joey Kovács!
LITTLE BOY: Present.

INTERMEDIARY: No presents!... "I'm here" is good enough.
SUPERNUMERARY: *(Right next to him.)* I'm here, I'm here! Zippo! *(Slinks away upon a look from Madarász.)*
INTERMEDIARY: One private-sector married couple, middle-aged: Árpád Lukasics, Mrs. Árpád Lukasics — partners in tax fraud.
DIE CASTER: What fraud? The only fraud here is what you're up to! And anyway, I'm a die caster...
MRS. DIE CASTER: We're here, all of a piece. Please go on! *(Hisses.)* Shut your trap.
INTERMEDIARY: One old lady, drunkard, nightclub washroom attendant: Mrs. Kálmán Fáth, widow!
GRANNIE WASHOUT: *(Smoking.)* Old in a pig's eye! *(To the crowd.)* I'm not even ready to retire. Still working at it...
INTERMEDIARY: *(Undaunted.)* One middle-aged, untrained gym teacher, unreliable, neurotic: Steven Palotás!
GYM TEACHER: I am, I am, I am.
INTERMEDIARY: One unmarried nurse, urological clinic, excellent qualifications: Martha Páncél!
NURSE: *(A somber slob of a woman, steps forth.)* And my husband! *(Drags him behind her.)*
CRIMINAL: *(A short man.)* Common law, common law!
INTERMEDIARY: Not indicated. Onward! One thief, repeated convictions, assault on officers of the law, disorderly conduct, rape, and what's this? I can't make it out. Doesn't matter. John Kis.
CRIMINAL: That's it, that's it!
GITTA GAMBS: *(A wispy administrator.)* May we sit?
INTERMEDIARY: Let's not. And don't touch anything!
BUTCHER: *(In an apron, seated with legs crossed.)* We already sat down. We're already seated. To hell with standing!
INTERMEDIARY: *(In one breath.)* You people have no idea of the danger. But never mind. To sum up: We have here butcher, teacher, physician, waiter, administrator, young girl, divorced lady, housewife, unwed mother, insurance adjuster. *(Bows.)* Two actors. *(Squints at document.)* Excuse me. Three. Why do we need three? Why do we need actors?... In a word up to fifteen or sixteen people. But I emphasize: IT CAN HAPPEN AT ANY MOMENT!

(Silence.)

NON-SOLOIST: *(Bursts out.)* What? What can happen?
BEGGAR: *(Elbows his way to the front.)* And a beggar. Excuse me. With a permit. A regulation permit. *(Shows it.)* I've had it for twenty years! A rare thing, this. They don't issue them very readily. But I have one! *(To Intermediary.)* Of course old man Deutsch is always overlooked, as if he didn't exist. Well, he does.

NON-SOLOIST: *(Shoves him away.)* Go away, be so good as to go home! Again I ask you please to tell us what it is that can happen!

(Silence.)

INTERMEDIARY: The trouble, that's what! And that would be a catastrophe. Don't you get it? *(Bluffing.)* Just look around you! *(The astonished crowd sees nothing.)*
BEGGAR: I can't get home from here. Where should I go?
INTERMEDIARY: We are at the scene of the tragedy! Look around!

(No one sees a thing.
Kozma ceremoniously turns a page of his newspaper.
The three graces stir.)

BETTY: Where's the cocoa butter? I'm listening, Hedi, go on!
HEDI: *(Sits up.)* There isn't any here. Maybe your daughter has some.
BETTY: Crystal, precious, rub some on me.
CRYSTAL: *(Stands up.)* You're always ordering me around. *(Crystal rubs lotion on her mother.)*
BETTY: Oh, but your fingers feel so good. The sun's heavenly! What luck, we could've had two weeks of rain. And this blessed quiet! I'll have a good rest. "Water nymph whose brown skin glows, in Budapest her radiance grows …" *(Squirms while humming.)*
HEDI: Only the wind! Before too. That whirring …
BETTY: The wind's the whole point! That's why I didn't bring the radio. We need a natural background. This is how I felt in Can. I'm telling you, that Can!
CRYSTAL: *(Somberly corrects her pronunciation.)* That's Cannes.
BETTY: What are you correcting me for? What does it matter?
CRYSTAL: It matters.
BETTY: More!
CRYSTAL: You're dripping already. Turn over on your stomach!
BETTY: Betty baby on her tummy. Whoop! … Rub it in. … Hedi, where were you? You started something. This sun's making me dimwitted, but it's so yummy. So go on.
HEDI: *(Is dizzy.)* I've completely dried out. I don't even know … *(Preoccupied, exercising her neck.)* Whatchamacallit.
BETTY: Crystal sweetie, give her some champagne! You have some too. Girls, aren't we going to get a bit tipsy? "Water nymph whose brown skin glows, in Budapest her radiance grows …" *(Yawns.)* Jesus, Mary, and Joseph! *(Drops back into a sunbathing position.)*

(Under the umbrella, Crystal pours drinks, totters back holding the tray, the ground is burning her soles, silence.)

CRYSTAL: How long should I hold it?
BETTY: *(Snaps out of her reverie.)* Let's drink! Afterwards Hedi can continue. I love Hedi's stories... *(Stops short.)* ... excuse me, no offense, but ... Bottoms up! *(Toasts.)*
HEDI: *(Embarrassed.)* Bottoms up.
CRYSTAL: Bottoms up.

(They drink and lie back.)

GYM TEACHER: *(Throws his hat on the ground and shouts.)* Let me go, I don't see a thing, but even if I did, let me go! I have to go: faculty meeting, quarterly. The Zsuzsanna Lorántffy School can't close down just on my account — all sixteen classes! What do you think? Not on my account. Besides, I have psoriasis and the dog hasn't been fed and the utilities company is after me. What should I pay them with? Well, today's payday. Today's payday. That miserable three thousand sixty-four forints... *(Covers his eyes, despair distorts his face; heaves a loud sigh.)*
INTERMEDIARY: *(Wipes his brow with a handkerchief.)* Silence! First the facts...
ANNIE MENOPAUSE: Today's not payday! Tomorrow is.
HEAD BOOKKEEPER: *(Yawns.)* Different strokes for different folks.
GITTA GAMBS: Ours was yesterday. Or was it the day before? *(Bewildered.)* I don't even remember... I don't remember anything!...
INTERMEDIARY: Please!
DIE CASTER: *(Fans himself.)* Salary is the way to go! No rat race, no tax auditors...
GRANNIE WASHOUT: The nouveaux riches ought to keep their mouths shut! Let him try living off *my* means. Let him scrub the toilet every day...
BEGGAR: Leben und leben lassen!
GRANNIE WASHOUT: Why, how did *I* get to the toilet from an aristocratic family?! I, who spent my girlhood in Baden-Baden...
INTERMEDIARY: *(Shouts.)* Please!

(Steven Palotás drops to the ground, groans in pain, clings with both hands to Martha Páncél's skirt.)

NURSE: What are you grabbing me for? Go grab your mother! What's his problem?... This one here's not well!
INTERMEDIARY: No panicking! I've told you, take care!
NURSE: *(Frees herself.)* Of what?
NON-SOLOIST: "To take care." Oh, come now! *(Feverishly.)* Who's taking care of you? Who took care of me? Who's taking care of the child now? The state, thank you! When did I last take a trip? Why did I marry my wife? I didn't even marry her — she married me! Queen of the Ball at Füred. A pig in the poke. I pulled her out! And why did my father lie about my having perfect

pitch, when I don't have perfect pitch, especially among postmen? *You* try making music with postmen, three hours at a stretch, with feeling. What was I trying to say?! *(Grabs his head.)*

CRIMINAL: *(Blurts out.)* Don't kill, don't steal, don't lie! *(To the crowd.)* I, if you please, served fifteen years in seven cells with characters like this! Can you imagine? *(Jumps into the arms of the nurse like a little monkey.)* Excuse me, sir ... don't beat me! You're the biggest frog in the pond!
SUPERNUMERARY: Zippo!

(Brief pause.)

ANNIE MENOPAUSE: Then, as a matter of fact, what are we doing here? Please tell me. I was really intending to go to the market today ...
BEGGAR: I put my hat here, voilà! I can't put it on any more. Let whoever sees it see it. *(Stands behind his hat, playing the harmonica.)*
INTERMEDIARY: I'd like to lay out the facts of the case and then ...
HEAD BOOKKEEPER: I can't lift my feet. No. No! People, it's as if I'd taken root ... What's going on?
VOICES FROM THE CROWD: Me too! Me too! What's happening?
BUTCHER: Ring around the rosey, pocketful of posies. Damn you all!
INTERMEDIARY: Don't touch anything — I told you! Doesn't matter. We have the appropriate means for assessing. That's why we came!
GRANNIE WASHOUT: *(Raging.)* What means?!
NON-SOLOIST: *(Raging.)* Assess what?!
HEAD BOOKKEEPER: *(Raging.)* Where are they?

(The crowd revolts, but cannot move.)

INTERMEDIARY: *(Weeps.)* This shouldn't have been entrusted to me, not this! Now they went and did it!
GITTA GAMBS: *(To herself.)* I don't remember! Not a thing ... My place of employment ... I don't even know that! I have an itty-bitty son ... no I don't. An apartment.
A husband.
Personal identification.
A girlfriend! ... but I have no girlfriends! *(Shouts to high heaven.)* Nothing! There isn't a thing! Not a thing! Nothing! *(Grows uncertain.)* Or is there?
MRS. DIE CASTER: My husband's like a rock. Look at him! He doesn't budge. Die-cast! *(Nudges her husband, who stands frozen.)* This one's done! Who did this? *(Swings her pocketbook above her head.)* WHAT HAPPENED HERE?

INTERMEDIARY: *(Agonizes.)* What happened was ... The reason for this ... I'll tell you ... The reason is that ... I'LL TELL YOU! *(Dies.)*

(Brief pause.)

NON-SOLOIST: Well, he's in no shape to tell us any more. He kicked the bucket! Ha ha ha. Ha ha ha ha haaa! *(His head twitches.)*
ANNIE MENOPAUSE: *(Screaming.)* Let's flee!
GRANNIE WASHOUT: *(Screaming.)* Let's run!
VOICES IN THE CROWD: Let's run! Let's run! Help!

(The stunned crowd struggles and writhes, then gradually stops, falls into a stupor. Silence. Kozma turns a page.)

BETTY: *(Sits up.)* Your turn, Hedi!
CRYSTAL: Don't pester her.
HEDI: She's not pestering me. You two were asking me how my husband died, that's all. But really, it's so ridiculous ... *(Props herself up on her elbows.)*
BETTY: Oh of course: Béla! Poor thing, poor thing ...
CRYSTAL: Don't listen to Mom ... she's drunk!
BETTY: Who's drunk?
CRYSTAL: So you left off with the air show on April fourth when all the smoke cleared.
BETTY: *(Gesticulating.)* No, no! She left off with when she was a cadre fresh from the village. They met at a Party crash course, he couldn't screw, no foreplay, and you were still an inexperienced little chickadee ...
CRYSTAL: MOM! *(Brief pause.)* She'll tell it.
BETTY: Well okay then! *(Opens a nail polish.)*
HEDI: But all that's true! The Goldberger Textile Factory sent me for further instruction as fledgling cultural secretary; at the social evening he asked me to dance. Two weeks later he gave me a ring; took me to his mother's; they slaughtered a pig. That's where the wedding was held too. And right away he got an apartment from our Party. In Pest! Middle of Gorky Lane! *(Muses.)* I was able to move there straight from the workers' hostel. The kitchen alone was as big as a ballroom. Still is. I have it. It's mine! *(Brief pause.)* Only somehow the thing didn't gel. There were problems on the emotional level. He'd come home evenings, he'd wear suits exclusively, "hi, pumpkin!" and a pat on the tush, that was his thing. *(Sighs.)* He kept me at home, I had to cook, I didn't have to work, he wanted a child at all costs. But he just couldn't produce one ... no matter how much he wanted to ... He couldn't! At the end we were reading books. He brought them from Yugoslavia. Illustrated how-to picture books! Then he died. *(Reflects.)* Could be it was all my fault. Evenings I'd be picking the dandruff off his lapels, every blessed evening. At night he

wanted cocoa in bed, brimming with sugar, he'd be glancing through the schedule in front of the TV till sign-off. In other words... *(Shrugs, looks off in embarrassment.)*
CRYSTAL: Glancing through what?
HEDI: The train schedule distributed by the State Railways, that's what. *(Brief pause.)* That's what. In other words...
BETTY: *(Polishing her nails.)* Happens. And then?
HEDI: *(Alarmed.)* And then this spring, at the holiday festivities, I mean on the anniversary of our liberation, as leader of the police detachment, he had to march out on the Danube embankment to supervise the goings-on. I mean, to supervise the comrades, a bunch of nitwits — needless to say. Béla was always complaining about them. But the big hubbub was over when, at three in the afternoon, on the deserted embankment — why he was still standing there is beyond me — a twenty-ton truck ran up on the sidewalk, even though there was no other traffic around, so the vehicle wasn't even passing anything — so I'm truly in the dark on this — and splat! Splat. In other words... *(Shakes her head in bewilderment.)*

(Silence.)

HEAD BOOKKEEPER: Maybe I'm still asleep! Sometimes my dreams are stupid, that's for sure. Sominex. *(Whimpers.)* Mommy, take me to the zoo! Let's look at the animals. Take me! I want some fun!...
NURSE: *(To the criminal perched on her back.)* Get down.
CRIMINAL: I don't dare.
NURSE: Get down!... Is there a doctor here? They said there was.
DOCTOR: There is. I'm a dentist. A dental surgeon. *(Dies.)*
DIE CASTER: I smell gas. *(Quakes.)* There's gas! I smell gas!
ANNIE MENOPAUSE: I don't even want to go to the market, really. I don't want anything anymore. How long till winter's over? No use my buying a coat... I'm still cold. I hate the streets, the melting snow drips on my head, my shoes slip and slide, people push and shove. I'm afraid to take the elevator alone. It's even worse with someone else. My son doesn't even write. *(Shouts.)* I still won't buy a television! *(Brief pause.)* I don't know which way I ought to be turning the radiator valve. The apartment's dark too. I'm cold! I wish it would warm up. This endless waiting!... *(Dies.)*
BUTCHER: *(Argues with his shadow.)* Why? Because I didn't buy that house in Pestimre? Well, I can't live in Pestimre! The tram lines don't go there, nothing does! It reeks of manure. From pigsties. Sties! I'm not moving to Pestimre, ever, may my mother rest in peace. I'd rather be miserable among you. Upon my life! *(Dies.)*
SUPERNUMERARY: I hate you all. I didn't want to be an actor, never did. Only my mother wanted it. They herd me around like a goose: Come in, go out,

come in again! Where should I go? I've already been there, you turds. How am I supposed to make a living? And then what if I'm already here ... voilà! Zippo! *(Dies.)*
MRS. DIE CASTER: Why did they bring me here? How could they do this? What did I do to deserve it? *(Dispassionately.)* They've already taken a tumor out of my womb. Removed one of my breasts. I wear a padded bra. *(Shows it.)* This is what it looks like. It's from Denmark. An illusion. *(Buttons up her blouse.)* And on top of it all he gets jealous! I'm on my feet sixteen hours at a stretch, I bend over backwards to please the customers, the suppliers, my daughter-in-law — and even so they report me every month! Whoever's fancy it strikes. For kicks! Only my childhood teddy bear understands. In bed at night. Teddy! Teddy! ... Teddy! Teddy! *(Dies.)*
GRANNIE WASHOUT: *(To the criminal.)* You look familiar to me, you hear?
CRIMINAL: Out of the question. Out of the question.
GRANNIE WASHOUT: But I do know you! We spent our forced relocation in the same place, pal. Of course. We were pushing our wheelbarrows side by side. Ever the jolly little baron, you were. I haven't gone completely soft in the head yet, you know. Help me, come here, lift me up!
CRIMINAL: What do you want?! Leave me alone. I wasn't even alive then.
GRANNIE WASHOUT: I'm going to collapse!
NURSE: Catch her!

(John Kis lifts Mrs. Fáth in his arms.)

GRANNIE WASHOUT: I want to depart in the arms of a man, you simpleton! Men have always been crazy about me, I'll have you know.
CRIMINAL: *(Totters.)* Is she heavy! For me this is too ...
GRANNIE WASHOUT: And I was crazy about the boys. I always weighed forty-seven kilos, like now. A small-boned girl. Good for playing around with. Good little chicken bones. And gizzards!
NURSE: Hold her!
GRANNIE WASHOUT: I had a governess, I'll tell the story now, because I had a governess, a French girl! A real French girl! She showed me how to do it with boys ... *(Weakens.)* How to do it nicely, sweetly, with finesse. How to do it when ... How to do it! *(Dies, slides to the ground.)*
NURSE: *(Quakes as if she were being shaken):* Get over here!
CRIMINAL: I'm not going anywhere anymore.
NURSE: Get over here!

(John Kis struggles to his partner, the woman lifts him in her arms, she calms down.)

CRIMINAL: This is like being in some dive.

NURSE: That's where you are.
CRIMINAL: The guy's completely soused. I'm spinning! What were we drinking, sweetie? It sure works!
NURSE: *(Rocks him.)*
"In an hour
Come up to the tower
Where I'll be waiting for you ..."
CRIMINAL: *(Beats about.)* Muzik, muzik! *(Dies.)*

(The beggar plays the harmonica.)

GITTA GAMBS: Maybe there is! Maybe everything's as it should be, only I've been left out of the mix. *(Looks at the sky.)* Here's the sky, here's the sun ... this is me, here's my skirt ... *(Haltingly pats herself.)* ... here's my leg, here's my body ... *(Comes to a realization.)* But it has no meaning. I don't need it. — Or do I?
NURSE: Look at the little rogue! He wanted to take what was his. So what? Unlike the rest of you, he didn't have a thing. Never had! He scrubbed the prison floors for fifteen years. The corridors!
GITTA GAMBS: *(Shouts.)* Or do I?
NURSE: Now who's going to tuck him in? Who's going to tuck him in, in my place?
GITTA GAMBS: *(Shouts loudly.)* Or do I? *(Dies.)*
NURSE: *(To the corpse.)* I'll stay with you, snookums! Lie down. *(Snuggles up to him on the ground.)* My little one, my pet. I'll keep you warm. We'll stay together. My regards to the astronauts! *(Dies.)*
BEGGAR: I know every tune! Try as they may, they can't do away with old man Deutsch. They've sent me to the front, to the concentration camps. I know every tune. *(Laughs, and shakes out the harmonica.)* Takes saliva, nothing else. And two good strong legs that work. And it helps not to show too much interest. The hat's empty now too. *(Picks it up.)* That's all right. Let them be wicked! These cheapskates will be gone anyway. They all go away sooner or later ... Others show up! Only old man Deutsch remains. Leben! *(Dies.)*
HEAD BOOKKEEPER: I want to wake up! I've had enough of this. *(Tries to remove his nightshirt, but gets tangled in it and—flailing with increasing vehemence—becomes a prisoner of the garment.)* I'm going to get up. Leave me in peace. Let me go, let me go! Leave me alone. Mom, Mommy, Daddy, don't help me, I can do it! It only works alone. I'll go away. I have to go away right now, one-two-three, I'm not going to ... *(Brief pause.)* Owah tagoo siam. Owah tagoo siam. Owah-tagoo-siam, owah-tagoo-siam. Oh what a goose I am. Oh what a goose I am ... *(Dies.)*
NON-SOLOIST: *(Dumps the ruined contents of his shopping bags and mutters.)* Everything's all mixed up together. Buggered up! Nothing salvageable ... Not a thing! And life is so expensive. *(Quaking, he rearranges the stuff on the ground.)*

Costs so much ... Money. I have to make this into one pile. Somehow. Everything. All together! *(Makes a mound of mud.)* You need luck to make it nice. *(Stands up.)* That's our job. That's what we're supposed to do. *(The little boy blows on him, he totters.)* Our job is to ... *(The little boy blows on him very hard.)* ... to ... *(The little boy blows on him very, very hard, he totters, then falls like a timber on top of the child, burying him.)*

(Silence.
Kozma turns a page of his newspaper.)

BETTY: *(Props herself up on her elbows.)* There was a big state funeral, wasn't there?
HEDI: There was. *(Sits up.)* The workers' militiamen sang rounds, fired off a salute, even the TV-news reporters came out to cover it for the third report, along with military honors ... Terrible! *(Bursts into tears.)*
CRYSTAL: *(Stands up.)* That's enough now. I'm bored.

(Searches under the beach umbrella.)

BETTY: She's always bored! My dear girl, get the hell away from here. Don't be making those faces. Go to the lounge. Every seat in there is already oily from your ass. I wonder how long before the custodian says something.
CRYSTAL: Give it to me.
BETTY: I won't.
CRYSTAL: You promised.
BETTY: I didn't promise anything.
CRYSTAL: You promised you'd let me have it in the afternoon.
BETTY: It's not afternoon yet. Go in the water.
CRYSTAL: Give it to me or I'll kill you! *(Pants.)* I'll slash open your ... I'll knock you down ... I'll strangle you! ... With a knitting needle I'll ... *(Shakes.)* Head first ... and I'll take a brick and I'll ... in your face, and ... your nails, and ... you alive ... and your entrails ... and ... I'll boil you in ... and kick you, and ... *(Chokes up.)*
BETTY: *(Calmly.)* And? Well? What else can you say to dear old Mommy?
CRYSTAL: Give it here, or I'm leaving for home right away!
BETTY: For where? *(Laughs, stops.)* What should I give you?
CRYSTAL: You know as well as I do.
BETTY: The hell I do, I haven't the foggiest idea.
CRYSTAL: *(Laments.)* I'll die!
BETTY: Die if you want to.
CRYSTAL: And you along with me!
BETTY: When Hell freezes over. The snow's on the clover ...
CRYSTAL: *(Interrupts.)* And the little elephant chirps beneath the eaves.
BETTY: *(Laughs.)* So, you remember it! *(Stretches out her arms.)* Come here, you

little globetrotter. There's no place like your mother. Let's kiss and make up. Come to Mama!
CRYSTAL: *(Bursts into a big laugh and kisses her mother.)* Give it to me, will you?
BETTY: Wait till nighttime! You gave it to me. We agreed, didn't we?
CRYSTAL: *(Shouts.)* I'm an adult. What are you ordering me around for? Don't forget, I'm not even Hungarian any more!
BETTY: *(Laughs tipsily.)* Well that's for sure! Nobody wants you to be either. *(To Hedi.)* And what're you crying for all the time? You ought to be glad ... I don't even understand you! *(With maternal attentiveness.)* You idiot. Seriously! *(Purrs in her ear.)* You're free now, you've made it, you're in the clear, you can stray anywhere you feel like. There's the car, there's the chauffeur, if you want, he'll even hump you. Does he hump?
HEDI: Excuse me?
CRYSTAL: How can you be so crude?
BETTY: *(Lashes out.)* Shut up! It's a natural need. *(To Hedi.)* Is there someone who humps you?
HEDI: Oh ... No, there isn't.
BETTY: Don't lie!
HEDI: *(Defensively.)* There isn't!
BETTY: Same here.

(Crystal screeches with laughter.)

BETTY: *(Drinks.)* It's so good for the skin, though. Smooths out the bumps, takes care of pimples ...
HEDI: *(Wistfully.)* I have two or three here on my back. *(Reaches back.)*
BETTY: You see? That's why! Don't worry, dear, we'll find some here at the resort ... or we won't. With all these bulging bikini trunks ... Can you guess whether I found any yet? ... Look at me!
HEDI: *(Flabbergasted.)* Here?
CRYSTAL: If you don't give it to me, I'm on my way.
BETTY: *(Slaps her across the face.)* It was a mosquito! ... Good-bye. Out of my sight! Now!
CRYSTAL: *(Gathers her things in a huff.)* I'm getting on the first plane ...
BETTY: *(Laughs.)* It's about time ... Parasite!

(Crystal rushes out.)

BETTY: Now she'll calm down in the shower. Poopsy can't make a move without me. You'll see, she'll come crawling back right away, and start begging again ...
HEDI: What does she want?
BETTY: What?! *(Looks away.)* Money. The princess needs money.
HEDI: Is she so hard up?

BETTY: West Berlin is no bed of roses either, my dear! What do you think? The Hungarian work ethic isn't fashionable there. Poopsy-types have no prospects there.
HEDI: Prospects?
BETTY: Eh, this isn't worth talking about, Hedi — let's drop the subject. *(Turns away.)* Besides, I'm glad she finally came home. I'm glad she could come home at all ...
HEDI: *(Doodles in the sand with her foot.)* Interesting, I thought ... *(Understands.)* Oh my.

(Brief pause.)

BETTY: Now you're catching on, you silly goose! Would they let her in here otherwise? *(Brief pause.)* And her with those god-given talents! She could have been anything: the Pioneer League wanted her, she won the children's drawing festival of India, she was a wonderful folk dancer, they took her to the World Youth Camp, she was involved with the Communist Youth League, her poetry recitations were gorgeous, she was an organizational genius, I got her accepted at the Econ School ... And she goes running after some jerk! After a good-for-nothing, because she fell in love with his counterrevolutionary cock! She lets herself be ruined, plundered, whacked out ... I was hard put trying to fix it so she could come home last spring.
HEDI: Gee, I got a different story from Poopsy.
BETTY: What story?
HEDI: Well that ... *(Irresolutely.)* her husband committed suicide out there. She had to put her child in an institution ... That's the only reason she came home. For a visit. A rest.
BETTY: *(Shrugs.)* That happens to be true. She wasn't lying about that. *(Drinks.)* He did, in fact, commit suicide. He was a neurotic. A neurotic lawyer and pop singer! *(Brief pause.)* It's just that first he ruined my daughter's life. Screwed it up ...*(Falls silent.)*
HEDI: *(Warily.)* Wasn't he some kind of poet?
BETTY: What difference does it make? He was a flake. An oppositionary louse. A troublemaker! He infected my daughter. She's a nervous wreck.
HEDI: So it's not true that ... *(Turns her eyes away.)*
BETTY: What?
HEDI: Never mind.
BETTY: I didn't say that! *(Drinks.)* I don't know that. Hey, want a good laugh, Hedi? *(Theatrically.)* I haven't been informed about that. The young lady doesn't deign to speak to me! *(Whispers.)* She's bananas ...
HEDI: Sick?
BETTY: *(Angry.)* There's nothing wrong with her. She's no more of a ninny than you are!
HEDI: *(Teary-eyed.)* You can say that to me? *(Puts her arm around her.)* My precious

darling, how good it is that I've gotten to know you!... It's tough for us, my dear.

BETTY: I'm fed up with her!

HEDI: Well, sometimes Poopsy's very impertinent, that's for sure! She's got a foul mouth, too, which I can't stand ... *(Drinks.)*

BETTY: Crystal was corrupted. *(On all fours.)* You know why?

HEDI: Why?

BETTY: Because she's a BASTARD. *(Slaps the ground.)*

HEDI: Bastard? Crystal?!

BETTY: *(Somberly.)* Crystal, of course. *(Stands up, applies cream to her face.)* She's Crystal because she was conceived under a chandelier. In the Parliament. On a desk.

HEDI: *(Titters drunkenly.)* Lizzie, no!... Come off it! Lizzie, not that...

BETTY: Absolutely. Just like that! Only you're too young to know about these things. And I might add that... *(Applies her facial cream.)* I loved her father. *(Reflects.)* Though I hardly even knew him. He was a thin little bespectacled man. First a minister of the church, then a minister of the state. Happens. Especially in those days... And all the typists were in love with him. I had the advantage. I was his stenographer. *(Sighs.)* Anyway, we couldn't leave the building then, because they were shooting... *(Shrugs.)* Hungarians at the Russkies, Russkies at the Hungarians ... eh, it's all behind me now. We sat across the desk from each other all night. His feet didn't even reach the floor. Ministerial armchair! The things that happened there, God almighty!... His eyes were bloodshot, pink as a white rabbit's. I don't think he'd slept in over a week. Maybe he was coming apart at the seams from the whole thing. I sure was. And how! New cadre straight from the farm. I was throwing up in the trash can. I don't want to go into details. *(Brief pause.)* At dawn I feel his hand under the table. Hey Hedi, I thought he wanted to cop a feel. And why not? Let him feel. I reached under the table too, and then ... *(In a choked voice.)* He pressed a Christmas bonbon into my hand. In November! When the Russians had already marched in. A little bonbon wrapped in red. *(Muses.)* Where'd he get it? Why? *(Muses.)* I climbed right into his lap. And from there onto the desk.

HEDI: *(Excitedly.)* And?

BETTY: What "and"? He got his. *(Muses.)* He deserved it. *(Gulps.)* Two years later. In closed court. He got his!

HEDI: Because of what he did to you? *(Inanely.)* Poor little Crystal. *(She catches on.)* What did he deserve?!

BETTY: To be hanged. That's what he deserved. He didn't deserve anything else. *(Pours water on herself and yelps.)* What else does a person like that deserve? Someone who, for all his priestly past, sics the crazed masses on the tanks, if you please; counteragitates even under martial law; plays the hero in open-top cars; incites with megaphones; when everything is already absolutely mum, when mum's the only thing possible, so we can finally learn from our mistakes, so the blood of children will finally stop being spilled here! Teenagers by the thousands were being blown up together with their Molotov cocktails, together with everything, so that we can be sunbathing here now, getting to know one another, running off to Vienna for scented toilet paper. I mean we don't even have to go get it, because it's being brought here! *(Loses her head.)* By now they're bringing in everything, from boutique fashions to the whole kit'n'caboodle, the Great Market-hall is bursting with meat, this is where the socialist bloc comes to stuff its face, the West too, and they *can* eat, as much as will fit in them, there's more than enough ... He's the cause of that too! He stirred things up to that point, only the jerk didn't realize! And he wouldn't shut his face, no matter how much they were begging him from the central office! I mean he could have been a minister again if he'd been smart. *(Winded.)* But he was a peasant. A priest! *(Imitates.)* "A subjective idealist!" A communist! *(Storms through the corpses, hits the side of the truck in rage, the chauffeur glances at her.)* What's a puny little bolshevik doing jumping around? It's socialism that's trying to get built here! *(Returns, drinks.)* And it will. *(Pause.)* As I live and breathe. And he should rot in the ground ... I don't even know where he's buried! Nobody does. *(Drinks.)* Only God Almighty and his secretary.

(Pause.)

HEDI: Who's this Molotov?
BETTY: Just catch rays, Hedi. Soak in that sun.

(Crystal enters silently along the path, carrying an enormous portion of ice cream in each hand, but she seems unaware of what she is holding; she stands in silence, smiling beatifically.)

CRYSTAL: *(Unexpectedly exclaims.)* How about it?
HEDI: *(Jumps up.)* Jesus Christ! Just like a cat. I mean ... I didn't mean anything by that. *(Quickly.)* What's new over there? I mean at the buffet?

*(Crystal does not answer.
Pause.)*

HEDI: Don't you want to lie back down here?

*(Crystal does not answer.
Pause.)*

BETTY: *(Sunbathes with closed eyes, or pretends to.)* What's up, Poopsy? Having fun? *(Brief pause.)* Having a good time? On top of the world?

(Crystal does not answer, then slowly nods.)

No departure after all? Where've you been, my little lamb? Tell your Mommy a story. We're starved for something ... What happened?
HEDI: We're bored, really. Throw out a topic ...*(Sits back down, perturbed.)*

(Crystal stands in silence.)
BETTY: *(Facing away, with closed eyes.)* Holding out on us?
HEDI: Leave her alone, Lizzie, she's not going to give us any. *(Brief pause.)* Even though it's dripping. Tsk-tsk, Poopsy! You could lick it at least...
BETTY: *(Shouts.)* Don't you dare give any away!
HEDI: How come?
BETTY: *(Opens her eyes.)* That's all she needs! Giving any away, even by accident ... I'd call the police!
HEDI: Police? That's weird ... *(Looks away.)*

(Pause.)

CRYSTAL: *(Yelps.)* How about it? How about an ice-cream pack, Hedi? I'll smear it on you. Are you Hungarian?
HEDI: How do you mean, dear?
CRYSTAL: Just that. You sneak around, nibble bacon rinds ... *(Reflects.)* You have a burp after dinner, glance through the Party daily ... *(Thinks.)* ... or the Women's Weekly, then you get into the tub ... *(Thinks.)* And just soak. Just for a rest. Then comes the ice cream.
HEDI: Ice cream?
BETTY: *(Sits up.)* This is what I'm talking about, my dear! This is the tragedy!
HEDI: Not a tragedy by a long shot ... *(To Crystal, with a false laugh.)* You give yourself ice-cream packs? For cosmetic purposes? Does it work?
CRYSTAL: It works! It's fashionable! *(Dumps the ice cream on Hedi's bosom and back, and immediately begins smearing it. Hedi squirms and screeches tipsily.)* This is all the rage now! The latest in Paris and Csepel. It's very cold, good and cold, stimulates the spine. Amanda Lear does it every day. So do all the German TV-reporter women. *(Smears furiously.)* The Hungarians too. Everybody in the world is cooling off, cooling off, searching for relatives and getting cold. We've been in the sun too long. Isn't that possible? We're fired up, we've got to chill out, we need tranquility, ice, lots of ice, a whole skating-rink's worth ... *(Stops.)* The only problem is that this is sticky. It clings! It drips. *(Tastes it.)* Too much salt.
HEDI: Ha ha.
BETTY: *(Cries out.)* Everyone has his cross to bear!

HEDI: *(Tottering.)* Why, don't be silly, it really feels good! Especially in this ungodly heat ... Lizzie, don't cry! *(To Crystal.)* Aren't you giving your mother any?
CRYSTAL: *(Over Betty.)* Who's this? My mother? *(Wonders.)* She's supposed to be my mother? Saltmother?
HEDI: Crystie, I'm dripping.
CRYSTAL: I'll lick it right up.
HEDI: *(Jumps away.)* Thanks, don't bother! I'll lick it off. *(Licks herself.)* Vanilla, strawberry. Mm! What's this, chocolate? *(Distances herself.)*
BETTY: *(Stands up.)* Hoarding on your own? *(Slaps Crystal on the back.)* You little wretch. Did you shoot up?
CRYSTAL: What's your problem, Mother? *(Smiles.)*
BETTY: *(Kisses her.)* Nothing. Really nothing! *(Drunkenly draws her daughter to her.)* Hedi, take a look at this girl: Did I deserve this from life? My just deserts? Should I call Budapest? *(Kisses her again.)* Poopsy, do you love me? Hedi, tell me now, what should I do?
HEDI: Don't do anything! *(Licks herself.)* Everything's sweet. All of me! *(Spins.)*
"I'm the one who's sweet!
I'd like a bite to eat!
I'm the naked emperor!
Caveat emptor ...!"

(Acts clumsy.)

CRYSTAL: *(Breaks forth.)* Mother, I love you only as much as I love salt! *(Brief pause.)* A hungry goat also licks salt. Salt pretzels, salt ice cream, salt Lake Balaton ... Everything's all salt here! How I'd like to lick you off, Hedi.
BETTY: Cut it out.
CRYSTAL: My bowels are on fire. The sausages are simmering. The commotion's on its way out. NO PASARAN! NO PASARAN!
BETTY: Yecch!
HEDI: What's she saying?
CRYSTAL: Back-loading automatic air pistol! *(Gives the raspberry, sobers up.)* Don't be alarmed. I'm a perfectly clean woman.
HEDI: Perfectly nuts ... *(Wipes her body with her hand.)*
BETTY: Are you trying to cause a scandal? Should I have you taken away?
CRYSTAL: Give it to me.
BETTY: *(Hurls a toilet case at her.)* Here!
CRYSTAL: It was in this? *(Throws herself in front of Betty, embraces her legs.)* Mom, Mommy, Mother dear! I'm no good, I'm ungrateful, don't be angry with me! ... My God, I don't have the nerve to look you in the eye! Know what? Let's escape to the Soviet Union! Let's leave everything behind, let's drink kvass, start a new life! I'm begging you, and "Ya kvam pishu, chivo zhe bolye,

shto ya magu yissho skazaty ... tyiper ya znayu vashem volye ... *(Gets stuck.)* naprimer ... *(Uncertainly.)* nakazaty."*

HEDI: What's she saying? What's she saying?

BETTY: What difference does it make? Who cares? Let her babble!

CRYSTAL: Thank you, thank you! "You're sweet, I'm crashing!..." *(Kisses her hand repeatedly.)* To Moscow! Let's go ...! *(Stands up.)* As soon as possible. I'm tired of this protectorate.

BETTY: That's enough.

CRYSTAL: I, in any case, am going.

BETTY: None too soon for me.

HEDI: And who's going to wash me off? Here you are having a jolly good time, and I'm sticky all over.

CRYSTAL: Don't wash it off! It nourishes the skin, it's full of vitamins. *(Presses the toilet case to herself.)* Oh, Moscow, Moscow! Moscow evenings! *(Laughs.)* I'll sleep. *(Runs off.)*

BETTY: And so it goes, Hedi! *(Blows her nose.)* Now at least you can see for yourself...

HEDI: Does she really want to go to the USSR?

BETTY: I don't know. Not very likely.

(Brief pause.)

HEDI: "Nourishes the skin!" What nonsense ... No problem, I'll survive. I'm dripping. The modern way! "Join the Pepsi generation." *(Plops down on her behind and agitatedly fusses around herself.)* Look at all the suntan lotion we've got! The packaging's so nice too. Neatso. Everything's neatso nowadays ... She left her glasses here! *(Picks them up.)*

BETTY: She'll come back for them.

HEDI: How strong are they? *(Tries them.)*

BETTY: Soda-bottle bottoms.

HEDI: *(Stands up.)* Terrible. *(Totters, throws down the glasses.)* Jesus Christ! Feels like I have sunstroke. That crazy sun! Aren't we going in the water? We'll take the ball ... *(Picks up a beach ball.)* Let's play catch in waist-deep water. *(Pensively.)* I never used to play ball.

BETTY: Neither did I. *(Starts forward, stops short.)* Eh, I don't want to go into this. It's muddy.

HEDI: True. It's marshy. The riffraff is polluting it. 'Cause they shouldn't all be using it at once. They all come here! Even the shit is discharged here. What's this going to be like in the year two thousand, huh? ... *(Falls.)*

BETTY: Rinse yourself off.

---

* Pushkin: *Eugene Onegin* (Tatyana's letter — excerpt, with poor phonetics.)

HEDI: You do it, Liz!
BETTY: Okay, straddle, little girl.

(Hedi stands straddle-legged, Betty douses her.)

HEDI: *(Shakes herself.)* Wow, is that cold! Like the blood of a fish, but it feels good. Boy, I needed that! My arm is all goose bumps... More! *(Rhythmically.)* "Budapest is in a daze, having caught the limbo craze..."
BETTY: *(With sympathy.)* It's not sun you need, dearie. *(Sighs.)* Drink some eggnog; you could do with a belt. *(Pours.)*

(Hedi trudges amid the corpses, repeatedly leaning down to rearrange their arms as if "straightening up"; she works diligently while Betty watches.)

BETTY: Hey, what're you doing?
HEDI: *(Working.)* Things have gotten so messy around here. And it looks like the wind is blowing the stuff over, too. I wouldn't want us to be bawled out at the end...
BETTY: We're no match for mother nature, my dear. But I suppose we can sweep it up... *(Helps.)*

(They work in silence.)

HEDI: A little activity'll do us good. I needed this, I really did. A rake or something would come in handy now.
BETTY: Our lowbrow background is showing, as always! This isn't the first time I've noticed. But that's as it should be... Let's not forget where we came from.
HEDI: I was brought up to be neat. I was put to work at the age of eight. Hoeing, cutting shoots, going to the well, gathering sheaves...
BETTY: That's when we were happy! *(To a corpse.)* Ugh, are you heavy! *(To Hedi.)* Just don't let the custodian know, you silly goose, otherwise the whole clubhouse will be laughing at us, you'll see...
HEDI: *(Stops.)* Honey, I'm dizzy.
BETTY: *(Stops.)* Working too hard.
HEDI: Grab hold of me!

(Betty catches her just in time, they stand a long time without a word, snuggle together in silence.)

HEDI: *(Hoarsely.)* We've got sunstroke. But... it's good.
BETTY: *(Laughs, quietly.)* What's good?
HEDI: Where's your daughter?
BETTY: Rotting on her sofa. She's forever rotting on her sofa. Staring at the ceiling!

HEDI: She's young.
BETTY: She was. *(Brief pause.)* She's faded. She burned herself out. Even her glasses are getting thicker. The studs don't want her anymore... *(Startled.)* Why do you ask?
HEDI: I never took dance class. Like others. I can't dance. Imagine.
BETTY: *(Snickering.)* And?
HEDI: Why, you can?
BETTY: And how! Why do you ask?
HEDI: Then teach me.
BETTY: Now? Here?
HEDI: NOW!
BETTY: But which dance? *(Laughs.)* There isn't even any music.
HEDI: We don't need music. I'll hum. Just show me how. At least there's no one here to laugh at me.
BETTY: *(Muses.)* How about the tango? Or what?
HEDI: One of those figure-skating kinds. A nice one.
BETTY: That can't be done now. That's different. *(Muses.)* Should I waltz?
HEDI: That's good too. But with me!
BETTY: *(Laughs.)* Then let's waltz... let's waltz!
HEDI: *(Harshly.)* Where should I stand?
BETTY: Stay there! Don't stand anywhere. Lift your hand. *(Maternally.)* Not that one! That's it, like that. Place your little hand in mine. *(Puts her arm around Hedi's waist.)* Don't squeeze, relax, I'll hum. Relax! Wait, don't worry. *(Hums.)* You just bring your left foot to your right one, then back again to the right with the left! TO THE RIGHT ONE!

(Tugs Hedi back and forth while singing.)

"Love is so illusory,
Illusion promising the moon,
Flirting with me playfully,
As fleeting as a rose in bloom.
Patience! So it counsels me,
Snow and sleet will melt away,
And mercy sweet will come my way."*

(They become entangled in each other's legs and fall; slowly and with difficulty they crawl on all fours to the mattresses and stretch out.)

---

* From *Sybill*, an operetta by Bródy — Martos — Jacobi

HEDI: It's hot.
BETTY: Sure is.

(Silence.)

(Kozma jumps off the hood, takes a leather briefcase from the driver's compartment, throws it down in front of him, strips naked, tosses his clothes into the compartment, sticks the briefcase under his arm, walks, and stops behind the ladies, watches them as they sunbathe with closed eyes, speaks unexpectedly.)

KOZMA: Comrades, is this mattress free?

(Betty glances back sleepily, then jumps up with lightning speed. Then Hedi comes to and practically flies into the air.)

BETTY: *(Obsequiously.)* Well, of course. Of course it's free.
KOZMA: *(With nonchalance.)* I'd like to settle down here, if that's all right with you ...
BETTY: *(Watches Hedi.)* Of course.

(Kozma treads on the mattress, takes suntan lotion from his briefcase, thoroughly and painstakingly applies oil to his body, puts on sunglasses; the women settle back into their places embarrassed, sitting more decorously than before.)

KOZMA: *(To Betty.)* I'm Kozma.
BETTY: *(Holds out her hand energetically.)* I'm Horváth.
KOZMA: *(Shakes her hand.)* Kozma.
HEDI: *(Frightened, upon Betty's signal.)* Mrs. Bartos ...
KOZMA: *(Shakes her hand.)* Kozma.

(Silence, Kozma sunbathes.)

BETTY: You're also a vacationer?
KOZMA: Well, of course. We came down. For a little relaxation.
BETTY: When did you arrive?
KOZMA: Now.

(He smiles at the women and suddenly lies back. Hedi wants to rush away, but, with a series of mute signals, Betty convinces her to stay.)

BETTY: Have you had lunch?
KOZMA: I generally don't.
BETTY: How about an aperitif?

HEDI: *(Embarrassed.)* A what?
BETTY: Oh Hedi! *(Stands up, harrumphs.)*
KOZMA: *(Sits up.)* Sure!
BETTY: *(Among the drinks.)* Vermouth? Champagne? Beer, eggnog, vodka — what'll it be? We've got it all!
KOZMA: WHATEVER. *(Quieter.)* Doesn't matter.
BETTY: *(Pours.)* Men are beer drinkers! Hedi, you're not drinking, am I right?
HEDI: *(Watches Kozma, then suddenly.)* No. I'll have some.
BETTY: *(Lying.)* Too bad, that was the last one. Good little girls don't drink beer. I'm not a good little girl. What'll we drink to?
KOZMA: To you, Comrades! *(Brief pause.)* But we can drink to peace too, as far as I'm concerned. And to the summer.
BETTY: To all of the above, Comrade!

(They drink.)

Family?
KOZMA: No. Don't want one.
BETTY: Don't be too sure!
KOZMA: *(Looks at her.)* A question of taste.
BETTY: Could put it that way.

(Kozma assumes another sunbathing pose; long silence and pantomime: the women are signaling to each other.)

KOZMA: How quiet we've become.
BETTY: Because there's nobody to entertain us.
HEDI: *(Lets this slip.)* How pale you are, my God!
KOZMA: I'll burn myself down soon enough!

(The women shriek in a fit of laughter, though when they discover that Kozma is not laughing with them, they immediately stop and turn serious.)

KOZMA: *(Unexpectedly.)*
 Hallo, what's this all about,
 Have you got me figured out?
BETTY: Come again?
KOZMA: Just talking to myself.
HEDI: We do that too.
BETTY: *(Angry.)* What's the matter with you? *(Drinks and lashes out at him.)* Comrade Kozma, you really could tell us about yourself! That is, unless that's classified... We've been here drinking, sunbathing, and being bored since

morning ... women's shift ... and ... and ... DRINKING. We're a bit pickled, so there — to use a folksy expression. You can tell us anything. *(Finger to mouth.)* Mum's the word!... And anyway, whoever's admitted here... Especially if he can come and go when he pleases, when the coast happens to be clear ... That's probably when you came.
KOZMA: I come whenever I want to.
BETTY: *(Drunkenly.)* There, you see, we don't shit in our pants over a county Party secretary ... That is, well, you know what I mean. Or if you don't ... Never mind! I've been a widow for twenty-five years, I know men inside and out! Not Hedi. She doesn't know anything. She hasn't even tried. She doesn't even know that ... NEVER MIND. We're an outstanding audience. Especially Hedi. *(Laughs.)*
HEDI: Aunt Lizzie!
BETTY: But I am too. I've seen it all. She hasn't yet. *(Brief pause.)* We're all ears!
HEDI: Comrade Kozma, don't listen to her. *(Whispers in his ear.)* She's soused. That's how *we* say it ...
KOZMA: Don't lean on me. *(Hedi pops away.)* Later!

(Hedi becomes silent, Betty chuckles, claps.)

As far as that's concerned, Comrades, I'll gladly regale you. And how!... There are no secrets between us. Go ahead and question me boldly. On anything! We struggled for the same cause, we're struggling for the same cause, and we'll continue to struggle for the same cause in the future as well ...
HEDI: What cause?
BETTY: You mean we're playing Twenty Questions? Oh boy, finally some amusement! An end to the boredom. Hedi, now aren't you glad you got your pass? ... I'll do a political screening on you, dear Comrade. Will I ever!... You're a godsend!
KOZMA: Could be.
HEDI: *(Fidgeting.)* Do we have to ask questions?
BETTY: I start! State apparatus? That was dumb; of course you're state apparatus. From the Communist Youth League?
KOZMA: No.
BETTY: Trade Union?
KOZMA: You're out of turn. *(Turns to Hedi.)*
HEDI: *(Happily.)* Oh, do I have to? *(Brief pause.)* What did you come down here for? *(Frightened.)* Bad question; that's not what I meant to ask. Don't get mad!
KOZMA: It's a good question. *(Brief pause.)* I came down because of you two.
HEDI: Because of us?!
BETTY: For our beauty? *(Suddenly sobers up.)* Is something wrong?
KOZMA: Wrong? No. Nothing's ever wrong.
BETTY: *(Stands up, ashen.)* Something connected with me?

KOZMA: You're out of turn again! *(Brief pause.)* But I'll answer anyway, providing you let Comrade Bartos also have her say. *(Betty sits down.)* ALSO.

(Pause.)

HEDI: I can't think of a thing. *(Sincerely.)* It's so exciting! Can we ask anything?
BETTY: Was that a question?
KOZMA: Yes! ... That answers both of you at once.

(Silence.)

BETTY: Are you with the police?
HEDI: *(Shouts.)* My husband was also with the police! A captain or a colonel. But at the time I was just a country bumpkin on the farm! *(Covers her mouth.)* What am I saying? I've had too much sun! Mr. Comrade Kozma, don't draw any conclusions ... We've had too much to drink! *(Brief pause.)* Though he said he was a colonel, or ... but I don't remember any more. *(Realizes.)* But they've got their own separate beach resort: a gorgeous restricted area. Though this one isn't open to the public either, is it? In other words ... *(Falls silent.)*
KOZMA: I'm not with the police. Not at all!

*(Kozma smiles at Betty.
Pause.)*

BETTY: The wind's up. Well, well ... *(Looks away.)*
HEDI: Do you think there'll be a storm?
BETTY: The sky's all blue. There won't be a storm.

(The untrained gym teacher drags himself on his belly, muttering, toward the sunbathers.)

HEDI: *(Stands up.)* Do you two feel it?
BETTY: *(Holds out her arm.)* Let it blow!

(The gym teacher raises himself to his knees, the women grab for their things, "storm's rising.")

GYM TEACHER: I've received it, finished, let's start, I gave it up, I swallowed it, I let up, I summoned him, sit down, stand up!, he pleaded, I shut him up, wash it up!, he washed it up, once again!, he fell, stand up! enough! once again! swallow it, I will not, I rammed it down, suffocate! look at me!, where's the pipe?, summon him, look at him!, you're the one, that's not true!, silence, enough, douse him!, I shut him up, he fell down, stand up!, take him out, that's a child!, that's no child, all bloody, take him out, take him, how old?, I don't know, drop dead, I shut him up!, hit the kidneys, once again, go on!, I pulled him up, let me go!, hit the kidneys!, where's the club?, get the record, he threw it up, I pulled him up, look at him! he didn't look, hit him, get the lights!, keep at it, go on, I finished!, down!, on all fours, get the buckets!, he whimpered, hit him!, he's dead, he's still alive!, he's dead, take him out, time for a change, keep at it!, go on, go on, go on, go on, go on ... *(Repeats it.)*

HEDI: *(Outshouts him.)* The glasses ought to be gathered up too! Liz, hurry!...
BETTY: It'll let up right away! It'll pass!... *(Grabs some things.)*
HEDI: Boy, is it raging!
BETTY: It's just passing through ... Happens all the time around here!
HEDI: I want to go inside the house! *(Sets off.)*
BETTY: Wait for me! *(Hurries.)*
GYM TEACHER: GO ON! *(Falls on his face; it is over.)*

(Silence.)

KOZMA: Where are you rushing off to?
BETTY: I told you ... just a gust. What's the big deal?
HEDI: There was almost lightning ... I thought there was going to be a storm.
BETTY: Not quite, my dear. Have a look: tranquility, sunshine, busily buzzing bees ... *(Sits back down.)*
HEDI: There aren't any bees around here! *(Sits back down.)*
KOZMA: ... and beautiful ladies! *(Smiles at Hedi.)*
HEDI: *(Flustered.)* Oh go on! ... Far from it.
BETTY: *(Cheerfully.)* Comrade, excuse me for calling you a policeman.
KOZMA: I'm not offended. *(Brief pause.)* Why, is "policeman" an insult?
BETTY: *(Alarmed.)* It's not an insult. Not at all an insult!

(Silence.)

HEDI: Who's next? Aren't we playing anymore?
KOZMA: You're next. Always the one who asks.
HEDI: *(Chewing her nails.)* Oh no, oh no ... *(Cannot think of a thing.)* Er, did you know my husband?
KOZMA: Better than myself.
HEDI: *(Cheers up.)* No kidding! Seriously? And how come?
BETTY: *(Pops up.)* My turn! *(Brief pause.)* You know, Comrade Kozma, we've been lying here for quite a while. It's possible we have sunstroke! There are indications: pains here and there, dizziness ...
KOZMA: Why don't you two ever go inside the house?
BETTY: You're not the one who's supposed to be asking questions! ... But never mind, I'll answer ... The reason I don't go inside the house is that everybody in there is like you. Everything and everybody! The formica dining room, the

German bowling alley, the internal-affairs agents playing rummy in straw hats ... Even the geranium patch stinks. For all their bother to trim it into a red-star pattern, they overwater it. I don't like state still-lifes, you understand? And Hedi doesn't go in because I don't. We share a room and she follows me around like a puppy. No skin off my back ... Poor thing! Such a novice! I feel sorry for her. *(Leans into Kozma's face.)* What of it?

KOZMA: *(Laughs.)* What do you mean to ask me?

BETTY: *(Flushed.)* If, as you said, anything goes, then it's all right to ask how much younger than me you are, and how many times over that counts around here? In other words, what's the proper tone for you to use? Or if you're such a big shot, what the hell are you doing on my daughter's mattress? Where's your own? Or did you climb over the wall, you little rascal, without getting electrified? And is the reason you're having us do all the talking, after insinuating yourself upon us, to make sure the gatekeeper's two white sheepdogs don't God forbid accidentally bite your cock off? ... But I won't ask you any of that, even though I was already an honest-to-goodness commie-brigade member, giving my all to the Party, when you, my little Kozma, were still craving your mother's tit. But never mind! For now I'll only ask this — and only because I'd so much like at least one person here today to be happy — so tell me honestly: Did you have a chance to check her out? ... *(Changes tone.)* Does this unfortunate Hedi appeal to you as a man? *(Sits on the ground.)* Oh boy, sir, I really did get sunstroke. My stomach's churning. But answer! *(Points at Hedi.)* Do you like her?

HEDI: Betty dear, let me take you in.

BETTY: ANSWER!

KOZMA: Of course. For sure! Very much so.

HEDI: *(Embarrassed.)* Really?! Why?

KOZMA: You remind me of my wife.

BETTY: Did she die?

KOZMA: She's alive. *(Gives Hedi the once-over.)* She's in the pink!

HEDI: *(Recoils.)* Who is?

(Kozma remains silent, smiles, gazes at Hedi.)

BETTY: *(Laughs.)* Well I'm going inside now! *(Struggles to her feet; to Hedi.)* Don't you dare budge! I can find my way in. You stay! *(To Kozma.)* You'll excuse me, won't you?

KOZMA: You're joking.

BETTY: You know, this belle is a brand-new widow.

HEDI: *(In a panic.)* Not *that* new!

BETTY: *(Laughs at her.)* Our Hedi! Come to think of it, dear, why were you given such a highfalutin name?

HEDI: *(Collapses.)* I was named for ... the countess who owned our village ...

BETTY: Oh, God! ... Well, again, you'll excuse me, Comrade, won't you?
KOZMA: Of course! We'll be seeing each other again.
BETTY: *(Harshly.)* I do hope so.
HEDI: Lizzie, don't leave me here!
BETTY: Don't worry, I'll be back.

(Betty departs.
Pause.
Hedi remains silent for a long time.)

HEDI: How about a swim?
KOZMA: *(Stares at her.)* Not me! No way.
HEDI: But it's nice! ... I mean the opposite shore. What I mean is the view! *(Begins panting.)* What do you want from me?
KOZMA: Rub lotion on my back!

(Terror-stricken, she scurries among the suntan lotions, then zealously applies some to the man's back, silence.)

KOZMA: You scum. Cur, lowlife ...
HEDI: *(In fear for her life.)* You mean do your shoulders too?
KOZMA: Brazen, aren't we, Hedi? Beach-whores rubbing lotion on just anybody, valderie-valderah? I don't even know where to begin. I ought to trample you underfoot right away!
HEDI: *(Rapidly applying lotion.)* You've got me mixed up with someone else.
KOZMA: *(Stands up.)* Have I? Got things mixed up? Dear me! A thousand pardons! *(Grabs her.)* So then isn't the entire second floor of 140 Gorky Lane yours, Hedi? Where you can lounge about in your imported nylon dressing gowns among your fifty-thousand varieties of nail polish? And aren't you the daughter of László D. Backwoods Nagy? Aren't you the worker prima donna with village mud between her toes? Who'd so much like her husband to be run over by some car, to be splattered all over the pavement ... but you'd throw in the number six tram to boot! "Car" nothing. A truck! A twenty-tonner at that! Isn't that so, hm?

(Hedi covers her eyes.)

But that's only what Hedi would *like!* A pipe dream ... so take care! Would be nice though ... that's for sure! ... To be rid of all the bother, rid of the little husband, that stupid jerk; to be the brand-new widow available for wooing, eligible for the Socialist Homeland's Merit-pension, raring to go window shopping. *(Raising his voice.)* And never to stand in front of that row of machines, to watch for when the thread breaks, together with the other kerchiefed whores, lasso-cunted textile-worker comrades! No. In your case: separate vacation resort on the shores of Lake Balaton, so you can flirt with every Tom, Dick, and Harry that happens along, whether a punk hooligan, a chauffeur, or whatever, while that busy-bee husband is diligently doing his Siberian duty to the Party in sub-zero temperatures, because *somebody* has to be with those eager-beaver youngsters, those valiant little guest workers, who're laying Hedi's oil lines — after all, the Friendship Pipeline is being laid for her too! — so the goose can have her scented West German bubble bath! ... You've got the gall?! With whom am I mixing up this trollop? Are you the one?

HEDI: *(Removes her hands from her face.)* I am.

KOZMA: And then you're enjoying yourself here on the beach? You won't even give me a little kiss? At least you could ask me: Dear sir, how did you get here from the great Soviet Union, from so ungodly a distance in such tiptop shape?

HEDI: *(Sincerely.)* How?

KOZMA: What business is it of yours how I got here? In a private airplane! I was dropped off in a parachute by Friendship! Do you know yet?

(Silence.)

Listen here, do you have any idea — did you ever have — where I work, and what the hell my work is? Tell me!

HEDI: *(Shrugs her shoulders.)* No.

KOZMA: Well, isn't that convenient, toots! In that case I won't ask any more questions. *(Brief pause.)* The hell I won't! ... How's tricks, Hedi? Tell me how long I haven't existed ...

HEDI: All right.

KOZMA: *(Laughs.)* Really?

HEDI: I burned your clothes on the stove. First your shirts and ties. Then all your suits, your militia uniform, your decorations, your production-drive-challenge pennants, and your filthy portfolios, the ones from those conferences! *(Brief pause.)* I burned your shoes, too, and I put all your socks underneath them so the leather would catch fire! There was such a stench that I had to open all the windows ... And this happened right on the first day, but I woke up at night and tore your personal I.D. to smithereens, all your I.D.! One of them cut my finger. *(Shows him.)* Right here! *(With pleasure.)* Then I stuck the quartz watches that the delegations gave you as tokens of friendship into a brass mortar and smashed them till they couldn't even be recognized because half the pieces flew away ... You've got nothing left at home.

KOZMA: *(With suppressed laughter.)* I don't need anything.

HEDI: *(Dreamily.)* Every noon your Mercedes takes me to the Hilton ... they said I could keep it for a six-month grace period ... the waiters already know me there, I have my own table. I eat what they bring me, they recommend the especially good things, because they're eager for tips! Afterwards I saunter up to the bar to hobnob with the artists! ... I show some leg.

KOZMA: Hobnob with whom?

HEDI: *(Gets into the spirit of it.)* Those who smell like roses, the Westerners, the bearded, the counts! *(Bursts forth.)* With the artists, the Bavarians! Who know how to communicate without having to say anything ... Chivalry is not dead! It's alive and well. *(Pensively.)* Good, soft music, the little illuminated globe turns, my ear is brushed by breath ... *(Stretches.)* ... And four thousand!

KOZMA: *(Shakes with suppressed laughter.)* That much?

HEDI: That much! But only if he's young and slim. Otherwise he can pay in dollars! Somebody inevitably turns up ... a count, who wants it right there in the hotel ... gets aroused ... but, you see, I want it on Gorky Lane. By the open window! So that's what the little count and I discuss over vermouth and cocktail snacks. But as soon as he gets into the back of the Mercedes, the little count knows I don't need it for bread! I baptized your bed every day, my dear.

KOZMA: *(Laughs.)* Screw you too!

HEDI: *(Ecstatically.)* Just you laugh, the joke's on you — every time I straddle their shoulders, as in those blue movies you used to drool over. But now it's all getting fleshed out in reality ... and I'm the one! With some Western stud wearing a gold chain, doing lots of foreplay from the "What and How-To" series. So quick, Béla, get yourself a pair of binoculars ... *(Runs out of breath.)*

KOZMA: I'm not Béla. Can't I laugh?

HEDI: Will you still be laughing when I tell you who my current lover is, you louse?

KOZMA: *(Curiously.)* Who?

HEDI: The little conductor, Herbert von Karajan, that white-haired darling, who comes to Hungary only for my sake, with his aquiline nose, incognito, I'll have you know. Without the country's or the TV's or anybody's being aware of his presence. And he always brings me tropical orchids, and he kisses my hand, and we dine by candlelight. He always autographs pictures for me, even though he's a count! But he's started studying Hungarian, from the dictionary, in case — this is what he said — he takes me out to his clifftop castle, where he has a manmade sea and trained black leopards, negroes, slaves, and there, on a solid gold four-poster bed ... *(Thrashes the man while sobbing. Kozma laughs.)* You cursed son of a bitch, you! ...

(Hedi falls to the ground weeping.)

(Crystal, screeching, buzzes down the path on a bicycle, without her glasses, rolling over the mattresses, she loses control and takes a great spill. Hedi recovers, jumps up, pats her face.)

CRYSTAL: *(Happily.)* Reckless driving! "Rote Armee-Fraktion!" Caution, I'm a ticking time-bomb! Long live Khadafy! ... *(Clambers to her feet.)* Interesting!

I feel terrific. What's this? *(Blinks.)* There's a man here? *(Totters to Kozma nearsightedly. Pats him.)* Way to go, Hedi! Herr, Herr! Congratulations, Hedi! Nice catch! So, the fish are biting today! There will be caviar too ... *(Sniffs him.)* Ungarische Sonnenmilch! ... Okay, enough of this ... *(Searches for her glasses on the ground.)* Where's my mother? Have you seen her by any chance? ... What gives now? Are you two smooching? *(Blinking.)* Why don't you answer?

HEDI: *(Jabbers wildly.)* I'm the one you're asking? Don't ask me! You're coming from where she went, she just went in, but go now ... *(Waves her hand.)* What do I know!

CRYSTAL: Excuse me, what are you saying? What're you getting in an uproar over?

(Short silence.)

HEDI: Well, in that case, allow me to introduce my husband! *(Covers her mouth with her hand.)*

CRYSTAL: Didn't he die? *(Stands up.)* I'm Crystal.

KOZMA: Kozma.

CRYSTAL: Really? *(To Hedi.)* You said he's called Bartos!

HEDI: Yes. Because now ... No! Well, yes, because ... No! Yes. *(Shakes her head no.)* Yes ...

KOZMA: *(To Crystal.)* Unbelievable woman. In truth, I've known her for about ten minutes, considering ...

*(Hedi madly rushes off.
Silence.)*

CRYSTAL: You're not her husband after all?

KOZMA: Whose?

(Silence.)

CRYSTAL: I can't see a thing.

KOZMA: Would you like to see?

CRYSTAL: I'm in the pink! Well, I'll be taking my leave ... I'll just find my glasses first. *(She stoops and rummages, hums, whispers, murmurs, as if she were alone.)* Warm, warm ... Hot! Cold. Cold ... *(Does not find them.)* "Everything turned out just as I knew it would ..." Not a thing, nothing! "You're suspiciously familiar to me, here we go again ..."

KOZMA: *(Picks up the glasses.)* Is this what you're looking for?

CRYSTAL: Could be.

(Crystal puts on her glasses, stares at Kozma and is taken aback.)

CRYSTAL: Won't this ever come to an end? *(Rushes to the drinks.)* The sweet face, the expression that was so popular in Budapest, and the courage, and the tufts of curly hair ... and then no results! A defecting balalaika ... *(Drinks.)* The free world isn't interested in a handsome Hungarian loser. *(Quotes.)* "Manic depression!" ... You should have died! You're a coward! Once a hick, always a hick. "Cock-a-doodle-doo!" ... You're worthless, a good-for-nothing, you just got under my skin, that's all ... You're a washout. They didn't buy you ... or me either. We're faceless! I'm not going to scrape you up off the floor anymore. *(Shouting.)* I want an end to this, an end! Cymbal crash, carrion stench, and silence; and enough now! ... So you didn't jump out the window after all? *(Comes to a realization.)* But that's what Radio Free Europe announced! ... *(Ponders.)* "Free!" "Europe!" ... They're free of us, in any case. *(Waves her hand jerkily.)* This is stupid! Scat! *(Drinks.)* Scat, get away from here! Shoo! Out of my sight ... I've seen quite enough of you, my love, my darling, my stupid Laci!

KOZMA: Are you speaking to me? ... Why do you drink so much after popping pills? ... After all, I'm only sitting here on this mattress ... *(Stands up.)* But not for long.

CRYSTAL: *(Hiccups.)* Come to think of it, I don't understand how you were allowed in here at all. *(Titters.)* A specter is haunting Europe ... FA soap! Footbath. Village smiles. U.N. refugee camps! ... Laci dear, why do you exist? Don't! I don't want to exist either. I want to go to the moon! I'll be the concierge there ... and I'll let in only those who can whistle. Whistle, my dears! Everyone whistle what he knows: The Yellow Rose or the Prison Anthem or the Internationale ... *(Tries unsuccessfully to whistle.)* Rise, rise! ... All the way to the moon! Let me love you there! Where there are no obstacles. Where there's still a possibility of freedom, of a blank private life ... A moonlight marriage, a moonlight family! *(Drops in front of Kozma, embraces his knees.)* I went to the Consulate ... know what? They were thrilled, delighted! They're just like you ... They had me sign all sorts of documents. You ought to get chummy with those guys. They sure do know their documents. The small print, the important questions, the red tape. — I couldn't care less about the lot of you. I get the estate, you take the kid. Do whatever you want with him: Sell him to some German who'll raise him to be a bureaucrat, a little moustachioed functionary! Berufsverboten ... you could get a lot of money for him, you hear? Business, my dear, business!

KOZMA: Pardon me, Comrade! *(Steps away.)* There's been some misunderstanding here ...

CRYSTAL: *(Grabs him.)* All I want by now is to be rich! Anywhere. Wherever it's permitted. Beach-front property ... yes! And palm trees, ice-cold hand-kisses, colored servants. Animals with big balls! A bank account, credit cards, a house

in Barbados, a heated tennis court in the basement, and ... and ... macho Jamaican bartenders! *(Shoves him away.)* Don't be following me around, you hear? What are you people talking about? *(Sings drunkenly.)*
"Ye stars that once returned my gaze,
Are now receding into haze.
I'm out of time — it passed me by,
Now I'm watching angels fly."

(Silence.)

KOZMA: Are you in fact a comrade, Comrade? Or are you still in the Communist Youth League? Don't be shy! The young workers' brigade is also a good thing! An elegant career lies ahead of you. Spilling your guts in public! *(Muses.)* Group therapy. Editing for television. "Let's go with this ... let's go with that!" Poetic presentations of the disco, of crowd control with dogs ... *(Muses.)* And the whole frisky, cheery office on top of it all! All those stiff, sniveling dolts, who stand up and beat their desks when they see you ... Be fruitful and multiply! "Youth! Politics! Culture!" Tune in the Communist youth broadcast, baby! The whole country's yours!

CRYSTAL: *(Stands up, quaking.)* Country?! What country? What do you people mean? ... There aren't any more countries, there's no such thing ... Everyone went to sleep. Every country will now get its sleep! *(Imitates snoring.)* Hegel is snoring, so is Marx ... Square! And Engels Square! ... Why do you think I came home from Berlin? Any idea? *(Howling.)* To catch up on my sleep! I want some peace and quiet, and a passport that's very much in order! It's not so urgent ... Makes no difference. *(With a wave of the hand.)* Let's have it all the same! It's can-do here. Things are good here. Hungary is the solution. Didn't you know? Why didn't you know? I want to be lazy, relaxed, and satiated. Law and order! Fried chickens hanging from the trees! *(Snickers.)* They've hung the trees full of chickens. Can't you tell? *(Sniffs the air.)* Smells of meat. A country with a sweetish aroma. *(Smacks her lips.)* I'll lick off the glaze. I'll win the jackpot. Any possible way. Here any way *is* possible! ... What do I know? I'll have a make-believe husband, and the surf in the summer and video in the winter ... Or I'll found a polite-society orchestra! That'll be the new wave. My own! *(Laughs.)* Then we'll cleverly balalaika away ... Business! Lawyers! Dance hall! *(Waves.)* And just you stare at the wall from morning till night. It'll be there in any case. It's a big wall! It doesn't interest me anymore. Finished! Absolutely! The whole rotten riffraff, your whole pompous horde, the swaggering and the bragging! ... Legal geniuses, sneaky martyrs: all rumbling down the drain ... together with you! And I'll be sitting pretty above it all ...

KOZMA: Couldn't have been easy, getting all that out, Comrade! I've got to hand it to you: Credit where credit's due.

(Offers his hand.)

CRYSTAL: *(Bursts into tears.)* Laci, Laci, my dear Laci...
KOZMA: Who's Laci?
CRYSTAL: I loved you, I loved you! *(Rages.)*
KOZMA: Really? Whom? *(In her ear.)* Where is that man? Where is he?

(Crystal freezes.)

How many times do I have to tell you: My name is Kozma. *(Brief pause.)* Comrade, I'd like to have a rest! ... I too have a right to rest here, do you understand? *(Looks Crystal in the eye.)* Still, what do you think? Who am I? Are you sure you know me?
CRYSTAL: *(Stares at him.)* I don't know! I don't know!
KOZMA: There, you see? But then you're not obliged to know everything, either ... Lucy!
CRYSTAL: Who? Who?
KOZMA: "Lucy in the Sky with Diamonds"!
CRYSTAL: You're an infiltrator! You've been ... *(Bangs her head against the ground.)*
KOZMA: *(Laughing.)* Pssst! You're an infiltrator too! Everyone here is an infiltrator. That's what makes this place so terrifically fortunate! ... In any case, I will not leave my homeland, not me. It is, after all, mine. So there! Like everything here. *(Brief pause.)* Am I right?
CRYSTAL: *(Aghast, stands up and backs away.)* But, of course, yes ... Who are you? *(Muses.)* Are you perhaps from above? From where?
KOZMA: Bull's-eye!

(Crystal totters, wavers, points about, cannot find words, shakes.)

Wouldn't you like to take cover in the shade a bit? You like the cool. *(Gestures toward the corpses.)* It's cool there! You'd calm down!
CRYSTAL: *(Calmly.)* Where should I sit?
KOZMA: *(Points about.)* It's up to you! Wherever it's nicest. Wherever it's softest.

(Soberly, Crystal locates a place for herself atop the corpse pile and sits down.)

CRYSTAL: Thank you. And excuse me! *(Brief pause.)* I'll soon be feeling better.
KOZMA: No doubt.
CRYSTAL: Aren't you hot?
KOZMA: I can take it. For a while longer anyway.

(The throng of corpses beneath Crystal stirs, rises, sinks, recoils.)

CRYSTAL: *(Points at the sky.)* Look, the swallows are migrating! How beautiful ...
KOZMA: *(Stands motionless.)* I'm glad you see them.
CRYSTAL: They're not swallows after all ... they're just sparrows. All those sparrows! ... Don't you see them?
KOZMA: Not me.
CRYSTAL: But there are so many! Millions of them! You still don't see them?

(Sudden silence, the field becomes still.)

KOZMA: *(Whirls around, shouts.)* WHERE?
CRYSTAL: *(Frightened.)* Nowhere, they've flown away! I don't know. They're gone. Even though it isn't autumn yet ...
KOZMA: *(Turns his back, sits down.)* We're getting there!

(Betty, tugging Hedi behind her, makes her way stumbling over the corpses lying across the pathway.)

BETTY: All this debris! The wind blew it here ...
HEDI: The gardener's not doing his job! *(Falls.)*
BETTY: Hedi, dear, be careful! *(Helps her up.)* Really! I'm going to have a word with the custodian.
HEDI: Watch your step, you too! Don't tread on any bristles, there're all sorts of things here ...
BETTY: You just give me your hand! Come on! ... *(Arriving in front of Kozma.)* Get out of here!
CRYSTAL: *(Shouts.)* Mother, you've got it all wrong!
BETTY: Did you hear what I said? Do you want me to summon Security?
HEDI: Lizzie, really now! ...
BETTY: Really now nothing. Didn't he pose as your husband? Didn't he beat you?
HEDI: *(Nods.)* No.
BETTY: No?
HEDI: *(Sadly.)* Only my husband. A lot.
BETTY: Is he your husband?
HEDI: Yes. I mean no. In other words ... Leave me alone!
BETTY: But that's what you said before. Isn't that what you said? Think back. You came over, I was standing in line at the buffet ...
CRYSTAL: Mother, watch it! He's from very high up! Somewhere high up ...
(Betty approaches her, becomes frightened.) I don't know where he's from either!
HEDI: *(Laughs out of distress.)* You either? Well now! That's a good one ...
BETTY: What is? *(To Crystal.)* You were here?
CRYSTAL: Yes.
BETTY: Where? *(Shouts.)* Where?

CRYSTAL: Here, where I am. Where else?
BETTY: Come on over here! ... Closer! ... Look into my eyes! Pull yourself together ... Who's this character?

(Crystal keeps silent.)

BETTY: I'm not asking you again!
KOZMA: No point anyway.
BETTY: You! Getting me in trouble? *(Slaps Crystal.)*
CRYSTAL: *(Returns the slap.)* Hit your dog!
HEDI: Uh-oh!
CRYSTAL: *(To Betty.)* Why, who is this? You don't recognize him?
BETTY: *(Takes a look at Kozma.)* Not me! Never saw him before ...
CRYSTAL: Me neither. That's the problem! *(Brief pause.)* He absconded, he came home ... *(Becomes uncertain.)* He didn't abscond, he was driven out ... He's a person. Anybody! I don't know. He's the one who ... doesn't matter! I love him to this day. In other words ... I love him. I love him!
BETTY: *(To Kozma.)* Is this true?
KOZMA: It's not true. Not a word of it ...

(Silence.)

HEDI: Oh no, oh no. *(Begins genuinely moaning.)*
BETTY: *(Gasps, blanches.)* What's going on here? *(Shouts.)* WHAT IS THIS?

(Hedi stops groaning. Silence.)

KOZMA: You mean: *Who* is this? Who could this be?
HEDI: You really shouldn't have hit her, you know! Don't cry, sweetie, your mommy's nervous ...
BETTY: And how! *(Brief pause.)* Who is this man?
KOZMA: "Is this Father Christmas lurking near?
    No, it's the Gestapo over here.
    Bearing gifts and tidings of good cheer?
    No, I'm bringing orders for you, dear.
    Oh but sir, this surely is a jest.
    Not at all, I'm here for your arrest!"
BETTY: *(Sheds tears, nods.)* Joey! Joey! Joey! ...

(Silence.)

HEDI: Come away from here, Crystal dear! Come quickly, come on ... Right now! *(Tries to pull her away.)*

CRYSTAL: Didn't I tell you? What's this about Joey? There's no Joey here!
HEDI: Let's calm down, that's the main thing ... to calm down! All of us. Come away from here!
BETTY: You two go away from here!
HEDI: *(Puts her arm around Crystal, they trample through the corpses.)* Of course, Lizzie, of course! We'll be just fine here in the shade. Right, Crystal? *(They sit down.)*

(Silence.)

BETTY: *(Quietly.)* Are you his son?
KOZMA: *(Imitating her.)* His son.
BETTY: *(Does not notice.)* He sent you?
KOZMA: *(Imitating her.)* He sent me.
BETTY: When did he die?
KOZMA: He didn't die.
BETTY: *(Disconcerted.)* Was he released only now?
KOZMA: *(Thinks it over.)* He wasn't released.
BETTY: *(Nods, says to herself.)* I was so sure they'd hang him ...
KOZMA: Well, if it had been up to you alone ... enough said ...
BETTY: How dare you adopt such a familiar tone with me! ... *(Laughs.)* You're beautiful. A chip off the old block! I knew from the moment I saw you. I suspected. The only thing I couldn't understand was why you're here ... *(Rapt in thought.)* Somebody must have told you my name.
KOZMA: Hey ... Comrade Horváth! Why did you cook up that parliamentary bonbon story? Does that make it nicer, smarter, more delightful? ... The world looks better through rose-colored glasses?
BETTY: *(Looks at him searchingly.)* Do you know everything about me? Everything?
KOZMA: There's no need for that.
BETTY: Then you don't know anything!
KOZMA: I? *(Laughs.)* Crystal, are you paying attention?
CRYSTAL: *(Obediently.)* I'm paying attention!
KOZMA: Who's your father?
BETTY: Don't do this.
KOZMA: Why not?
CRYSTAL: We never talk about that!
KOZMA: We will now.
CRYSTAL: Some minister of state. Former. Supposedly. Then again ... *(Falls silent.)*
KOZMA: Minister of state? Nonsense. Your father was a baker! A kneader at the bread factory at Zugló. A big, blue-eyed boob, a village cadre. Strong as an ox! Your eyes are blue too. So are mine.
CRYSTAL: *(In a panic.)* Even so, you can't be my brother!

KOZMA: No? *(Turns away.)* Your mother lied!
BETTY: Not me. I mean about that, yes ... but not about this! I mean ... *(Shakes her head.)* I don't understand! *(Stares at Kozma.)* Simply inconceivable.
KOZMA: Shall I explain it?
BETTY: I'm the one who ought to be doing the explaining here!

*(Silence.
Betty heaves a sigh. The little boy climbs out from under the corpses, runs to the truck, climbs into the driver's compartment, honks the horn, then shouts.)*

LITTLE BOY: Why is it stopped?
BETTY: *(Bursts out.)* I have nothing to be ashamed of! From the Democratic Youth Federation, to the student hostel, to the school of commerce. A village girl in Budapest! They didn't even want to let me leave home, because there wasn't anything to eat. *(Corrects herself.)* There was! *(Corrects herself.)* As long as we had land. *(Corrects herself.)* But I denied that we had any. *(Shrugs.)* I had to. The peasants were doing shorthand in school! The kulak children of so many poor people ... And the palaver, the palaver! I shot my mouth off in every possible circle ...
KOZMA: And?
BETTY: And ... then ...
KOZMA: Then?
BETTY: Then a state security agent began courting me. While Joey was holding my hand under the desk ... *(Brief pause.)* They flunked him, even though he was smart. *(Corrects herself.)* Not true, he was a cabbagehead. Only handsome. The baker! *(Corrects herself.)* He was smart, only it got out that he had had a bastard kid! A while back. By a charwoman: lumpen element. They found out. Kicked him out. The governing body of the school voted unanimously. And that state security agent married me. *(Kozma looks at her.)* I mean, I married him. Even though by then Joey and I had ... *(Falls silent.)* We held the reception at the Blue Star ... Even Joey came. He brought his child. How did they get in?! Why?! *(Shouts.)* I didn't know I was pregnant with Crystal! ... *(Utters with difficulty.)* By Joey ... *(Corrects herself.)* I did know. He didn't know. The state security agent. And Joey was only a bagger at the market, because they didn't take him back at the factory. *(Heaves a sigh.)* Then came the revolution. *(Corrects herself.)* Counterrevolution. *(Tiredly.)* Revolution. I don't care, doesn't matter. *(Corrects herself.)* It does matter! *(Brief pause.)* Doesn't matter. — The last time I saw him was at the demonstration on the twenty-third, then he was swept away by the crowd. *(Corrects herself with clenched teeth.)* Not the last time! *(Slowly.)* The last time I saw him was at the hearing in the summer of 1957. *(Corrects herself.)* And the November of the previous year — the whole month! *(Brief pause.)* In other words, the officer said to me: "Little girl, you went astray, soon you'll be giving birth,

repentance is showing, too ... now we will bring you face to face. There's a whole world out there for you." They led me over, Joey was standing there. All I had to say was: YOU'RE THE ONE.

(Falls silent.)

HEDI: *(In a deranged manner.)*
"Whither, fishers, whither
Have you aimed your tiller?"
Sometimes they don't even give me an advance, they just take me away! They even forbid my using a razor, I can't even shave! Westerners like their pussy fuzzy! They like fuzzy pussy! *(Laughs.)*
CRYSTAL: Who's "the one"? Sleep, sleep! Pleasant dreams, rosy angels! Stars, stars! *(Tries to hide.)*
LITTLE BOY: *(Shouts.)* Why is it stopped? Why doesn't it move?
BETTY: They caught the little boy too, the poor little chump! Because he's the one who was throwing the Molotov cocktails, isn't he? ... I, to be sure, was thrown right into school! Once again. *(Smiles.)* By sixty-one I already had a rock-solid position in Atád. INDEPENDENT! No one can understand it. *(Brief pause.)* They handed me his belongings: his father's chain, his little shirt, pants ... Why to me?! Because! I don't have the foggiest idea! Because all the blue-eyed people died! *(Muses.)* My husband had blue eyes too, such rotten blue eyes ...
KOZMA: *(Grabs her.)* Really? He too had blue eyes?
BETTY: *(Stares at him.)* You can't be alive. But then in that case ...
KOZMA: *(Shouts.)* No?
CRYSTAL: *(Screams.)* Enough! I want to sleep! The end!

(Betty writhes, emits inarticulate sounds, Kozma does not release her from his grip.)

HEDI: *(Deranged.)*
"On what do fishes feed
When nets define their need?"
Salmon, caviar, hazelnuts. Turtle sandwiches, French champagne, crab ... Fuzzy pussy!
CRYSTAL: I can't fall asleep! To sleep! ...

(Crystal again tries to hide among the corpses, but cannot; the arms, legs, bags prevent her; she rummages like a gopher; Betty wrestles with Kozma; they roll across the ground tumbling over each other.)

KOZMA: Now you see it, now you don't. You're quite sunburned, Betsy! Don't believe her, girls, not even the questions she asks have any truth to them ...

Your husband's here and you won't even give him a kiss. How many kinds of death did you invent for me, my dear? How many times did you mentally have me buried? Too bad for you I'm still here. Alive. *(Leaves Betty.)* Or maybe I'm not alive. Maybe I'm under the ground after all. Under twenty meters of ice, like some shadow. Like the mammoths! *(Points about.)* This too could be a mammoth grazing ground! That too. And you are still the wolves here. So, what's going to happen? Tell them how I ended up beneath the ice! Your husband. When the trains from Budapest still used to go beneath the ice ... Let the others learn! I don't even know.

BETTY: *(Pants.)* That's what State Security advised. Ordered! It was an order.

KOZMA: Well now this could be the truth. It's getting there!

HEDI: But what, after all, is this State Security? *(Repeats it laughing.)*

CRYSTAL: *(Under the corpses.)* To sleep! ... To sleep! ...

KOZMA: It doesn't exist any more. Now there's something better. She's all that's left of it ... she remained as chronicler. All alone. Holding the front lines!

BETTY: *(Points at Kozma.)* That's what he was, too! Good thing it was done away with. Nothing like that is possible anymore today, that's for sure ...

KOZMA: What's not possible, dear?

BETTY: He bowled me over with his high pay, with all the wining and dining, with the car for his exclusive use ... What could a stupid peasant girl know?! Even the smell of your skin disgusts me. *(Brief pause.)* All I had to do was inform on what he's up to, what he says about whom, in the kitchen, in his sleep ... The swine! I was glad they did you in.

KOZMA: Now you're talkin', Comrade!

BETTY: Who are you to talk?! *(Shouts.)* An eye for an eye, a tooth for a tooth! And yes, I cheated on you with the baker. A thousand times, with gusto! I wanted to be his wife, that's how they were able to blackmail me! *(Changes.)* Why didn't you drop dead? Him they did in! But why his little boy? I couldn't help that! *(Corrects herself.)* And what if I could? Everybody here with any mettle died. Only whores stay alive here. And you!

KOZMA: *(Stretches.)* And meantime I haven't aged a bit!

BETTY: Right, so it seems! *(Makes a sudden realization.)* I mean ... *(Her blood runs cold.)* How can this be?

(The three graces stare stupefied at Kozma.
Anagnorisis.
Silence.)

KOZMA: Comrades, you may continue sunbathing! *(Prepares to leave, packs.)*

HEDI: *(In a panic.)* Please don't leave, please have a seat. Say something, you two!

BETTY: Please stay, keep us company.

HEDI: A Kozma lived near us. I know people by that name ...

BETTY: *(Demented.)* Of course, stay. I didn't mean it that way either! It would be better if you stayed.

(Silence.)

KOZMA: Well, all right! *(Smiles at them.)* A bit longer then!... So as not to leave any bad blood between us. *(Sits down.)* Won't you come closer? It must be uncomfortable back there...

(The women venture forward.)

After all, this is all yours! I'm just freeloading here ... by your gracious leave.
LITTLE BOY: *(Honks the horn.)* When are we leaving?
KOZMA: *(Without looking back, with outstretched arm.)* I'm coming right away!

(Brief pause.)

HEDI: *(Cautiously.)* To whom did you say that just now?
KOZMA: To everybody who's here. *(Points about.)*
HEDI: *(Points there.)* To these here? *(Looks at the corpses, puzzled.)* That's a possible interpretation, true. I'm the one who said we ought to rake them up. Or throw them in a pile and burn them.
KOZMA: You'd burn them, really?
HEDI: *(Frightened.)* Why ... that's customary!
BETTY: It's not our problem. That's what gardeners are for! *(Approaches Kozma.)*
CRYSTAL: *(Calls out.)* Mother!
HEDI: I just... It just sort of occurred to me! Property of the state. Then the whole thing will rot away all by itself.

(Brief pause.)

LITTLE BOY: *(Calls out loudly.)* Why is it stopped?
BETTY: *(To Kozma.)* Who *are* you?
HEDI: *(Tries to pull her away.)* You see, Lizzie, they've gotten you all mixed up too! Loose lips sink ships. The sun was a bit much.
BETTY: Who are you?
HEDI: *(In a panic.)* Comrade Whatchamacallit, don't misunderstand, Lizzie didn't mean anything by it, she's just worked up, she's talking gibberish ...
BETTY: *(Calls out.)* Who are you?
KOZMA: *(Looks her in the eye.)* It's me. *(They stare at each other, Crystal steps behind Kozma, who turns around immediately and looks her in the eye.)* Me. Who else? *(Turns around and looks into Hedi's eyes.)* Yes. I am the one.
CRYSTAL: I see. *(Takes off her glasses and throws them away.)*
HEDI: So then, yes.
BETTY: You! *(Steps up to him.)*
CRYSTAL: *(Screams.)* Mother!

LITTLE BOY: *(Calls out.)* I want to go home! I want to go home! I want to go home! I want to go home! I want to go ...

(The three women hurl themselves at Kozma and kill him in an orgasmic frenzy. They then clamber to their feet and hurriedly bury the corpse under the beach articles: mattresses, pails, bags, umbrella, and towels. Finally they collapse at the base of the mound.

Silence.

The little boy honks the truck's horn three times, the corpses stir, sit up and stand up.)

GITTA GAMBS: I'm alive.
INTERMEDIARY: Then we've done it ... Golly! Excellent. I never would have believed ...
GYM TEACHER: Sweet motherland! *(Stands up.)* What time is it?
NON-SOLOIST: The things a person gets mixed up in all the time!
ANNIE MENOPAUSE: Whoever thought this up should have been sent here!
BEGGAR: Gott sei Dank. The main thing is: it's over.
HEAD BOOKKEEPER: You think so?
INTERMEDIARY: Don't you see? Everything went like greased lightning. Hats off to you people!
GITTA GAMBS: I'm alive.
DOCTOR: Any need for a doctor?
SUPERNUMERARY: No need! ... Anybody got a comb?
CRIMINAL: I have! *(Does not hand it over, combs himself, sings.)*
"I find no love whene'er I go
To th'underworld. Yet even so
I go for I just can't say no ..." *(Pesters the nurse.)*
NURSE: Don't pester me or I'll haul off and let you have it! ... So then, what now?
GRANNIE WASHOUT: What else? A smoke! *(Lights up.)* How 'bout a ciggie, little Baron?
MRS. DIE CASTER: *(Calls over.)* Árpád, the supplier is coming tonight!
DIE CASTER: Nicht vor dem Publikum, Gizi!
GITTA GAMBS: I'm alive.
INTERMEDIARY: No false modesty! Ladies and gentlemen, we've accomplished our task. Congratulations, I'm very pleased with each and every one of you ... *(Shakes their hands, pulling up those who are still sitting.)* With you ... with you too ... with you, my dear, for the selflessness, diligence, and forthrightness demonstrated by every one of you. You passed with flying colors and that's that! You're a reliable group, you are.
ANNIE MENOPAUSE: That's for sure.
INTERMEDIARY: *(To the non-soloist.)* Even you, sir, though you are a blusterer.
NON-SOLOIST: I never uttered a single ...

INTERMEDIARY: Because keep in mind: Deeds speak louder than words. And you delivered! *(To the gym teacher.)* So did you.
GYM TEACHER: *(Afraid.)* What did I do?
INTERMEDIARY: You did what you were called upon to do. That's what. And you did it with precision! In an organized manner! Smoothly and expediently! You're promising people, you are... Community spirits!

(Silence.)

NON-SOLOIST: That's good.
GRANNIE WASHOUT: Yes indeed.
GYM TEACHER: A person does what a person's got to do.
SUPERNUMERARY: ZIPPO!
CRIMINAL: Thanks. Then when do we go home?
INTERMEDIARY: Right away! *(Gestures grandly.)* Let us retire to the truck and settle down in comfort... *(The crowd scrambles to the truck.)* Let's pick up after ourselves, let's give Grannie a little boost from behind, upsy-daisy... splendid! That's the ticket! We'll be on our way presently. *(He too jumps up.)* People! In a difficult and tragic situation you have acquitted yourselves solidly and reliably! I shall write a special report on precisely that, citing everyone of you individually, by name...
CRIMINAL: Not me.
MRS. DIE CASTER: Me neither!
LITTLE BOY: *(Points at the three women from the steps of the driver's compartment.)* What's over there?

(Silence.)

What's that there? Who're they?

(Silence.)

ANNIE MENOPAUSE: Aren't they with us?
NON-SOLOIST: They're sunbathing.
HEAD BOOKKEEPER: Somebody's not well over there.
NURSE: Not our concern.
BUTCHER: I'll buy a house after all. I'll spend some time in the summer house, an' everything'll be okay...
DOCTOR: Does somebody need a doctor?
NON-SOLOIST: No!... They didn't ask for one.
DIE CASTER: Let's go already, what are we frittering away the time for?
CRIMINAL: Hallo, ladies, do you need anything? Ladies!
GRANNIE WASHOUT: They're asleep.

DIE CASTER: *(To the criminal.)* Can't you see they're asleep?
INTERMEDIARY: What's this here? What's this? I didn't see it before ...
GYM TEACHER: Nothing.
BEGGAR: Vacationers. Let's go!
SUPERNUMERARY: I don't want to act any more! I'm fed up!
GITTA GAMBS: I'm alive, I'm alive, I'm alive!
CRIMINAL: *(Shouts.)* Do you need any help? Do you need any help?
NON-SOLOIST: Why don't we get moving? What the hell's going on?
INTERMEDIARY: *(Pounds the outside of the empty driver's compartment.)* Step on it, boss! Let's get going!

(Silence.)

What's the matter?

(Silence.)

NURSE: Why isn't it moving?
BUTCHER: When are we leaving?
NON-SOLOIST: Won't it start?
GITTA GAMBS: What happened?

(The little boy gets into the driver's compartment, randomly switches controls on the instrument panel; the wheels of the truck spin in place in the dust.)

(After a while, blackout.)

END

On the Editor

Eugene Brogyányi studied at the Cooper Union and New York University. He is a founder and Artistic Co-director of the Threshold Theatre Company in New York City. He has written on Hungarian theatre, has translated many contemporary Hungarian plays, and in 1983 received an award from the Translation Center at Columbia University. He is currently working on an English-language volume of plays by Géza Páskándi.